SEVEN DAYS,
MANY VOICES

SEVEN DAYS, MANY VOICES

Insights into the Biblical Story of Creation

EDITED BY

Rabbi Benjamin David

✦

CENTRAL CONFERENCE OF AMERICAN RABBIS

Library of Congress Cataloging-in-Publication Data

Names: David, Benjamin, 1977- editor.
Title: Seven days, many voices : insights into the biblical story of creation
  / edited by Rabbi Benjamin David.
Description: New York, NY : Central Conference of American Rabbis, [2017] |
  Includes bibliographical references and index.
Identifiers: LCCN 2017021125 (print) | LCCN 2017021904 (ebook) | ISBN
  9780881232998 | ISBN 9780881232905 (pbk. : alk. paper)
Subjects: LCSH: Creation--Biblical teaching. | Bible. Genesis--Criticism,
  interpretation, etc. | Reform Judaism.
Classification: LCC BS1199.C73 (ebook) | LCC BS1199.C73 S48 2017 (print) |
  DDC 296.3/4--dc23
LC record available at https://lccn.loc.gov/2017021125

10 9 8 7 6 5 4 3 2 1
CCAR Press, 355 Lexington Avenue, New York, NY 10017
(212) 972-3636

www.ccarpress.org

Contents

Introduction

The opening words of the Torah are iconic, and they mark the start of an iconic narrative, namely the Torah's account of how God created our world. Centuries later, these words continue to carry power and resonate broadly. However, those first six days, presented twice in Genesis, tell of much more than the beginning of day and night, skies and seas, animals of earth and air; they provide us with a touchstone to return to once and again over the course of our lives. When we dare to investigate the intricacies of the Creation text we come to see not only ourselves, but the imperatives with which we live as Jews: to care for the natural universe, to take responsibility for ourselves and those around us, to lift up the Sabbath as a holy day, and to always remember our ever-profound origins.

Why this book? Why now? In an age of dire pace and frenzied obsession with technology, holding fast to our beginnings matters greatly, for us and our children. Rather than fixate forever on what's next, and whose social media status garners greatest attention, Creation has us consider who we are at our most fundamental. They are verses to which we are meant to pay attention. The Talmud thus expounds on Ecclesiastes, "The wise man, his eyes are at the beginning" (2:14), by equating wisdom with the one who "inquires from the world's beginning, from the six days of Creation and thereafter" (Babylonian Talmud, *Chagigah* 11b). Centuries later Rashi will argue that while the Torah's corpus of mitzvot begin in earnest in Exodus 12, where we find an early iteration of the festival calendar, it is in Genesis that God's grandeur and might are first declared without question.[1] The Creation accounts thus accomplish, among so much else, establishing the very God who will exist in covenantal relationship with the Jewish people.

We might also argue that never before have there been greater misgivings regarding Creation. At a time when considerable skepticism is aimed at religious institutions and tradition at large, the early chapters of Genesis are easily cast aside as antiquated, even irrelevant. And yet, even when placed beside the realities of scientific discovery and evolution, those chapters remind us in the most succinct fashion of precisely what is so ennobling regarding religion and religious life: ritual, poetry, coexistence, tradition, and the underlying belief so many of us carry in a benevolent Creator manifest in our daily lives. It is true that if the Creation story is going to withstand the test of time, it is not only because of its literary prowess and magnitude, but because it consistently renews our commitment to faith itself.

Finally, this book seeks to highlight the range of thinking that exists when it comes to Creation, particularly within Reform Judaism. Among Reform Jews past and present there are innumerable understandings of and responses to Creation. I am proud to align myself with a denomination that accommodates and celebrates such diversity of thought. This book presents some of that great diversity to the reader, including a range of present-day rabbis, cantors, thought leaders, and scholars from both within and beyond the Reform Movement, who each inhabit their own unique ideological and theological environs. If the Creation narrative draws particular misunderstanding, even mistreatment, then part of the book's aim is in fact to redeem Creation and show how thoroughly it allows for readings of significant intellectual nuance and depth. Some authors present us with Creation as it relates to life in Israel, while others link Creation to rabbinic literature, the sciences, climate change, Jewish history, personal practice, overnight camp, and nature. Many of these readings speak directly to the world that we live in at this very moment, one of multiculturalism, ever-changing geopolitical realities, and very much an increasingly threatened natural environment. To be sure, the Creation accounts, because they are so widely read and have been treasured by so many different faith groups across time, invite a multiplicity of responses, perhaps unlike any other section of our sacred text. The verses practically call out to us, *darsheini*—"interpret me"—and the hope is that this book presents readers with a new understanding of and appreciation for Creation.

I came to this project not as an expert on Creation, but as greatly curious when it comes to Creation, as I imagine we all are. My aim was to engage as many great minds as possible and to allow them to fill the pages of this book with their perspective and wisdom. I learned so much over the years that it took to bring this anthology to completion. I hope that you will find it to be as informative and enlightening as I do. Readers will find that the book is divided into seven distinct sections, one for each of the world's first days. Within each section are six essays, each of their own unique styling. I am eternally indebted to the book's many contributors for their hard work and their willingness to take part. A special thank you is due to Rabbi Hara Person at the CCAR Press for her inimitable vision and expertise. I thank Rabbi Don Goor and all the members of the CCAR Press Council, as well as Rabbi Steven A. Fox, for their belief in this project. Thank you as well to Sasha Smith and rabbinic students Andrue Kahn and Hilly Haber for their dedication to this wonderful project.

Lastly, to my wife Lisa and our family, thank you for supporting me . . . from the beginning.

Note

1. *Pentateuch with Rashi's Commentary*, ed. M. Rosenbaum and A. M. Silberman (New York: Hebrew Publishing Company, 1870), 2.

Note about Translations

For consistency, all translations used within this volume are from *The Torah: A Modern Commentary*, General Editor, W. Guther Plaut, Revised Edition, General Editor, David E. S. Stein (New York: Reform Judaism Publishing, an imprint of CCAR Press, 2005, 2006, 2015). The translation of Genesis was done by Chaim Stern. The translation of Exodus through Deuteronomy was created by Rabbi David E. S. Stein based on the NJPS translation and done with permission of JPS. The only exception are several essays where the author's commentary is significantly based upon a different translation. In those cases the translation used is noted.

Acknowledgments

While there was One author of Creation, this collection was a team effort. The book would not have been possible without the expert guidance of Rabbi Hara Person, with whom I interned as a rabbinic student many years ago, and now have had the pleasure of working with as a colleague. She is a gifted editor, an unwavering guide, and a true rabbi. I also owe a debt of gratitude to Sasha Smith, CCAR Press editorial assistant, and to HUC-JIR student interns Andrue Kahn and Hilly Haber for their commitment to this far-reaching project. Thanks also to the rest of the CCAR Press team, including Ortal Bensky, Carly Linden, Debbie Smilow, and copy editor Debra Corman, and of course Rabbi Steven A. Fox, CCAR Chief Executive. Thanks also to xxx, members of the Worship and Practice Committee, for their careful review of the manuscript. A special thank you goes to the many religious leaders who contributed essays to the collection and whose remarkable insights gave the book great shape and breadth. Thank you to my congregational community for their constant inspiration and partnership. Most of all, thank you to my wife, Lisa, and our beautiful family, whom I love deeply. Finally, I would like to dedicate this book to my grandmother, Ann Strauss, who grew up in Nuremberg, fled Nazi Germany as a teen, and went on to see her grandson become a father, a rabbi, and now an author.

SEVEN DAYS,
MANY VOICES

Day One

✦

LIGHT AND DARKNESS

*When God was about to create heaven and earth, the earth
was a chaos, unformed, and on the chaotic waters' face there
was darkness. Then God's spirit glided over the face of the
waters, and God said, "Let there be light!"—and there was
light. And when God saw how good the light was, God divided
the light from the darkness; God then called the light Day, and
called the darkness Night, and there was evening and there
was morning, the first day.*

Genesis 1:1–5

1

Cosmic Disorder

RABBI OREN J. HAYON

*When God was about to create heaven and earth, the earth
was a chaos, unformed, and on the chaotic waters' face there
was a darkness. Then God's spirit glided over the face of the
waters, and God said, "Let there be light!"—and there was
light. And when God saw how good the light was, God divided
the light from the darkness; God then called the light Day, and
called the darkness Night, and there was evening and there
was morning, the first day.*

Genesis 1:1–5

History's greatest story opens on a scene of cosmic disorder: the universe is *tohu vavohu*, formless and shapeless. The Bible makes a point of insisting that what existed before Genesis 1 was not vacancy or nothingness, but instead a vast primordial jumble. Before God's first utterance, the cosmos was all murky shadows and jagged edges; all color was muddled into an unseen, violent blur. And so God begins the work of Creation by deftly extending one divine hand like a mighty sieve, straining and sifting. The process of universe building emerges from God's impulse to impose order on disorder, to sort solid from liquid and light from dark.

3

What drove God to do this work? What singular urge inspired God to reach into the *tohu vavohu*, before the first photon ricocheted from one surface to another, before color and texture were ever known? What impulse was God obeying when God delicately extracted luminous scraps from that shadowy mixture, forming them into sun and moon and assigning them their celestial functions?

We might imagine that God was behaving like an expectant parent, eager to create new life that would bear God's image and carry on the divine name. But instead (as the classical commentators agree, with rare unanimity), the primary motivation behind God's work of Creation seems to have been not the formation of human life, but the construction of ethical discernment and the establishment of a sustainable system of justice.

Rabbi Naftali Tzvi Yehudah Berlin, in his nineteenth-century scriptural commentary *HaEmek Davar*, notes that, significantly, the name for God used in the Creation narrative is *Elohim*, which carries a subliminal connotation of God-as-Judge in the classic interpretive tradition. Accordingly, the framework of Creation that begins here ought correctly to be understood as the first phase of God's project of establishing justice on earth. With the innovations of Genesis 1, God encodes law, judgment, and justice into the genome of the universe.

The Rabbinic tradition urges us not to overlook the particular mechanism by which God initiates the work of creating the cosmos: God's first action is to produce a current of wind, which sends ripples shuddering across the dark surface of the water.[1] Surely it cannot be coincidental, the Sages point out, that the climactic moment of Israel's national liberation will arrive in precisely the same way. Later, in the Book of Exodus, the slaves are invited into freedom through a portal in the waves, formed when a mighty east wind shapes the waters of the sea into two great shimmering walls that soar and thunder opposite one another (Exodus 14:21). The thunderous drama of water roiled by wind symbolizes—both in Genesis and in Exodus—God's presence propelling the force of divine justice into the fluid structure of human civilization.

These insights about God's reasons for initiating the work of Creation do not, however, help to unravel the mystery behind the Torah's account of the sequence of Creation. Specifically: Why begin with *light*? Why should the first sentence ever spoken by God in Hebrew Scripture be a rather mundane pronouncement calling light into being—rather than, say, life, or virtue, or peace? And how do we make sense of the fact that light is created before the sun that transmits it?

When we read Creation as an allegorical record of how justice was introduced to the world, none of these questions presents us with a difficulty; we must simply first acknowledge that what the Torah calls "light" in the first verses of Genesis is not visual light as we know it in our everyday lives (we arrive at this conclusion naturally, following the fact that this "light" is created before the sun, moon, and stars come into being in Genesis 1:14–18). Instead, what is created in Genesis 1:3 is an intense, purified energy; beyond simply providing illumination to the physical world, this substance was created to serve as a highly potent catalyst for humans' moral insight and ethical perspicacity. When people perceive clearly what is right and just, even in our modern lives today, we are, in a sense, seeing by that first "light" that God released at the beginning of history.

The universe's first light was so powerful and so precious, however, that God fretted over the possibility that human corruption and shortsightedness might someday threaten its purity and safety. And so, the Sages taught, "When the Holy One observed the generation of the Flood and the corruptness of its deeds [see Genesis 6:5–7], God removed a portion of the divine light from the world and hid it away for the righteous. And now, whenever God pauses to contemplate the trove of concealed light [*or ganuz*], God rejoices, as it is said: 'The light of the righteous brings joy' (Proverbs 13:9)."[2]

This evocative illustration produces a bittersweet reaction in us: God is not optimistic about humanity's ability to root out wickedness and dishonesty from our society. But, on the other hand, at the times when human history is at its most debased, God is still able to return to the hidden store of holy light that was secreted away at the beginning of time, which brings comfort to the divine heart at times of darkness. In a sense, God is the One who remains uniquely able to see in the dark, so to speak: only God can discern through the clutter and welter of *tohu vavohu* an underlying moral design that binds and unifies all of humanity. Even when the human world is at its darkest, its most desperate, its most morally debased, God can be soothed by gazing at the *or ganuz*, which reminds God about the bright potential of justice, which was injected into Creation at the universe's beginning.

Still, one wonders, why should God tolerate moral darkness at all? Given that the impulse to create came about as an expression of God's inclination toward justice, it is difficult to understand why God would tolerate any injustice whatsoever and why, in the system God created, light should ever be prevented from penetrating to every dim corner.

The Sages insist that this is the wrong question. It is not the case that God simply *permitted* darkness to seep in around the edges of God's bright creation; in fact, God actively *created* darkness as a separate commodity with unique characteristics of its own. As evidence, they present a verse from Isaiah in which God proclaims, "I form light and create darkness" (Isaiah 45:7). This divine pronouncement fortifies God's identity as the ultimate Source of all: both darkness and light, wickedness and virtue, corruption and purity.[3]

Given the assumption that light and dark are independent substances, and given the principle that two independent substances cannot occupy the same space at the same time (one can easily imagine those ancient Rabbis delightedly working their way through these concepts, one step at a time, like mathematicians laying out a difficult proof), then it necessarily follows that good and evil must always remain distinct from one another. And so Isaiah's verse comes to forestall the possibility of our concluding erroneously that darkness and evil exist only in the places where God fears to tread or that suffering can creep insidiously into the world because there are spaces in which God fails to pay attention. Instead, we are reminded: God is the point from which both light and darkness originate. Both good and evil emerge from God's creative impulse, and as they fill the world, swirling and spiraling and mixing in varying ratios, the human conscience may be drawn by turns toward gratitude, humility, elation, or grim resignation.

We must recognize that this teaching can lead us toward troubling conclusions as well. Can we believe that a benevolent God created the seeds of human suffering? Why was God unwilling or unable to incline the world against vice and depravity? If God began the work of Creation by forming light—by which we mean the capacity for righteousness and moral sensibility—then why would God not conclude Creation by banishing darkness? The Rabbis offer this reliable (if tepid) consolation: just as one's eyes become increasingly sensitized to light during night on earth, the human soul's innate thirst for fairness and morality yearns even more desperately for justice, to God's great delight, when it is confronted by evil on all sides.

Upon the sprawling backdrop of *tohu vavohu*, Creation begins with the gathering of tiny sparks that are drawn lovingly, painstakingly, out of the dimness. In each minuscule winking ember—no matter how forcefully the inky darkness presses toward it from all sides—the light of God's justice continues to glow. Even at the times when God's nearness seems fleeting, in the places where injustice appears to dominate, we can sense the Holy One's nearness by immersing ourselves in the work of justice. This work is illuminated by the *or ganuz*, the primeval light God concealed eons ago, which still shines on humanity's deeds of compassion and fairness. Committing ourselves to justice, even in a world that is indifferent to goodness and mercy, we feel the presence of God. That presence reassures and comforts us, like the warmth on a pillow left by a loved partner, who even now awaits us in an adjoining room, desperately hoping that we will open the door separating us and leap into an embrace to which we are desperately, constantly, silently invited.

Notes

1. Rashbam on Genesis 1:2.
2. BT *Chagigah* 12a
3. Shadal on Isaiah 45:7.

2

—

Creation

Responsibility, Blessing, and Sanctity

RABBI DR. YEHOYADA AMIR

God then surveyed all that [God] had made, and look – it was very good!

Genesis 1:31

At first glance the biblical Creation narrative (Genesis 1:1–2:3) looks to be no more than a mythical depiction of the coming-into-being of the universe, namely a problematic, archaic alternative to scientific theories. If that is actually the case, then there is very little a modern or postmodern Jew can learn from it. For questions of nature and biology, geology and cosmology, we tend to turn to the best of scientific research, to the best of human endeavoring to explore the world and life. Archaic perceptions might be a subject for historians of ancient culture but are no challenge to the scientific comprehension of the natural world. Furthermore, even when we step forward and explore the moral, philosophical, and religious question such scientific theories might raise, it is not necessarily the ancient depiction of Creation that we would tend toward, but rather to the contrary, the best of the contemporary insights concerning physics and biology, sociology and psychology. Asking the Book of Genesis *how* the universe came into being, *when* it took place, and other similar questions seems to be no more than a mere fundamentalism, betraying both our sense of truth and our faith.

A second, more sensitive look at that narrative would reveal other layers to us. Behind the mythical story of the "how," and even beyond the revolutionary monotheistic idea that the one and only God is the Creator of heaven and earth, the Creation narrative tells us something about the value of the world, the merit of life, and our place and role in the universe. It aspires to create the infrastructure for our religious and moral orientation, to award us with mitzvah and responsibility. This layer is of unique value to our generations. It does not compete with the scientific worldview but rather wishes to provide us with that which science and research could never express.

The nouns and facts of the Creation narrative might well represent an outdated perception and perhaps represent an ancient, irrelevant image of the world. Let us turn instead to the Hebrew verbs it makes use of, to the ladder on which it climbs up. The second word of the narrative is *bara*, loosely translated as "created." In Genesis 1:1 this verb describes the whole of Creation. The very beginning of the dominant verb on that ladder is *h-y-h*, or "be": "The earth was a chaos, unformed" (1:2); "God said, 'Let there be light!'—and there was light" (1:3). This indifferent "be" receives its value by the divine approval of the deed of Creation: "God saw how good the light was" (1:4). The divine commanding voice is also the approving instance. The created being, manifest in the light, is declared as valuable, as good. This valuation is the kernel of the entire story; it will appear again, fully or partially, throughout the days of Creation.

The second day marks the climbing of a further rung on the ladder. On top of "be" now comes *l'havdil*, "to divide" or "to make distinct." The created being has a purpose. It is there in order to be made distinct. The idea that there is purpose, namely that things are there "in order," exceeds all that which modern science and modern philosophy of science dare say. It is the primary step toward the notions of value and meaning of natural being, a realization of the perception that that which science analyzes and constitutes is, on another level, a creation of God.

The third day marks an essential escalation. Creation is no longer passive but rather an active player. God commands that the earth itself "bring forth":

> God said, "Let the earth grow vegetation, seed-bearing plants, fruit trees on the earth that bear fruit, each true to its type, with its seed in it!—and so it was. The earth brought forth vegetation, seed-bearing plants, each true to its type, and trees bearing fruit, each true to its type, with its seed in it. (Genesis 1:11–12)

The biblical narrative tends to be short. Here, to the contrary, we read a long sequence of details, repeated twice in a seemingly unnecessary manner. We are told what the command was, and we learn that "so it was," that the order was executed fully. However, a closer look reveals that this is not the case. Indeed, the order was executed, but not fully. Two midrashim deal carefully and sensitively with these verses. In the first (*B'reishit Rabbah* 5:11), Rabbi Y'hudah bar Shalom pays special attention to the trees. The divine order was to bring forth "fruit trees . . . that bear fruit." The earth brought forth "trees bearing fruit." According to the midrash, the difference is substantial. The divine intention was that the trees would actually be "fruit trees," edible and sweet. However, the trees the earth brought forth are not edible, only their fruits. Rabbi Y'hudah criticizes sharply this partial fulfillment of the divine order: "The earth transgressed the commandment."

In the other midrash (Babylonian Talmud, *Chulin* 60:1), Rabbi Chanina bar Pappa focuses on the grass. He focuses on the phrase "true to its type," interpreted by him as a demand that each of the created species will have its own separate place—that they would not blend. In the divine order this command appears only concerning the trees; in the depiction of its realization it appears in regard to the vegetation as well. In response, Rabbi Chanina offers an imaginary description of the vegetation, listening carefully to the divine order and learning, beyond its literal meaning, what God wills. Trees grow naturally separated, not blended. If, nevertheless, God bothered to emphasize that the trees should be brought forth "true to its type," argues the vegetation, one should learn how important it is that species have their own place. They apply that principle also to themselves, though not literally commanded to do so.

The first midrash depicted the earth as transgressing the divine order; the second one depicts the vegetation as a creative partner, implying active reasoning. Both are symbolic metaphors, wishing to learn from this detailed description that once Creation is active, the story is no longer solely a story of the divine creative will, but rather of a balance between Creator and Creation, between intention and realization. Created reality represents the divine will and, at the same time, natural, worldly quality. Those layers of reality correspond to each other but also differ from each other. Our task is to design our human orientation in the world in accordance with this gap, taking account of the tension between nature and Creation, science and faith.

The fourth day brings up a verb of a new quality. The sun, moon, and stars are there not only to "lighten" the day and the night and to "separate" them (Genesis 1:14), but also to "govern" them (1:16). Asking about the function of the various phenomena, in the manner science teaches us to, is important and valid. Nevertheless, we ought to view the created universe also from the perspective of the responsibility of ruling, echoing that which God's will planted in it. When proceeding to the fifth day this new quality becomes explicit and clear. For the first time, concerning life, comes the verb *vay'varech*, "blessed" (Genesis 1:22) That which was implied by the notion that the lights are there in order to rule is now expressed fully. Life is not merely a fact, a concept, but rather a value-concept; life is blessed, it carries a blessing. "Be fruitful and multiply," commands God, "fill the waters of the seas, and let the birds multiply in the earth" (1:22). This marks a much higher confirmation than the primary "good" we met on the first day. Blessing life is the grounding for human responsibility to preserve life and avoid redundant suffering of living creatures. The taking of life blessed by the Creator should never be an indifferent act.

Biblical scholars are united in arguing that the usage of the verb *b-r-a* concerning the making (on the fifth day) of the "great sea monsters" (Genesis 1:21) is no more than a direct polemic against Mesopotamian pagan myths, and not an integral part of the Genesis narrative itself. If so, then we should look at its two interconnected essential appearances: on the first day, concerning "heaven and earth," and on the sixth day, pointing to the making of humanity. The common translation of *bet-reish-alef*, "to create," hardly expresses that which the Hebrew expresses in the biblical narrative. Creation and creativity (and their equivalences in languages such as German, French, Latin, and Greek) can well be attributed to human deeds and artistic works; *bet-reish-alef* marks the absolute uniqueness of the divine act, to the transcendence of God's deed in creating the universe on the one hand and humanity on the other. Only God creates in this way; the universe and the human are direct and explicit creations of God. "So God created the human beings in [the divine] image, creating [them] in the image of God, creating them male and female" (Genesis 1:27). This multifold repetition is only one of various linguistic means marking the profound uniqueness of this creation over anything else in our narrative.

God's declaration of the will to do so, and its dialogical form, is another powerful means: the statement conveys that this creature, contrary to any other part of the universe, carries "God's image." The divine blessing also exceeds all that which we already met. Not merely "be fruitful and multiply," but also "fill the earth and tame it" (Genesis 1:28). It is in this spirit that the sixth day reaches its climax with the festive declaration that "God then surveyed everything that [God] had made, and look—it was very good!" (Genesis 1:31).

Nevertheless, neither the narrative nor the sequence of escalating verbs come here to the climaxing completion. It is not "everything" that ends the process of Creation. It is on the seventh day, Shabbat, that "God had completed the work that had been done, ceasing then on the seventh day from all the work that [God] had done" (Genesis 2:1). The blessing to humanity and the confirmation of the whole of Creation as "very good" do not exhaust that which the Bible wishes to tell us about the value and meaning of the world. We are the last, supreme creation; life and blessing are given to us; the world and its fullness are there for us. However, all of that is true only in essential connection to a superior dimension, one that is not "given" to us; a dimension that awaits us, awaits our commitment and devotion.

The mark of this dimension is found in the unique verbs of the seventh day's narrative. They start with "ceased" and "rested." Between these two, we meet again the verb "blessed," this time referring not to a specific existing element but to time itself. And then, from the womb of the blessing of time is born the last and supreme of the Creation verbs. God not only blessed Shabbat, but also made it holy, awarded it with sacredness. The blessing is a given, marking the value of life and the commandment to choose life. It is a supreme layer of the partnership between humanity and God. It calls upon us to confirm in our life that which God has confirmed. Holiness, *k'dushah*, is of a different quality. If blessing is rooted in the deed that marks the end of Creation, holiness is anchored in the rest, pointing toward the future. We are commanded "to make" Shabbat (Exodus 31:16) in the same manner by which God made it: resting and sanctifying the day. The blessing constitutes the human scientific and moral autonomy; the sanctity exceeds this autonomy, reaches out beyond all that we may reach. Powered by God's blessing, we are responsible to determine the meaning and value of the weekdays of our life; when entering the sanctified Shabbat we submit ourselves to a superior layer, beyond and above our deeds, a layer that might award our decisions and deeds with a transcendental "Amen." This is the layer that points out to the mystery of God's presence in the Creation, that places us in an "I-You" relationship with God. Without the weekdays we cannot live; we cannot struggle to realize the image of God carried by our being. Without Shabbat our life would be no life; the universe would not be God's world, and our soul would not be "the candle of God" (Proverbs 20:27).

3

"In the Beginning" of BT *B'rachot*

Another Creation

ALYSSA M. GRAY, JD, PHD

God then called the light Day, and called the darkness Night, and there was evening and there was morning, the first day.

Genesis 1:5

B'reishit

The medieval sage Rashi (1040–1105) famously (at least among those interested in Jewish Bible interpretation) notes the grammatical difficulty of the first word of the Torah, *b'reishit*, and proposes a reading that makes its way into the Jewish Publication Society (JPS) translation: "When God began to create heaven and earth. . . ." The King James Version of the Bible (KJV) renders Genesis 1:1 as the majestic "In the beginning God created the heaven and the earth," which implies (as Nahum Sarna has pointed out) that *b'reishit* marks the beginning of time and consequently that God is beyond time and space.[1]

Sarna's understanding of KJV is consistent with the comment of the Italian Jewish commentator Ovadyah S'forno (ca. 1475–1550), who writes that *b'reishit* means "at the beginning of time . . . for there was no time preceding it." To S'forno and the later KJV, Genesis 1:1 and the entire Creation account that follows it mark a radical rupture in the life of God. God and God alone is all that connects what follows "in the beginning" and the timeless unknown that preceded it. Just as the Bible portrays God's rupture of the fabric of reality to allow for God's creation of time and space in Genesis, the seminal, classical Rabbinic works the Mishnah (redacted ca. 200 CE) and the Babylonian Talmud (BT; known as the *Bavli*, redacted ca. 600–700 CE) implicitly portray God as having ruptured the fabric of their own reality in the destruction of the Second Temple in 70 CE. The Rabbinic project itself is implicitly constructed as another creation; unlike Genesis 1:1 this later act of creation is entirely in human hands and is an effort to heal the wounds of the loss caused by its precipitating rupture—not only human wounds, but also divine wounds.

Mei-eimatai

However read and interpreted, Genesis 1:1 is a declarative statement. By contrast, *Mishnah B'rachot* 1:1, the jumping-off point for both the Mishnah and the *Bavli*, opens with a question: "From when [*mei-eimatai*] is the evening *Sh'ma* recited?" The Mishnah's first answer to "From when?" is opaque: "From the time the priests enter to eat of their *t'rumah* until the end of the first watch." This response poignantly evokes a reconstructed Rabbinic memory of a quotidian aspect of priestly routine in the Jerusalem Temple, lost for a second and final time in the destruction of 70 CE. The priests of the Temple would enter to eat their meal of *t'rumah* (the mandated agricultural gift to them from the people Israel) at the end of the day.[2]

The Mishnah—and indeed, both Talmuds—thus opens like the Bible with a tacit acknowledgment of rupture, but unlike the Bible,

it also opens on a tacit yet unmistakable note of loss. For the Rabbis who composed these works, the image of priests entering to eat
t'rumah toward evening, at the conclusion of their ritual purification,
is an anachronism. The *Bavli* takes up the interpretation of *Mishnah
B'rachot* 1:1 in its opening pages and connects this mishnah to Genesis
1:5 ("and there was evening and there was morning") through shared
reference to evening preceding morning. Just as Genesis 1:5 is a moment in the healing of a rupture in God's life through the creation of
space and time, the *Bavli*'s use of it to interpret *Mishnah B'rachot* 1:1 is
a moment in the Rabbinic healing of a rupture in the life of God and
the people Israel through the Rabbis' creation of a new way of Torah
and a distinctively Rabbinic approach to daily time.

Erev, Arvit/Arvin, and Genesis 1:5

Like Genesis 1:5, *Mishnah B'rachot* 1:1 also refers to "evening" (*arvit*
or *arvin* in different versions). The *Bavli* sensibly asks why the mishnah opens with the evening rather than the morning *Sh'ma* (Rabbinic
law having already established that the *Sh'ma* is to be recited daily as
part of the morning and evening prayer services) and offers two possible scriptural supports (BT *B'rachot* 2a). The first, introduced by "the
Tanna is relying on a verse," is from Deuteronomy 6:7: "when you
lie down and when you get up." "Lie down" (evening) precedes "get
up." The second, introduced by "and if you like I can say that he [the
Tanna] learns from the creation of the world," is from Genesis 1:5:
"and there was evening [*erev*] and there was morning [*boker*]." The literary parallel is striking. The written Torah begins with the creation of
the world, and the first day of that creation concludes with a mention
of *erev* before *boker*. Here, in *Mishnah B'rachot* 1:1, the entire Rabbinic
compilation known as "the" Mishnah also begins with *erev*. The *Bavli*'s
commentary on this invites us to ponder Genesis 1:5 in relation to
Deuteronomy 6:7 and *Mishnah B'rachot* 1:1. Genesis 1:5's *erev* is thus
"Rabbinized," appropriated for use in the distinctively post-tannaitic

Rabbinic project of understanding *Mishnah B'rachot* 1:1. But there is more. The written Torah's *erev . . . boker* marks the completion of a day, a stage, of Creation. The *Bavli*'s use on *B'rachot* 2a of Genesis 1:5 as a justification of why the Mishnah places the evening *Sh'ma* before the morning *Sh'ma* is not an end but a beginning, the beginning of a longer analysis of the evening *Sh'ma* (BT *B'rachot* 2a–9b), the morning *Sh'ma*, and prayer, and indeed, it is the beginning of the entire *Bavli*. The *Bavli* uses the shared focus on *erev* in Genesis 1:5 and its own opening commentary on *Mishnah B'rachot* 1:1 to help introduce its particular Rabbinic project—a new act of creation, this time a human creation.

The *Sh'ma* and the Rebuilding and Destruction of Jerusalem—and God

The *Bavli* wrestles with the opacity of *Mishnah B'rachot* 1:1, "from the time the priests enter to eat of their *t'rumah*." Only one detail need concern us: the *Bavli*'s quotation (following the *Tosefta*) of the biblical book of Nehemiah 4:15–16 as part of its strategy for fixing the meaning of the Mishnah's "time the priests enter" (BT *B'rachot* 2b). Nehemiah 4 recounts how, during the return of the Israelites from Babylonia in 539 BCE, the non-Israelite inhabitants of the area around Jerusalem were determined to use any means, including violence, to stop Jewish efforts to rebuild the walls of Jerusalem; the builders had to be armed and prepared to fight. Verse 15 states that "half were holding lances, from the break of day until the stars appeared," while verse 16 states that "we may use the night to stand guard and the day to work." The *Bavli* chooses verses about the rebuilding of Jerusalem after its destruction by the Babylonians in 586 BCE—another, earlier "beginning"— in order to fix the earliest time the evening *Sh'ma* may be recited. On the surface the verses may help in fixing that time, but the choice of verses reveals a deeper, richer analogy between the rebuilding of Jerusalem and the evening *Sh'ma*. Rabbis and other Jews of late antiquity might not be rebuilding Jerusalem and a third Temple, but they are rebuilding nevertheless: recasting the Second Temple ideological and cultural complex of God, Temple, and Torah into the Rabbinic way of God, prayer, and Torah through the ritualization of evening *Sh'ma* recitation and the Rabbinic discourse around it.

God is notably missing from the rebuilding efforts of both Nehemiah 4 and BT *B'rachot* 2b, but appears on 3a as part of the interpretation of the term "watch" in *Mishnah B'rachot* 1:1. The *Bavli* there quotes an allegedly earlier passage in which Rabbi Eliezer says that at each of the three watches of the night God sits and roars like a lion, citing Jeremiah 25:30 (which does not mention lions). Jeremiah 25 is a prophecy of Jerusalem's destruction; the immediately preceding verse 29 specifically says that God is going to bring evil on the city. Significantly, verse 30 mentions that God roars from "on high" and "makes His voice heard from His holy dwelling" about "His [earthly] abode," which the *Bavli* understands as an allusion to the earthly Temple.

Rabbi Eliezer is likely thinking about the more recent Roman destruction of the Temple in 70 CE, not the earlier destruction of Jeremiah's time at the hands of the Babylonians. The *Bavli* thus boldly (albeit quietly) associates God with the Roman destruction of Jerusalem in 70. For those keeping score, the *Bavli* has thus far (*B'rachot* 2a–3a) put together texts and imagery that associate destruction with God (Jeremiah 25) and rebuilding (Nehemiah 4 and the discourse about the *Sh'ma*) with humans. The *Bavli*'s linkage of God with destruction takes a sharper and darker turn further down the page on 3a, where Rav Yitzchak bar Sh'muel quotes Rav's tradition about exactly what words God roars at each of those three watches of the night:

Woe to the children on account of whose sins
I destroyed My house and burned My sanctuary
And exiled them among the nations of the world.[3]

Rav represents God as speaking in God's own voice. These are the first words that God utters in the *Bavli*, and they are far from the stately majesty of God's first words in Genesis 1:3, "Let there be light." The *Bavli*'s God is in mourning here, sorrowing for God's exiled children and bemoaning God's own destruction of the Temple. On BT *B'rachot* 3a, the *Bavli* makes God Godself take the step of associating God with destruction.

The *Bavli* sharpens this tradition even more toward the bottom of *B'rachot* 3a. Rabbi Yosei encounters Elijah the prophet in one of the "ruins of Jerusalem." *Inter alia* Elijah asks Rabbi Yosei what he heard in the ruin, and the rabbi responds that he heard what sounded like the sigh of a dove, proclaiming the words of the lament attributed to Rav earlier on the page. Elijah emphasizes that this woeful proclamation is made three times every day, and he adds a critical new datum: when the people Israel enter synagogues and study houses and make the liturgical response "May God's great name be blessed," God nods God's head and says:

Happy is the king whom they so praise in
His house. Woe to the father who exiled His
children, and woe to the children exiled
from their father's table.[4]

According to Elijah, God refers to Jewish places of prayer, such as synagogues and study houses, as "His house," hence, as the equivalent of the destroyed Jerusalem Temple. And in Elijah's version of God's lament—unlike the version of Rav and Rabbi Yosei—God appears almost (dare we say?) regretful over the destruction of the Temple in 70 and the resulting exile ("Woe to the father . . ."). Moreover, Elijah's version of God's lament adds the critical point that the people Israel provide comfort to God through their liturgical response "May His great name be blessed." In sum, God is associated by the *Bavli* and by

Godself with destruction and even possibly regret over that destruction; by contrast, the *Bavli* associates the people Israel with healing (God!) through prayer and earlier with the rebuilding of the earthly Jerusalem (via Nehemiah 4:15–16).

As in Genesis 1:1, BT *B'rachot*'s God is a God who has experienced a rupture in God's divine life. But Genesis 1:1's divine rupture is the creation of all that is, including time. BT *B'rachot*'s divine rupture is destruction, loss, and regret. In Genesis, God is the creator. In BT *B'rachot*, the people Israel are associated with creation and God with destruction. In Genesis 1, God is self-contained and self-sufficient. In BT *B'rachot*, God needs the comfort provided by Jews' blessing God's name in their synagogues and study houses.

The Rabbinic Redemption of Darkness

On BT *B'rachot* 3a, God roars in anguish during the hours of darkness, a stark contrast to God's serene separation of light from darkness, naming of darkness as "night," and observation that all this was "good" (Genesis 1:4–5). BT *B'rachot* redeems darkness through the image of King David awakening every night at midnight to study Torah when the north wind would make music from the harp hung above his bed. Other traditions have him composing psalms during the night (BT *B'rachot* 3b). Presumably God's nightly roaring at the three watches of the night overlaps with David's psalm composition and Torah study; again, God is associated with lament over destruction, while at those very moments of divine anguish the proto-Rabbinic David is associated with creation, through his engagement in Torah. Elsewhere (BT *Chagigah* 12b), Reish Lakish teaches that the one who studies Torah at night will be blanketed by divine protection during the day. The Rabbis and ultimately the *Bavli* redeem the darkness by sanctifying the study and creation of Rabbinic Torah by night.

In sum, the *Bavli* uses *Mishnah B'rachot* 1:1 to portray the Rabbinic project as a multifaceted human creation that heals the divine and human wounds caused by the loss of the Temple. In the shadow of the memory of the Temple, the *Bavli* uses Genesis 1:5 to link the divine Creation to its own distinct, wholly human, and providential creation. In place of Genesis's powerful poetry focused solely on God, the Rabbis place their dialectic, their weavings-together of sources, their powerful poetry of the human intellect and spiritual striving as the new, transformative, and wholly human act of creation.

Notes

1. Nahum M. Sarna, *The JPS Torah Commentary: Genesis* (Philadelphia: Jewish Publication Society, 1989), 5.

2. BT *B'rachot* 2a–b suggests that the priests in question are those who had become ritually impure, had immersed to remove their impurity, and had to wait until nightfall before being eligible to eat *t'rumah*. This understanding is presented as the plain meaning of the mishnah by Rashi (s.v. *mei-eimatai*) and later Mishnah commentators.

3. My translation.

4. My translation.

4

Creating Worlds
One Day at a Time

CANTOR AMANDA KLEINMAN

And there was evening and there was morning, the first day.

Genesis 1:5

There is an old Jewish joke about a man who, while admiring the beauty of nature, feels especially close to God:

> "God," the man asks, "what are a million years to You?"
> "A million years are but a second to me," God replies.
> "And, God," the man continues, "what are a million dollars to You?"
> "A million dollars are but a penny to Me," God answers.
> "So, God," the man asks, "can I have a million dollars?"
> "In a second."

This joke, perhaps loosely based on a line of Psalm 90, "For a thousand years are, in Your eyes, like yesterday when it has passed, and like a watch in the night" (Psalm 90:4), hints at ambiguities in the Jewish conception of time. The Bible, in particular, is full of references to time that are difficult to take literally: early biblical figures routinely live for centuries, Sarah gives birth to Isaac after the age of ninety, and our Rabbis tell us that according to the Torah, our world is not yet six thousand years old. It is probably the biblical concept of a day, however, that has been most heavily scrutinized. The biblical day, particularly as the measure of time in the Creation story, has been debated for millennia. The twenty-four-hour day as we understand it, through the lens of science, becomes problematic when applied to the biblical narrative of Creation. If the changing location of the sun in relationship to the earth defines our concept of a day, how could three days of Creation be recorded before God brought the sun, moon, and stars into existence on the fourth day?[1] And if, according to scientific understanding, human beings are the product of billions of years of evolution by natural selection, how are we to believe the Bible's account that God created human beings after only six days? Rabbi Shlomo Yitzchaki (Rashi), the esteemed eleventh-century Jewish commentator, sums it up: the Torah's account of the creation of the world "says nothing other than: explain it to me!"[2] Rashi is right: the Bible's Creation story, while written so as to provide an understanding of the origin of our world, ironically leaves the present-day reader with more questions than answers.

Many biblical commentators, scholars, and scientists have attempted to reconcile the biblical day with the voluminous evidence that suggests that the creation of our world cannot be measured in days, but rather eons. While some commentators favor a literal reading of time as presented in the early chapters of Genesis, others reject completely the biblical presentation of time. In between these two extremes, however, we find a wide range of nuanced opinions, each of them authentically representative of the Jewish tradition. Most of the Rabbis and Jewish exegetes believe that the day presented in the Creation narrative, and throughout the Torah, does not necessarily correspond with the twenty-four-hour day as we understand it;

instead, they view the Creation narrative as a series of creative acts of indeterminate duration culminating in a period of rest for God that the Jewish people emulates in the observance of Shabbat.

On the surface, the first day of Creation as presented in the text, on which God separates light from darkness and calls a "day" into being, seems to function so as to establish a concrete period of time; perhaps, as our Rabbis suggest, the day is not meant to represent only a concrete period of time comprising a certain number of hours, but also a discrete period of time representing the potential for a creative act. It is striking that the Torah's first use of the word *yom* (day) is not in reference to the measure of time it denotes throughout the rest of the Torah. After God creates light and separates the light from darkness, we read, "God then called the light Day, and called the darkness Night" (Genesis 1:5). In its first use, the word "day" becomes synonymous with "light." Day, then, becomes associated with God's first creative act, calling into being the natural element that brings the initial semblance of order into an otherwise dark and shapeless world. It seems contradictory, or at least confusing, to define a "day" as both the light alone and as the entire span of time encompassing a single rotation of the earth. Considered instead as the name given to the progression from darkness to light, *yom* comes to represent not only the span of time measured in a day, but the creative process that transition entails. It is appropriate, then, that the Jewish day begins with evening and continues with morning; each day becomes a new opportunity for creation, for bringing light into a world of darkness. This daily creative process is reflected in the *Yotzeir Or*, the prayer praising God as Creator of light and darkness: "In Your goodness You daily renew the act of Creation."

The Torah makes clear to us that our lives are measured and given meaning by their shortest cycles of time, that our small daily actions and decisions can profoundly affect our world. Each day carries tremendous weight, and each day offers us an opportunity to emulate

God by bringing the light of our own divinely inspired creativity into the world.

It is fitting, then, that the day becomes the Torah's core measure of time, the constant reminder of the creative potential each of us carries within, no less than the heroes and heroines of the Hebrew Bible. Their journeys are most often measured in days, rather than in weeks, months, or years: Laban takes a three-day journey away from Jacob (Genesis 30:36); the Israelite spies spend forty days scouting the land of Canaan (Numbers 13:25); following their escape from Egypt, the Israelites journey for three days into the wilderness before complaining about the lack of water (Exodus 15:22). Even the Israelites' forty years of wandering in the desert (to which they are condemned by God for their reluctance to enter the Land of Israel) correspond to the number of days the spies spent scouting the land before rejecting it: "You shall bear your punishment for forty years, corresponding to the number of days—forty days—that you scouted the land: a year for each day" (Numbers 14:34). For each of the forty days, the spies had a new opportunity to develop a different perspective on the Land of Israel; the punishment of the Israelites, therefore, reflects each day of missed opportunity.

The Bible also measures the course of human life in days—in striking contrast to our usual frame of reference, years. We are commanded to honor our parents "that [we] may long endure on the land" (Exodus 20:12). Another way to translate the Hebrew would be "so that [our] days may be lengthened." In Exodus, Moses reminds the Israelites that through loving God and heeding God's commandments, "[they] shall have life and shall long endure" (Deuteronomy 30:20). God here is referred to as "your life and the length of your days." The final line of Psalm 23, the Jewish tradition's famous words of comfort, reads, "Surely goodness and mercy will follow me all the days of my life," and concludes, "and I will dwell in the House of the Eternal for many days" (Psalm 23:6). It is striking in all of these instances that the Bible refers to extended periods of time as "days" when they might be best described in years.

So too are the lifespans of biblical figures often recorded not only in years, but also in days: for instance, at the time of Abraham's death, we read, "These are the days of the years of Abraham's life" (Genesis 25:7). The authors of the Torah wanted us to view the lives of our ancestors as comprised of days. It's not an arbitrary literary choice: their method of accounting is intended to suggest to us our potential for renewal with each new day of life. Indeed, many of our biblical figures achieve that creative potential late in life. Consider Abraham and Sarah, who create new life in Isaac only after they "were well advanced in years (literally: progressed in days)" (Genesis 18:11).[3]

Thomas Cahill, the author of *The Gift of the Jews*, suggests, apropos of our theme, that the great innovation of the Jewish people was to break free of a widespread ancient understanding of time that Cahill calls "profoundly cyclical." The cyclical understanding of time subjugated humanity to the cycles of nature, preventing us from being able to exercise any real creative power, to make any sort of impact on our world.[4] And our lives are, in fact, profoundly cyclical, comprising tens of thousands of days, which, despite changing seasons and circumstances, can often seem indistinguishable from one another. Days become subjugated to routines of work, family, and school; years repeat the same cycle of seasons and repeating observances. Our Bible recognizes this cyclical function of time: "What has been is what will be, and what has been done is what will be done, and there is nothing new under the sun" (Ecclesiastes 1:9). Our cycle of holidays acknowledges that "Jewish time" is, at least in part, cyclical. But the Jewish tradition *also* acknowledges time's linear direction, time's *progress*, moving us forward, from point A to point B, so to speak. While day follows day in endless succession, Judaism teaches that no two days need be the same.

The very first verses of the Torah remind us that we have the power to influence the never-ending cycle of time with each setting and rising of the sun. The day, that most basic measure of time, seemingly dictated by nothing more than the earth's rotation with respect to the sun, actually becomes something upon which human beings can make their mark. Just as God uses each day as an opportunity to create, so too do we, human beings made in God's image, seize a regular opportunity to create and to influence the direction of our world.

The end of the Book of Lamentations, recited throughout the High Holy Days and each time we return the Torah to the ark, perfectly captures the tension between the cyclical and the linear, the repeating and the innovative: "Renew our days as in the past" (Lamentations 5:21). The sun rises and the sun sets, but each day is a brand-new world unto itself.

Notes

1. James L. Kugel, *How to Read the Bible* (New York: Free Press, 2007), 49–50.

2. Rashi on Genesis 1:1.

3. With thanks to Rabbi Jonathan Blake for pointing out this example and helping to structure this section.

4. Thomas Cahill, *The Gifts of the Jews: How a Tribe of Desert Nomads Changed the Way Everyone Thinks and Feels* (New York: Nan A. Talese, 1998).

5

The Why and the How of Creation

Harmonizing Genesis and the Big Bang

RABBI GEOFFREY A. MITELMAN

And God said, "Let there be light!"—and there was light. And when God saw how good the light was, God divided the light from the darkness; God then called the light Day, and called the darkness Night, and there was evening and there was morning, [the] first day.

Genesis 1:3–5

I'm going to let you in on a secret: the Bible is not a scientific textbook.

Now, this might seem obvious on an intellectual level, but when people read the opening chapters of Genesis, emotions come into play. Some people know and embrace this version of Creation. Others reject this version of events, casting it aside as make-believe. Some even try to read Genesis in a way that matches with the latest science. And still others create silos where science and religion separate into two different spheres.

We grapple with the relationship between Genesis and the big bang, a relationship that at its core takes on the question "Where did we come from?" As such, we face a challenge: the Bible says one thing, and science says another. So how do we make sense of Genesis 1 in light of big bang cosmology?

In order to do that, we need to start with a few basic beliefs Reform Judaism holds about the process of Creation. First, we believe that the best (or perhaps the only) way we can accept factual claims about the world is through science. Second, we believe that the Bible was written by human beings in a particular context and time, with a certain level of scientific knowledge, and that its literal meaning needs to be translated and interpreted for today. And third, even if the Bible is not to be taken literally, it is still to be taken seriously. So starting with those assumptions, we can examine some different ways to talk about the relationship between Genesis and the big bang.

My organization, Sinai and Synapses, presents four different ways we can talk about science and religion in general. The first three are the most common ways Jews try to understand the relationship between the big bang and Genesis. All three, however, are problematic, often because the understandings of both science and religion are too simplistic. Before we address how we can better understand both Genesis and the big bang, let's first take a look at the more problematic understandings of this relationship.

In Conflict

This first model is the one that gets the most attention in the media and the blogosphere. Here, either science or religion is correct, and if we accept one, then we have to reject the other.

While those in the fundamentalist Christian community who buy into this model tend to choose religion over science, in the Reform Jewish community, these "conflicted Jews" will choose science over religion. The common refrain from those in this camp is that the stories in Genesis are purely fictional—the big bang is the way we can understand the universe, and we don't even need to engage in what the Torah teaches. Indeed, when I was a congregational rabbi, I would constantly hear the refrain "I don't believe in God. I believe in science."

But the problem here is that this model creates a false dichotomy and a deep antagonism between science and religion. And since most Reform Jews view themselves as rational and scientifically minded, this model creates a caricature of Judaism, and so it needs to be rejected. After all, if Genesis is just a bunch of Bronze Age myths that don't really tell us about the world as it is, then why should we care?

So while the conflict model embraces the science, it doesn't help us engage the Torah in a sophisticated way.

In Concert

This model is, in many ways, the flip side of the conflict model. Here, the goal is to read Genesis in a way that helps us reconcile Genesis and the big bang. The common refrain for this model is "We don't know how long a day is. The Psalmist even says, 'A thousand years in [God's] sight are like a day that has just gone by' [Psalm 90:4], so I can read the Torah in a way that doesn't violate my scientific sensibilities."

On one level, this model might seem to work, as it seems to allow us to embrace both science and Judaism. But it also requires a lot of mental gymnastics—it's trying to fit a square peg into a round hole. This model is an attempt to fit science into the biblical narrative, but the problem is that Bible isn't meant to be read scientifically. Indeed, rather than believing that the Bible was one human attempt to understand origins of the world, this model assumes that the Bible is literally true and so then tries to squeeze science into the biblical narrative.

While the concert model allows people to accept the Bible, it still leads people to read the Bible too simplistically.

In Contrast

Here, science and religion live in separate spheres. In this model, the refrain is "I use science as my source of truth and knowledge, and I use religion as my source of ethics, meaning, and purpose. They don't need to intermingle."

This model, in my experience, is the most common one in the Jewish community. It allows people to have both science and Judaism but doesn't lead to the mental gymnastics the concert model requires. And on a day-to-day level, most people can live happily without science and religion interacting.

But when Reform Jews do start to think about the big questions in life—such as "Where did we come from?"—religion and science begin to rub up against one another. We don't want to reject the Torah, but we don't want to read the Torah literally, either. So when we start to ask, "Where did we come from?" we face the problem that the big bang and Genesis offer two different answers to big questions, and so we end up bifurcating our sense of identity, keeping our science and our Judaism far away from each other.

In Contact

So how do we reconcile Genesis and the big bang? Well, we know that we shouldn't read Genesis for factual information about the origins of the universe. But a better understanding of the science can help us rethink why we still want to read Genesis.

There's often a misconception about the big bang. It doesn't actually tell us how the universe started. Instead, it tells us what happened immediately *after* the universe started. As astrophysicist Adam Frank describes it:

> Most folks think of the Big Bang as a description of the Universe's creation but that was never really the case. The Big Bang was always a theory of after creation. It describes what

happens after the Bang and it does so in exquisite detail. In Big Bang theory you begin with a super-hot, super-dense fireball that contains all Space, all Time, all Matter and all Energy. There is no "outside" the fireball because Big Bang Theory takes all those "alls" seriously. The super-hot super-dense fireball is all existence. Big Bang theorists just assume its existence and then they just let it go.[1]

In many ways, the way we understand the big bang theory is similar to the classic midrash that asks why the Torah starts with a *bet* and not an *alef*. After all, *alef* is the first letter and starts everything, so why does *b'reishit* start with a *bet*?

The answer, Rabbi Levi says, is that "the *bet* is closed on three sides and open only on the fourth. This teaches that one should not question what is above or what is below, or what came before, but only what transpired from the day of the world's creation forward" (*B'reishit Rabbah* 1:10). While the Rabbis might have viewed these as prescriptions, for us they might be descriptions—the only thing we can currently understand is what has happened *after* all time, space, matter, and energy began.

In his book *Judaism, Physics and God: Searching for Sacred Metaphors in a Post-Einstein World*, Rabbi David Nelson talks about how the big bang has offered him new metaphors for his view of Judaism. Since, as Reform Jews, we shouldn't read the Bible as a literal, factual, scientific account, we should instead see how scientific metaphors for God can be *useful*.

As one example, we can read the *Sh'ma* in the light of the big bang. Usually, the *Sh'ma*, proclaiming that God is one, is taken to mean that there is only one God, rather than two, three, or more. But as Nelson says:

The oneness of God can now be understood as indicating that everything, the totality of being itself, is, in a sense, God.

"God is one" may now be taken to mean that "God" is a term that signifies the unity of all existence in a single point of time, space, and nascent matter. The very term *singularity*, which has become a commonplace of contemporary physics, might be seen as a modern Jewish metaphor for the traditional Jewish idea of oneness. Can we imagine a new translation of the *Shema* in a contemporary prayer book generated by the metaphors of science? "Listen, O Israel, *Adonai* is our God, *Adonai*, the Singularity!"[2]

Understanding the big bang gives us a new way to read the most important prayer in Judaism. The big bang helps us appreciate our deep unity, our common humanity, and even our connection with the universe as a whole.

And just as we can read the *Sh'ma* differently in light of big bang cosmology, we can read Genesis differently, too. Here are three examples:

1. The key phrase in the Genesis story is one that the big bang can't address: "and God saw that it was good." Leaving aside God for the moment, we can all agree that while science can tell us what *is*, only human intentionality and action can determine what *should be*. If the universe is "good," then we have certain responsibilities to safeguard and protect Creation.

2. Along those lines, the second law of thermodynamics tells us that from the big bang until today, the natural tendency of the universe is to go from order to chaos. The only way to move from chaos to order is to direct energy toward that task. And that's exactly what we see in Genesis 1, where each day ends with *vay'hi erev, vay'hi voker*, "there was evening, there was morning." The word *erev* also connotes "randomness" (as in *eirev rav*, "a mixed multitude" (Exodus 12:38), and *boker* connotes "order"

(related to the word for "to distinguish," *levaker*). In Genesis, then, God reverses the natural entropic order of the universe, implying that God intentionally moves from chaos to order. And so if we view ourselves as being "in the image of God," then our job, too, is to overcome the universe's natural inclination to move toward chaos and instead strive to create more order.

3. One thing that science has shown us is that (in Carl Sagan's words) "we are all star stuff." Everything that exists in the universe—you, me, the book you are holding in your hand—is the result of the big bang. And so that means that we all come from the same source. In the end, we are all one.

Ultimately, we may never be able to scientifically answer the question of how the universe began. We keep getting closer and closer, now coming to understand the first billionths of the universe, but we still can't get to $t = 0$, the very instant the universe began.

Instead, we can read Genesis as a way to remind us of our common unity, as a way to create more order in a chaotic world, and to ensure that the actions we take are "good." While the big bang can help us better understand ourselves and our world, it is upon us to use that understanding, in conjunction with Genesis 1, as a way to create more peace, justice, and goodness in our lives.

Notes

1. Adam Frank, "Beyond Genesis: Is Science Past the Big Bang Already?," *Huffington Post*, January 5, 2012, http://www.huffingtonpost.com/adam-frank/before-the-big-bang_b_1179837.html.

2. David W. Nelson, *Judaism, Physics and God: Searching for Metaphors in a Post-Einstein World* (Woodstock, VT: Jewish Lights, 2005), 19.

6

Light and Darkness

The Human Condition
in Buddhist and Muslim Texts

RABBI JOSHUA M. Z. STANTON

And God said, "Let there be light!"—and there was light. And
when God saw how good the light was, God divided the light
from the darkness; God then called the light Day, and called
the darkness Night, and there was evening and there was
morning, [the] first day.

Genesis 1:3–5

So much is implied in these succinct sentences from the Torah that
we often overlook their significance. We are as though blinded by the
concept of light and its myriad uses within our commentaries. Jewish
scholars have for millennia reflected upon and debated these verses,
each adding to the interpretive literature. Yet in creating continuous
chords of dialogue across centuries and continents, our scholars often took on the assumptions of those who came before. Sometimes it
proves most helpful to venture beyond the bounds of our own com-

mentaries, if for no other reason than to gain a new vantage point and understand the assumptions of those who came before us. Why did God need to create light? Why was it good? If light is good, why should nighttime exist at all? How does the concept of light fit within the broader motifs of the Creation story?

This essay will focus primarily on Muslim and Buddhist understandings of light and darkness, corresponding to the first day of Creation in the Torah. I approach these sources with the humility of a person who is increasingly versed in sacred Jewish texts, but only aspiring to understand those held dear by other traditions. Even from this limited base of knowledge, I sense that there is much to be gleaned, particularly about the more universal use of light (or the lack thereof) as a symbol of humanity and its state of being.

Buddhist Discussion of Light

One of the more beautiful—and challenging—aspects of Buddhist thought is that it calls into question the notion that time is linear. If the universe is eternal, there cannot possibly be a beginning, much less a notion of Creation itself. Birth and death are relative and recurrent, while the universe is enduring. This difference merits study in its own right, evoking long-pondered questions about whether Creation really took place *ex nihilo* (from nothing) or with God as a divine shaper of matter that existed eternally.[1] From this perspective, the darkness and light in the Torah's first day of Creation can be seen as temporary states of being within a universe that never truly ends.

Even looking beyond questions about the nature of time, Buddhist texts have a great deal to teach about the phenomenon of light and the link between physical light and the human state of enlightenment. Mahayana Buddhism is one of the two major schools of Buddhist thought and the one most commonly practiced around the world. Its focus is on personal enlightenment, using the Buddha as the quintessential and eternal source of wisdom that transcends the physical realm and enables people to break a cycle of rebirth and suffering. As the *Avatam-saka Sutra* (a major set of Mahayana teachings) notes:

> The realm of the Buddhas is inconceivable;
> No sentient being can fathom it. . . .
> The Buddha constantly emits great beams of light;
> In each beam of light are innumerable Buddhas. . . .
> The Buddha body is pure and always tranquil;
> The radiance of its light extends throughout the world; . . .
> The Buddha's freedom cannot be measured—
> It fills the cosmos and all space. . . .
> The Buddha body responds to all—none do not see it.
> With various techniques it teaches the living,
> Sound like thunder, showering the rain of truth. . . .
> All virtuous activities in the world
> Come from the Buddha's light.[2]

In working to understand this text, one must first separate the notion of the Buddha as a historical figure from the Buddha as a figure of philosophical and even metaphysical significance. The Buddha can be seen as a symbol of complete enlightenment, connected to the unending universe and able to transcend time, rebirth, and the very human reality of suffering. The Buddha is light in a temporal world that might otherwise have darkness, emblematic of wisdom that radiates like a star, whose followers seek to become illuminated by its rays.

Insofar as this text (among many other teachings within Mahayana Buddhism) relates to the Torah's story of Creation, it raises fundamental questions: Is the story of Creation actually about growing human awareness of the world? Is the Torah's story of the first day less about the physical creation of light itself than of growing human awareness of the natural patterns of darkness and light with each passing day?

Could Creation on the first day be about the earliest stages of human enlightenment rather than light itself? These enduring questions cause us to look past light and to wonder anew about the degree to which humans have grown in self-awareness and understanding of the wider world.

Muslim Discussion of Light

For those who have not yet read the Quran (or even opened its pages), its text is composed of poetic verse, whose beauty in Arabic is reputed to be singular. The nuance of language is lost upon those of us who are reading it in translation. Much is also lost on those who do not have a thorough understanding of the context in which it was written or through which it has been transmitted. Even with these clear limitations to my grasp of it in mind, its poetic use of light and darkness merits our attention.

In a thorough analysis of the topic, Moroccan scholar Khalid Berrada explores the use of light and darkness as key metaphors in the Quran, suggesting that "light and darkness are two concrete domains" that help human beings gain clearer understandings of "Allah . . . the prophet [Muhammad] . . . the holy Quran . . . and many positive qualities."[3] Berrada then traces uses of these metaphors from the Quran into Sufi texts (from schools of mystical thought and practice), as well as common expressions in Moroccan Arabic.

Citing a particular chapter and verse of the Quran (Sura 24:35), he translates:

Allah is the Light
Of the heavens and the earth.
The parable of His Light
Is as if there were a Niche
And within it a Lamp:
The Lamp enclosed in Glass:

The glass as it were
A brilliant star:
Lit from a blessed Tree,
An Olive, neither of the East
Nor of the West,
Whose Oil is well-nigh
Luminous,
Though fire scarce touched it:
Light upon Light!
Allah doth guide
Whom He Will
To His Light.[4]

Muslim scholars parse these verses in different ways.[5] Some focus on the first portion, understanding God to be the source of all physical light. Others focus on the second portion, understanding God to be the source of all human enlightenment. In both metaphors, darkness would come about only from the absence of God, the source of all light—spiritual or physical. Human beings are helpless without God's presence and unable to navigate a darkened world.

Of significance to those studying the Torah, this verse from the Quran presupposes a human connection to God. Light might have existed long beforehand, but a key purpose of light now resides within God's relationship to human beings. Light for its own sake is an intrinsic good, but its purpose can be most fully realized in the presence of humanity.

Another stark aspect to the verse is the acknowledgment that not all humans will be enlightened. God chooses among them, bringing some closer to truth—even as others languish in its absence. Perhaps intended as an allusion to the challenges Muhammad faced in the early days of the Muslim community he established, light is construed as a divine privilege, not simply a reality for all people.

Conclusion

Even a cursory study of Buddhist and Muslim texts indicates that the metaphor of "light" might have more universal significance. These two traditions, originating far from each other and presenting entirely different worldviews, both connect light to goodness and wisdom—whether associated with a concept with God or the ultimate in human potential (or both). It is perhaps unsurprising that "light" and "enlightenment" would be so common, given the former's very physical association with human life: without light we cannot see, and the absence of sight can be frightening for us as people. Light can mean safety, security, hope, enlightenment, connection, or transcendence.

Even as Islam and Buddhism present disparate understandings of light, sacred texts within both traditions suggest that light is inherently good. The universally positive connotations with light can be applied to the Torah to great effect, notably because the idea of light is introduced in the Torah on the first day of Creation itself. God creates light on the first day, establishing the basis for connection with people, among people, and within all of Creation. Taken metaphorically, light enables us to rise above the human condition, replete with suffering, limited knowledge, and conflict. Light is thereby established as the point of reference from which all else stems in the story of Creation. It gives credibility to the idea that God is in fact good.

God creates light. Light is good. Therefore the Creator of that light is probably good, as well.

Notes

1. Moses Maimonides and other medieval Jewish scholars living in majority-Muslim realms grappled with similar questions. This came as classical Greek philosophical works were translated into Arabic, bringing into discourse *Timaeus* and other Platonic dialogues pertaining to the origins of the world and role of humanity—in addition to works by other cornerstone Greek scholars.

2. Paul Williams, *Mahayana Buddhism: The Doctrinal Foundations* (New York: Routledge, 2009), 134.

3. Khalid Berrada, "Metaphors of Light and Darkness in the Holy Quran: A Conceptual Approach" (2006), http://www.flbenmsik.ma/data/bassamat/basamat1/Berrada.pdf, 46.

4. Ibid., 49–50.

5. Ibid., 50–51.

Day Two

✦

SKY AND WATER

God then said, "Let there be an expanse in the midst of the waters, and let it divide water from water!" So God made the expanse, separating the waters beneath the expanse from the waters above the expanse—and so it was. God then called the expanse Sky, and there was evening and there was morning, a second day.

Genesis 1:6–8

7

The Second Day

A Pilot's Perspective

RABBI AARON PANKEN, PHD

God then said, "Let there be an expanse in the midst of the waters, and let it divide water from water!" So God made the expanse, separating the waters beneath the expanse from the waters above the expanse—and so it was. God then called the expanse Sky, and there was evening and there was morning, a second day.

Genesis 1:6–8

The second day of Creation supplies the world with a new device never seen before: an "expanse" that separates two domains, the heavens and the waters, from one another. This expanse, which God made to divide the heavens from the seas, once had a far more distinctive name. "Firmament" was the venerable word, from an old Latin term in the Vulgate (the authoritative fourth-century Latin translation of the Hebrew Bible), *firmamentum*, or "something made solid." As is often the case, it arose from a Greek translation (στερέωμα, *stereoma*, or "firmness") of the original Hebrew *rakia*, "something that is beaten or stamped out," like a sheet of metal an artisan has flattened into a thin layer to divide one area from another. Portrayed here as decidedly solid, later in Genesis (7:11 and 8:2), we learn that rain can descend from the heavens through windows or sluices, offering the fascinating possibility of trans-expanse communication: water could come down, and in certain very rare instances, people could go up.

In the Genesis Creation story, though, this impenetrable barrier separates the heavens (*shamayim*) from the waters (*mayim*). In Hebrew, both words are plural, and they sound remarkably similar—as if they are two connected sides of the same coin. Even in a time when the only thing produced by humans capable of rising up to heaven was smoke, their phonological connection speaks to the perception of close proximity between the domains of humanity and Divinity. And yet, at the same time, the Creation story makes it clear that it is only God who can decide precisely who or what gains entry to the heavens above.

In the early days of postbiblical literature, the idea of human beings ascending to heaven to access hidden secrets was all the rage. In bizarre and fascinating writings known as ascent apocalypses, we read stories of certain special individuals who journey to a world beyond regular mortal access. While in heaven, they go on celestial tours and later return to earth with otherwise inaccessible skills, knowledge, information about the future, news of the end of days, and other special wisdom that they obtained during their journey. Enoch, Elijah, Moses, and just a few other characters were granted such supernal experiences, succeeding in their desire to gain divine knowledge in a way that even the subsequent mythical Prometheus would have envied.

As a rabbi and student of ancient texts *and* a pilot, I admit to feeling a deep connection to these ancient ascent stories. We moderns, who leap routinely heavenward in complex tubes of beaten metal with sophisticated machinery, life-sustaining pressurization, and electronic wizardry unimaginable to the premodern mind, are often pretty blasé about what it takes to leave the earth's surface, climb a mile into thin air, and land a thousand miles distant. In fact, we all too often fall asleep or focus on the lack of legroom and the stultifying in-flight entertainment rather than on the utterly astounding act of aviation we are involved in committing. Considering it has only been about a century since our species figured out how to do this at all, each and every flight still represents a remarkable achievement, unfathomable until so recently, and that ought to fill us with awe and amazement, capturing our attention and respect. Certain aspects of flying fill me with awe every time, no matter how long or short the flight, whether I am in the cockpit or next to the bathroom in the last row of coach.

Focus, for a moment, on the wing of an aircraft, a small but critical expanse that separates the air above it from the air below it. Why does it actually enable that aircraft to fly? The answer is a complex combination of Bernoulli's principle, the relative pressures above and below the wing, and how the camber (shape) of the wing interacts with the particles of air that rush around it. Precise balances must be achieved between lift and weight, thrust and drag, for a craft to move controllably forward, up or down, left or right. Despite many attempts at eloquence, explaining this to even the most sincere questioner results in eyes glazing over long before understanding sets in. This is nothing new in aviation. In fact, it took Wilbur and Orville Wright, our first true aviators, years of watching birds fly and crafting experiments to validate their basic hypotheses before they finally captured the essence of controllable flight. They, of course, were building on hundreds of years of abject failures and partial successes that preceded them, and they, too, had their own record of incidents and accidents before finally soaring across the coastal North Carolina sky into history.

Just like God's act of Creation, the act of flight itself is remarkable. Even after more than a hundred years of doing it with some regularity, to ignore the colossal achievement of flight is to commit an infraction that Abraham Joshua Heschel warned of in his *God in Search of Man*: "Indifference to the sublime wonder of living is the root of sin."[1] The wonder of flying reminds me that there still exists a division between the heavens above and what is below. We can comprehend and control parts of our world, but certainly not all of it. We can fly, for a time, in the heavens, but in a highly limited, transitory, and imperfect manner supported by endless amounts of technology that could leave us vulnerable at any moment. Forgetting this is tantamount to indifference; remembering, an act of righteous faith.

Focus, for another moment, on the intense harmony that must be achieved by the unstintingly complex mechanism that is an aircraft, the balance between going above and returning to below. On the nice days, dozens of systems must align nearly perfectly to get you safely and comfortably from here to there: propulsion, navigation, communication, pressurization, landing gear, flaps, ailerons, elevator, seats, windows, lavatories, lighting, pilots, flight attendants, and so on. When flying over high terrain or on extended overwater operations or at very high altitudes, at night, in the clouds, onto short or more difficult runways, or through significant weather systems that contain precipitation or lightning, the complexity spirals ever higher, and the task of the pilot grows more challenging. Granted, most of the aircraft we fly today are quite capable of managing these challenges, but nothing that requires such a complex balance should be taken for granted, especially when the risks are so significant.

In the complexity of the mission lies another expanse we must cross: the expanse of reaching for expertise. Bringing oneself squarely up against a challenging task one learns to perform is a vital part of being fully human. Flying is but one of these sorts of tasks—it could just as easily be conducting an orchestra, deciphering a page of Talmud, painting a still life, building a congregation, racing a sailboat, performing surgery, designing a skyscraper, dancing a ballet, writing a novel, or building a computer—the truth is we become fully human when we commit our entire selves to something that is hard and worth doing, when we know our limits, and when we take pride in what we achieve.

The harmony that results from diverse parts that function together suggests a oneness to the universe that is both human and beyond humanity, existing both below the expanse and above it at the same time.

Focus, for a final moment, on one lesser known form of aviation: soaring, also known as gliding. Unpowered flight was actually the first way that humanity flew, long before the Wright brothers concocted a way to attach a lightweight engine to a flimsy airframe. In soaring, one mounts a sleek aircraft that has no mechanical system of propulsion. A powered aircraft tows you up from a grass runway to a few thousand feet over the airport, whereupon the glider pilot releases the towrope, and glider and pilot sail free to employ the air around them to remain aloft as long as possible. By circling in rising columns of thermal currents, utilizing the lift generated by wind crossing ridges, and riding large-scale waves of climbing air cascading off massive mountains, glider pilots manage some staggering achievements. World-record glider pilots have climbed (engineless, remember!) to altitudes higher than fifty thousand feet, traveled more than fourteen hundred miles from takeoff to landing, and remained in the air for more than fifty-six hours straight.

As a glider pilot substantially below world-record level, I have personally circled in rising columns of air with families of hawks, climbed over ten thousand feet in just a few minutes in strong thermal lift, and remained aloft for hours traveling miles and miles powered only by the air. Such flights have opened my eyes to the wonders of our atmosphere in ways that I never learned in twenty years of powered flight and helped me recommit to addressing the world in a way that does not harm it, but embraces it. To be able to understand clouds and wind, lift and sink, terrain and airflow well enough to do this makes me feel as if I have access to secret knowledge; as if I have, like an ancient, gone on an ascent to the heavens and returned with secrets that surpass regular humanity. Once one has soared, one can never quite look at clouds and the sky in the same way again. Each glance at sky above fills me with a deep and abiding sense of gratitude that God has created a world in which this is possible for mortal human beings.

For the remarkable ability to fly, with all its beautiful complexity, and for entrée to the secret knowledge of an aviator in the heavens above, I am profoundly thankful. The Creation story in Genesis reminds us, at its core, that God's handiwork is a gift God shared with us, which implies a duty of care and an invitation to investigate. Safe inside beaten metal thousands of feet above our normal dwelling place, we effortlessly cross expanses unimaginable to our ancestors, learning and growing as we go. This gift of ascent within God's Creation, whether literal or figurative, is one we can never fully repay.

Note

1. Abraham Joshua Heschel, *God in Search of Man: A Philosophy of Judaism* (New York: Farrar Straus and Giroux, 1955), 43.

8

Holding the Waters at Bay

RABBI MIRA BETH WASSERMAN, PHD

When God was about to create heaven and earth, the earth was a chaos, unformed, and on the chaotic waters' face there was darkness.

Genesis 1:1–2

In popular imagination, God's creation of the world is a whiz-bang, knock-down, dizzying work of wonder, as in a mere six days the Creator conjures a universe out of thin air, pulling stars, forests, and elephants into being like rabbits out of a hat. This image of God as magician, making something out of nothing, has a long history. For Christian theologians, the belief in *creatio ex nihilo*—creation from nothing—has been a point of faith for long centuries. More recently, theoretical physicists have reinforced this concept of "creation in an instant" through the very language they have chosen to describe the "big bang." Take a closer look at the verses in Genesis, however, and a different picture emerges. The reality God confronts as Genesis begins is not one of empty nothingness waiting to be filled, but rather a deep, dark, roiling chaos that fills everything. In the account of God's separation of the waters on day two, God's so-called "creation" of the world is so remote from popular notions of an instantaneous bang into being that a close reading cannot but complicate our very conception of what "creation" means.

Here is the account of God's activity on day two:

> God then said, "Let there be an expanse in the midst of the waters, and let it divide water from water!" So God made the expanse, separating the waters beneath the expanse from the waters above the expanse—and so it was. God then called the expanse Sky, and there was evening and there was morning, a second day. (Genesis 1:6–8)

On the second day of Creation, God does not make anything new. Before making anything new, God must make space for it, by clearing away the stuff that exists already. At the start of the day, ocean fills all space, and God divides these limitless depths into two separate bodies of water. Damming these waters off, God creates a wide expanse that is left open and empty in the middle. In the biblical account, this act of separating the primeval waters is not presented as preparatory or preliminary to God's work of Creation, but rather as a central act of Creation in itself, worthy of its own day of the week.

Biblical scholar Sara Japhet has pointed out that contrary to the image of God as Artist that sometimes comes through in poetic accounts of Creation, here, in the terse prose of Genesis 1, creation is much more mundane.[1] God is the one who makes order, clearing away the mess to make a place that is habitable. God is a homemaker, tidying up. On day two, God takes charge, setting limits to chaos, imposing order. Creation is not merely making new things, it seems; creation also means contending with what is, rearranging materials that are already there.

Even though the primordial ocean that precedes Creation is mentioned right at the very beginning of the biblical account, in most translations into English, these waters are overshadowed by a grand opening line that focuses on the Creator alone: "In the beginning, God created the heavens and the earth." When we read this verse as a headline for the entire Genesis account, it is easy to forget the darkness, the chaos, and the unfathomable depths that were already there before God got started. The medieval Jewish commentator Rabbi Shmuel ben Meir (Rashbam, a grandson of Rashi) argues that the real point of Genesis's opening line is precisely to describe what existed before Creation. Rashbam's commentary runs the first two verses of Genesis together, so it reads, "When God began creating the heavens and the earth, the earth was roiling chaos, and there was darkness over the depths, and God's breath hovered over the waters."[2] A close reading of Genesis's opening lines—in any translation—brings us face-to-face with waters that precede Creation.

What are these waters that God must clear away to make room for our world?

Critical biblical scholars have shed light on these mysterious depths by comparing Genesis to another ancient Creation myth, the Mesopotamian *Enuma Elish*.[3] Like the opening verses of Genesis, the *Enuma Elish* begins with a description of waters that precede the creation of the world:

1. When in the height heaven was not named,
2. And the earth beneath did not yet bear a name,
3. And the primeval Apsû, who begat them,
4. And chaos, Tiamat, the mother of them both,—
5. Their waters were mingled together,
6. And no field was formed, no marsh was to be seen.[4]

In this myth of Creation, the heavens and the earth are identified as the children of two watery gods: Apsû, the god of fresh water, and Tiamat, the goddess of the ocean depths. Their waters are mingled, filling everything. It is this image of a chaotic and watery beginning that most resembles the Genesis story. As the *Enuma Elish* unfolds, the differences between the two Creation stories multiply. In sharp contrast to the solitary God of Genesis who creates alone, the *Enuma Elish* is filled with multiple gods who bicker, battle, and struggle for dominance. When younger gods arise to kill Apsû and threaten Tiamat, she creates eleven fierce monsters to help fight her enemies. Eventually, Marduk, an upstart god who controls the wind, overpowers Tiamat and slays her. It is here that the images of Genesis and the *Enuma Elish* once again converge, as Marduk, now the chief god, divides the ocean-body of Tiamat in two:

> 137. He split her up like a flat fish into two halves;
> 138. One half of her he established as a covering for heaven.
> 139. He fixed a bolt, he stationed a watchman,
> 140. And bade them not to let her waters come forth.

Pushing half of Tiamat's body upward and half of it downward, Marduk sets limits to water, making a space for heaven and earth in between. While Genesis allows us to imagine God's separation of the primeval waters as a mundane picture of good housekeeping, in the *Enuma Elish*, where these waters are personified in the fierce and all-encompassing Tiamat, the division of Tiamat's depths is an act of war and domination.

Though the violence of Mesopotamian mythology is largely absent from Genesis 1, vestiges of a story of a cosmic battle between God and the sea do survive in other parts of the Bible. When the Psalmist praises God "who drove back the sea with Your might, who smashed the heads of the monsters in the waters" (Psalm 74:13, new JPS translation), the image calls Tiamat and her monsters to mind.[5] In the biblical imagination, heaven and earth are sandwiched between the upper waters and lower waters that God separated on the second day, and God's ongoing work of sustaining Creation means keeping these powerful waters securely dammed. This picture of the cosmos explains what happens in the time of Noah, when God feels regret about Creation—the flood that God inflicts on the world is literally the un-doing of Creation, the release of the very waters that God gathered up on the second day.

There is a story of cosmic struggle in the biblical account of Creation that is almost but not quite concealed by the ordered pattern of the narrative of Genesis 1. The measured way that the story is told, full of rhythmic repetitions and the regularity of one day following another, projects a vision of the world as safe, and ordered, and rule-bound. The work of the biblical writer in telling the story of Creation in this concise and controlled way corresponds to the image of the Creator within the story, where God acts to impose limits and regularity and order on a reality that is a disordered, encompassing, threatening mess. In the Bible, the forces of chaos are constrained, but never completely defeated. Contrary to popular imagination, the biblical God cannot make danger or evil disappear. The roiling waters persist, above the heavens and below the earth, and this means that God must continually fend off forces that threaten to engulf the world. Since the time of Noah, the persistence of the world has depended on God's ongoing effort to shield us from the abyss, to hold the waters of chaos at bay.

The ancient mythology of divine struggle that stands behind the Genesis account of day two is valuable not because it offers a persuasive account of how the universe is structured—we can look to modern science for such investigations—but because it offers a story that continues to resonate with human hopes and fears. Every day, in my most humdrum activities, I find myself struggling to fend off forces that threaten to overwhelm: mountains of e-mails, heaps of laundry, piles of dishes, more tasks than any one day can hold. Taking the story of God's struggle against the sea to heart, I feel a kinship with God's tireless work, and also with God's ultimate incapacity to make the chaos simply disappear. In God's ongoing effort to hold the waters at bay, I see a reflection of my own human limits. I can't take away the troubles and pain of the people I care about; I can't protect my own children from fearful things. But the story of God's ongoing effort to sustain Creation invests my own earthbound efforts to make a difference—to build a family, to create community, to safeguard the environment—with dignity, and grandeur, and holiness.

While Genesis is not science, its story of a world imperiled by threatening waters has new urgency and immediacy today because of the realities of global climate change. Chaos is seeping back into the world, along with seawater. As ocean levels rise, habitable lands flood, and superstorms grow ever more lethal and unpredictable. The world tilts closer to the primordial chaos imagined by biblical myth. God's work in separating the waters is no longer simply a story of a distant past; it is a glimpse of a very proximate future, in reverse. To do the work of stemming the tide, of holding the waters at bay, is the critical work of our time. Redemption won't happen in an instant, but Creation didn't either. As imagined by the Bible, it is arduous work to make, sustain, and protect our world, and God's efforts are steadfast and constant. Ours can be no less.

Notes

1. Presented in a class lecture at the Hebrew University, Jerusalem.

2. My translation. The division of Scripture into verses happens rather late in the text's development, so Rashbam's rendering of Genesis 1–2 into a single unit might indeed reflect an earlier reading. By his time, however, the Masoretes have already established a tradition of breaking his proposed unit into two. The new Jewish Publication Society (JPS) translation offers something close to Rashbam's version, though it keeps the accent on God's creative activity rather than on what comes before: "When God began to create heaven and earth—the earth being unformed and void, with darkness over the surface of the deep and a wind from God sweeping over the water—" (Genesis 1:1–2, new JPS translation).

3. Etched in cuneiform on seven tablets that were discovered in the ruins of the palace of Ashurbanipal in Nineveh, the *Enuma Elish* tells the story of a divine struggle to overpower a sea goddess that culminates in the creation of the world. The tablets were discovered in 1849 and upon their publication were widely taken as evidence

for a view of the world that stands behind the Genesis story; when George Smith published the first translation in 1876, he called it *The Chaldean Account of Genesis.*

4. *The Enuma Elish: Seven Tablets of Creation*, trans. Leonard William King (1902), http://www.sacred-texts.com/ane/stc/index.htm.

5. In addition to Psalm 74:12–15, see Psalm 89:9–12 and Job 9:13 for more accounts of God subduing sea monsters. The two that are named in the Bible are Leviathan and Rachab.

9
—

Separating the Waters

RABBI KINNERET SHIRYON, DD

God then said, "Let there be an expanse in the midst of the waters, and let it divide water from water!"

Genesis 1:6

One of my fondest childhood memories is of stealing away into our station wagon on a rainy day. I would lie down in the back of the car and close my eyes so that I could better concentrate on the sounds of the rain pattering on the rooftop of the car. I found it very calming.

The rhythmic drops must have put me into a kind of meditative state, allowing my thoughts to wander at first and then focus on a specific idea. I remember that it cleared my mind, centered me, and gave me direction.

Today, as a mature adult, I understand the special pull of a rainy day, of escaping into our parked car outside. I recapture this meditative state every time I swim my morning laps. I have always had a unique relationship with water. When I hike across different landscapes, I am drawn to the nearest body of water. Whether it is a pond, a well, a stream, a spring, a river, a lake, a waterfall, a sea, or an ocean, I will inevitably remove any footwear and step into the water source.

Water has a primeval pull that connects me to the source of life and fills me with a sense of contentment and joy. Perhaps it is the universal experience of all living creatures who are nurtured in their mother's amniotic fluids. Life begins in water. The globe is made of over 70 percent water. Our human bodies are made of over 70 percent water. Water is more than a mixture of hydrogen and oxygen molecules; it is the source of all life. Human beings can survive for days, even weeks, without food but can die in a matter of days without water. In Hebrew there is an expression for water: *mayim chayim* (living waters). Water is not only the spring of life, but it also sustains life. The British poet W. H. Auden wrote, "Thousands have lived without love, not one without water."

In Hebrew, the words *mayim* (water) and *shamayim* (heavens) have an etymological relationship. The word *sham* translates as "over there." Literally, the word שמים, *sham-mayim* (heavens), means "the waters over there." On the second day of Creation we learn about the creation of the firmament (the separation of the waters above from the waters below):

> God then said, "Let there be an expanse in the midst of the waters, and let it divide water from water!" So God made the expanse, separating the waters beneath the expanse from the waters above the expanse—and so it was. God then called the expanse Sky [*shamayim*], and there was evening and there was morning, a second day. (Genesis 1:6–8)

The relationship between sky and water is powerful. One of the most obvious connections between the skies and bodies of water is color. On gloomy days the dark clouds and gray skies color the water of the sea. Dark seas are a mirror for the ominous clouds storming above. Clear days of blue skies are also beautifully reflected in the sea or any other body of water. The color *t'cheilet* (sky blue) decorates various Jewish symbols, representing the Divine Presence. On the tzitzit of the tallit, we are instructed to attach a *p'til t'cheilet* (cord of blue) in order to recall God's various religious obligations. Once we look at the sky-blue fringe, we connect to the Divine and remember the mitzvot (religious imperatives, or commandments) so that we may fulfill them. On the background of the ark in our modest synagogue in Modi'in, Israel, the dominant color is sky blue, which sparks a visual association to sky and water and to the Divine Presence in the world. The depth of the sea and the infinite expanse of the sky bring forth a sense of *Ein Sof* (literally meaning "no end," or the Infinite One), one of the many names of God in our tradition.

There are many levels of meaning to the Creation story and its individual days. The second day of Creation teaches us about the special relationship between sky and water. According to the biblical narrative, they were originally one entity until God divided them. This is a divine act of separating a chaotic mass into a natural order that eventually will provide habitats and sustenance for life. Sky and water are also symbols of the infinite possibilities of life.

I have a personal ritual that I developed over the years while swimming every morning. When I enter the water and begin to swim laps, I am usually bombarded with a chaotic mass of thoughts, worries, and dilemmas that I face daily. As I continue to swim back and forth in a rhythmic fashion, the chaos of my brain begins to quiet, the frenzied thoughts begin to separate out into coherent categories, and I find myself focusing on one specific challenge. Perhaps the water, the meditative rhythm of my strokes, or the combination of them both allows me to find order in the chaos. I have composed many sermons while swimming in the mornings; I have also found solutions to a variety of tribulations in the life of the community as well as in my personal life.

Water is fluid. My strokes in the water are fluid. Together they provide a fluidity of thinking that is untenable in other settings. In the order of God's creative energy, I see a fluidity of events springing forth from the separation of the waters below from the waters above. Immediately following this separation, on the third day of Creation, we witness how God separates the collected waters from the dry ground, allowing for the Creation process to continue.

After the first ten minutes of lap swimming, when my mind is recreating a semblance of order, I begin a series of aquatic blessings. I call them *b'rachot babreichah* (blessings in the pool). There is serendipity in the fact that both words share the same root letters: *b-r-ch*. The word for knee in Hebrew is *berech*. One of the customs of prayer in Judaism is the bending of the knee at various intervals of proclaiming God's name. When you swim, you are in a constant position of gently bending your knees! I have fashioned a series of benedictions that allow me to thank the Source of Life, *Ein HaChayim*, for all the many blessings in my life. The framework of my benediction stays the same, but the content changes from day to day. When I contemplate the connection between sky and water in the primordial scheme described in the Book of *B'reishit* (literally, the Book of Beginning) and my morning blessing cycle, I am not surprised by the notion that I prefer to swim outdoors, where there is a natural meeting of both sky and water. While I am in the water, with the sky above me, I feel a oneness with the universe and a oneness with the Creator. I face new beginnings each day in the water with sky hovering above.

Just as God created order out of chaos, I too sift through the chaos and challenges of daily life to make order and to open myself to new understandings.

I find an important lesson in the second day of Creation, which teaches us that although we tend to compartmentalize our lives, which perhaps also helps us to create order, we should be conscious of the infinite flow of life. Life is not just a collection of different compartments; it is all part of a continuous flow, like the rivers that flow into the sea.

Day two is the only day in the rendering of the Creation story on which we do not read the encouraging words "and God saw that it was good." Why is this blessing missing? The medieval commentator Rashi teaches us that the process of separating the waters is not completed until the following day; therefore, God did not recite a blessing over an incomplete project. I suggest that the blessing comes when we realize the connections between the different parts of life. Indeed, the blessing appears twice on the following day when the gathering of the waters allows for the seed-bearing plants of the earth to bear fruit. The connections between the waters of the earth and the waters of the skies reflect the reality that we are all tied together in the flow of life. Once we realize those connections, we can make this world a better place for all, with the hope that our efforts will also bear fruit.

מודה אני לפניך עין החיים המבדילה בין מים למים ומכניסה אותנו לזרם החיים.

Modah ani l'fanayich, Ein HaChayim, hamavdilah bein mayim lamayim umachnisah otanu l'zerem hachayim.

I thank You, Source of Life, for separating the waters and bringing us forth into the flow of life.

Amen.

10

The Night Sky

RABBI SCOTT NAGEL

So God made the expanse, separating the waters beneath the expanse from the waters above the expense—and so it was. God then called the expanse Sky, and there was evening and there was morning, a second day.

Genesis 1:7–8

Stars are a funny thing. They speak to us of infinite distances. Most of us cannot possibly fathom the distance between us and the nearest star, yet it is possible to feel personally connected and, at times, even intimate with them. Stars also speak to us of the infinite nature of time. The light we see from them now was created millennia ago and will be around millennia after we are gone. The stars can make us feel small, if not even insignificant, in the grand cosmos of being. Yet, as we are able and privileged to witness them in their magnificent beauty, we feel part of something truly amazing—something not fully understandable, something larger and more meaningful than the self. Jews are intrinsically connected to the stars. In those stars we can find Judaism. In those stars we can find God. In those stars we can find ourselves.

Jews have had an interesting relationship with the stars from the very beginning. In Genesis 15:5 we read, "Taking him [Abram, who will become Abraham] outside, [God] said, 'Turn your gaze toward the heavens and count the stars, if you can count them!' And God promised him: 'So shall your seed be!'" One of the reasons we feel so connected to our biblical ancestors, like Abraham, is because we feel so much of what they felt, such as the smallness and wonder they felt when they looked at the stars. God recognizes Abram's, and all of humanity's, inability to truly fathom the expanse of the universe. The Torah uses the "stars of heaven" along with "sands of the sea" to symbolize a number uncountable by humans. Yet, unlike the sands of the seas that wash and blow away, the stars are set in their course and can be counted upon always to be there when we look up.

When we look up, the stars appear almost identical to the night before and the night before that. Ancient star maps are almost identical to the night sky today. So, while their numbers are unfathomable, it is the stars' nature as constants in their place in the sky during each season and their predictable movement through the year that make them the perfect symbol for the Jewish people and its progeny. The consistency of the stars speaks to the everlasting endurance of Jews and Judaism through time and uncountable difficulties. We are a constant in the world, always there, unable to be erased, shining even in the darkest of times. Like the stars, we have been called to bring light into the world. The eternal mission of the Jewish people is to be an *or lagoyim*, "a light unto the nations," which means that we are called upon to be a constant guiding force for good and righteousness in a world that can often be dark.

The mission of the stars is much the same as our own. We are taught that God created the stars in order to create order. The stars guide our times and seasons. In Jewish time, a new day begins at night only with the appearance of three stars. Shabbat begins on Friday night and ends with the appearance of three stars on Saturday night. This remains true for our holiday observances, including Rosh HaShanah and Yom Kippur, Passover, Sukkot, Shavuot, and even Chanukah and Purim. It is the stars that enable us to find order in the world.

Psalm 19 begins, "Let the heavens declare the glory of God," and they do. The stars proclaim God's power and wisdom. There is constant light and order in the universe. God asks Job and, by extension, all of humanity, in Job 38:31–32, "Can you tie cords to Pleiades [constellation of the Seven Sisters] or undo the reins of Orion [another constellation]? Can you lead out the *Mazzarot* [heavenly bodies] in their seasons, conduct the Bear with her sons [Ursa Major and Ursa Minor, otherwise known as the Little Dipper]?" The answer to these questions is of course, "No." Only God could arrange something as spectacular as the heavens. There is order in the patterns of the stars, and that order is a gift from God.

Stars are light in the darkness. Human beings have been using stars to navigate on land and sea for millennia. In Judaism the stars are even used to navigate Shabbat and the festivals. According to the Talmud, "When [only] one star [is visible], it is day; when two [appear], it is twilight; three, it is night. It was taught likewise: When one star [is visible], it is day; when two [appear], it is twilight; three, it is night. Rabbi Yosei ben Abin said: Not the large stars, which are visible by day, nor the small ones, which are visible only at night, but the medium sized" (BT *Shabbat* 35b). Thus Shabbat and the festivals end only when three medium-sized stars are visible. Stars provide the means for us to travel on the right path in the world at large and in Judaism.

Staying on the right path is what God calls us to do in order to draw near. Finding our way in the world strengthens our personal relationship with God. This concept is introduced in the Mishnah in Tractate *Avot* (2:2): "Beautiful is the study of Torah with *derech eretz*, as involvement with both keeps one from sin." *Derech eretz* literally means "the way of the land." In total there are about two hundred references in the Mishnah and Talmud to *derech eretz* that teach us about decent, respectful, and thoughtful behavior. These practices showed humanity how to navigate the world morally and ethically, and they still inform our values and moral today. These ideas are constants, like the stars.

Ancient Jews believed that stars not only gave us the ability to navigate through the world, but also guided us as individuals. There was hardly a debate among scholars about whether the stars held influence over us. What they did discuss was *how much* power the stars actually held. It was generally believed that each person has a corresponding star in the sky and that the position, size, color, and appearance of that star at a person's birth helped to determine that person's character, career, and life path.[1] The Talmud states in several places that every person has a celestial body (*mazal*), that is, a particular star that is their patron from conception and birth (BT *Shabbat* 53b; BT *Bava Kama* 2b). In fact, when we wish each other *mazal tov*, we are actually wishing that each other's *mazal*—that is, star—be in a good place. When we look to find God in the stars, it makes them all *mazalot tovim*, "good stars." We find good in the stars, and we wish for good in the stars. The stars are always there for us, unchanging in our experience. What changes is our perception of them.

Our perception of the stars changes under individual circumstances such as time, weather, and even location. It can even give us insight to the fact that the planet we are on is moving through space. Like prayer, stargazing can be a solitary or group activity. Like prayer, stargazing can bring us closer to each other and closer to God. I remember the first time I became aware that looking at the stars was a way to draw near to God. I was in the Negev desert sitting at the edge of a cliff in incredible darkness with someone I hardly knew. When our eyes adjusted to the dark, the view was so spectacular that each of us could hardly breathe. We were sitting on the edge of eternity and could barely speak, but at the same moment we uttered: *Baruch atah, Adonai Eloheinu, Melech haolom, oseh maaseih v'reishit*, "Blessed are You, Adonai our God, Ruler of the universe, who makes the works of creation." God was in that place, in those stars, and we knew it.

The desert is the perfect place to stargaze. There is little light pollution, and there are few great buildings or trees to obscure the view in every direction. The horizon is wide open. In a place like this, we too can become wide open to the experiences of the infinite. The stars can bring us to such an experience no matter where we actually are.

Stars are powerful forces for memory and feeling. They can lift us up and transport us to another place and time. There is a summer camp song, "Stars in the Sky," that speaks to the power of seeing the stars at night:

> Stars in the sky, stars in the sky
> Bring the summer right back to me
> Tell me you'll try, tell me you'll try
> To think about me whenever you see those
> Stars in the sky
> Rabbi Larry Milder[2]

Camps and deserts are great places to stargaze because they are often away from densely populated areas. These are places where we really can appreciate the stars. Experiencing the stars at summer camp is particularly special because it is part of the overall experience of creating unique and meaningful moments and connections with others. The stars become sacred because they are experienced as a whole—each individual star is different, each produces its own light, but it is the experience of them together that makes the display awe-inspiring. Such is the experience at camp—all of our experiences are higher and amplified through sharing them with others.

The desert is almost the opposite; the open expanse and the lack of other people remind us to feel small and humble. The desert reminds us of our limits and fragility. It helps us to find the blessings in our abilities and all that we have. In the desert, the stars call on humanity to find the sacred within.

Outside of the wilderness of places like the desert or summer camp it is becoming increasingly more difficult to see the stars in the night sky. The glare of the lights of businesses and the pollution of humanity are literally obscuring the view of thousands upon thousands of stars. In normal situations, the human eye can see only a fraction of the stars that were visible just a few decades ago. This is particularly true in regions where most of us live. Light scientists believe that a child born in a first-world nation will have only a one in ten chance of witnessing a truly dark sky in their lifetime. People who live in cities can only see about five hundred stars on any given night. Compare that with the potential of seeing fifteen thousand stars in more remote locations![3] The difficulty in accessing the stars in modern times mirrors the difficulty many feel in accessing God. This is one of the greatest contemporary struggles: to remember, and to believe, that the stars, like God, are always there—even if we cannot see them.

The power of the night sky calls us to put ourselves literally out there in an unusual, uncomfortable, or novel situation. It calls us to be willing to sit on the edge of a cliff or travel to the wilderness. It is about waiting for our eyes to adjust to all the darkness around us so that we may see the individual points of light. In those stars we can find God. In those stars we can find ourselves.

Notes

1. Joshua Trachtenberg, *Jewish Magic and Superstition: A Study in Folk Religion* (New York: Behrman House, 1939), 250.

2. From "Stars in the Sky," track 8, *American Psalm*, by Rabbi Larry Milder, January 8, 2004.

3. Rebecca Ruiz, "World's Best Places to See the Stars," *Forbes Magazine*, June 2008, 17.

11

Water Conservation as Biblical Imperative

RABBI KEVIN M. KLEINMAN

God then said, "Let there be an expanse in the midst of the waters, and let it divide water from water!" So God made the expanse, separating the waters beneath the expanse from the waters above the expanse—and so it was. God then called the expanse Sky, and there was evening and there was morning, as second day.

Genesis 1:6–8

When I am thirsty, I get a drink. I do not think about where my water is coming from or if it is clean. I simply go to the tap, turn it on, and fill up my glass. I am fortunate enough to live in the northeastern United States, in one of the regions of the world where people have access on a daily basis to free, clean, drinkable water. However, according to reports generated by the United Nations in 2013, 85 percent of the world's population lives in the driest half of the planet; 783 million people living in these countries do not have access to clean water, and almost 2.5 billion people do not have access to adequate sanitation.[1] In

2010, the direness of the situation led the United Nations General Assembly to recognize that water and sanitation should be a human right.[2] In this essay, I will provide a biblical context for water as a basic human right based on how water conservation was a necessity in ancient Israel, in order to provide a modern Jewish context for advocating for water rights for all of earth's citizens today.

Water conservation and the equitable distribution of clean and affordable water are worldwide humanitarian concerns and among the most pressing social and environmental justice issues of our day. The Jewish values of *pikuach nefesh* (saving a life), *hachnasat orchim* (welcoming the stranger), and *bal tashchit* (not wasting) are biblical principles that can guide and inform our modern thoughts on how we can best care for earth's most precious resource, water. According to the first chapter of the Book of Genesis, water was separated from the heavens and stored on the earth's surface by God during the second day of Creation, before God created animal and plant life. This shows how the writers of the Bible understood just how fundamental water is to the survival of all of planet Earth's inhabitants.

For millions of people around the world, access to clean and affordable drinking water is a matter of life and death. Chief among Judaism's core values is *pikuach nefesh*, the protection of human life. There are many commandments in the Torah that mandate feeding the hungry, underscoring the importance of saving the lives of the most vulnerable members of our society. Farmers were obligated to leave the corners of their fields for the needy to gather produce (Leviticus 19:9–10). These same farmers were forbidden from picking up what they dropped or didn't harvest in their first walk through, leaving it for the downtrodden to glean and use for themselves and their families (Leviticus 23:22). Water was, of course, vital and necessary to grow these crops, making it possible to perform these lifesaving mitzvot in the first place. Without proper rain and ground water storage and distribution systems, the entire community would be at risk for starvation and other maladies. It was vital to our ancestors' survival that they use water wisely.

The Torah gives examples of providing water to those on long journeys and to their animals as the ultimate symbol of welcoming the stranger, the Jewish value of *hachnasat orchim*. When three sacred messengers come to visit Abraham and Sarah's tent by the oaks of Mamre, Abraham runs to greet them and says, "My lords, if I have found favor in your sight, please do not pass your servant by. Let a little water be brought; then wash your feet and recline under a tree, and let me bring a bit of bread and you can restore yourselves" (Genesis 18:3–5). Abraham's compassion leads to the promise of the birth of a child. A few chapters later, Abraham charges his servant with the task of finding his son Isaac a wife from the land where he was born and bring her back to the land of Canaan to marry Isaac. The servant devises a test to ensure that he find a worthy wife for Isaac. He stops his camels at the well outside the city of Nahor and prays to God to let him find a maiden who, when she sees him and his camels, will offer all of them a drink of water. The woman who would offer him and his camels a drink of water after their long journey is the one whom Isaac is destined to marry. Upon seeing the servant approach the well after his long journey, Rebecca steps forward to offer him and the animals water, and thus a deal is made for her to become Isaac's wife (Genesis 24). In the Torah, offering water was a gesture of welcome as well as recognition that sojourners would need to be refreshed on the road and once they reached their destinations.

The Torah prohibits the needless waste and destruction of food through the commandment called *bal tashchit*. The biblical reference to not cutting down fruit trees during a time of war (Deuteronomy 20:19–20) gets extended in Rabbinic and medieval literature to apply to food, energy sources, clothing, and water. A Talmudic passage states, "A person should not dump out water from his cistern when others are in need [of the water]" (Babylonian Talmud, *Y'vamot* 44a). From this, we see that the biblical principle of *bal tashchit* applies to water.

When one person has enough water and another person does not have enough water, intentionally wasting that water is morally fraught. The ethical thing to do, according to Jewish tradition, would be the converse—to share the water with those in need.

Water can be seen as the most important natural resource to those living in the Land of Israel, a country with high water scarcity levels—both in Torah times and today.

Israel is an arid climate. The rainy season is in the winter. Rain is stored in aboveground waterways and belowground aquifers and must be carefully conserved throughout the growing season. In the modern State of Israel, farmers have invented irrigations systems that minimize the amount of water wasted while watering the fields. Inventors and engineers have developed technologies to desalinate the salt water of the Dead and Mediterranean Seas. Water conservation is a top priority among the varied ecological issues faced by Israel today.

The ancient Israelites were primarily subsistence farmers; they did not have the technologies that are so helpful to modern farmers today. They grew wheat, barley, figs, grapes, olives, pomegranates, and grapes—known as seven species native to the Land of Israel (Deuteronomy 8:8). They raised livestock—cattle, sheep, and goats—to milk, to eat, and to bring as offerings to the Temple in Jerusalem. Unlike modern-day farmers, Israelite farmers depended wholly on the rain falling in the right increments at the right time of the year in order to have a successful crop, or any crop at all. Too much rain or too little rain could have a detrimental effect on crop yield and could threaten their livelihood or, even worse, their lives. The Torah has stories of great floods and severe droughts—both with detrimental outcomes to people, animals, and the land itself. Our ancestors, and many throughout the world today, literally lived and died in direct proportion to the amount of water they had available at any given time to drink, feed their animals, and water their crops.

Water has a mystical quality. Human beings cannot simply make it rain by looking up into the sky. We are dependent on the forces of nature and the right weather conditions for rain to fall from the clouds above. Today, we understand the scientific nature of the water cycle. Water evaporates from the earth's surface and forms clouds in the atmosphere. When the clouds get heavy enough, it begins to rain. The biblical Israelites placed their faith in God to bring down rain from the heavens above. God, in turn, put the responsibility back on the Israelites. If the Israelites obeyed God's commandments to treat one another with dignity and let justice prevail over hatred and bigotry, then God would provide the proper amount of rain in the right season. If they partook in idolatrous practices, then the rain would be withheld (Deuteronomy 11:13–21).

The Torah's weather forecasting system is baffling at best. How could one person's actions truly impact the weather for their entire community? What if one person was obeying the commandments while another was disobeying? This theological framework stems from a deeper belief held by the ancient Israelites that God was the source of everything, that God's will manifested in natural and supernatural phenomena. It is consistent with the development of radical monotheism that formed the basis of Israelite religion, even though it might be troubling to the modern reader. After all, according to the very first stories codified in the Torah, God created the heavens and the earth, the water and the stars, and all things that make up our beautiful planet. God then placed earth's precious resources into human hands to till and tend, to guard and protect (Genesis 2:15). We became God's partner as nature's stewards, but only once we understood the ultimate power that God manifested to bring the earth into being in the first place.

The biblical authors put such care into choosing the words that would inspire awe and a deep respect for God's Creation as a means to inspire their community to take utmost care in preserving the life-giving resources of food and water, as seen in the text above. Reading this narrative closely, we can envision a horizon line above an ocean. Water seamlessly stretches for miles and miles, and yet, there is a clear separation between the waters of the sky, called in Hebrew *shamayim*, and the waters of the surface of the earth, called *mayim*. Water is a fundamental building block in the creation of the universe in the first chapter of Genesis, just as water is a fundamental building block of all life. The Creation narrative of the Torah is the ancient Jewish explanation for how the world came into being. Religious mythologies often compete for authenticity in the modern public eye with the ever-expanding scientific research that also explains the origins of planet Earth and our solar system.

At times science and religion are at odds with one another, and at other times they can complement each other. For many years, scientists believed that for the first hundreds of millions years of the earth's existence our planet was dry, and that water came later than the formation of the earth itself when the earth came into contact with "wet" asteroids.[3] A 2014 study by the Woods Hole Oceanographic Institution asserts the opposite, that the earth's oceans were present as the planet itself was being formed 4.6 billion years ago.[4] This groundbreaking study identifies primitive meteorites called carbonaceous chondrites as the source for the earth's water. It shows that water was, from a scientific as well as a religious point of view, present at the very moment the earth itself was formed.

Water is the primordial source of life on earth. All of our planet's species depend on water for our survival. Yet, only a small percentage of all the water on earth is accessible as clean water sources. Nearly 98 percent of the earth's water is in the oceans. Freshwater makes up less than 3 percent of water on earth, and over two-thirds of this is tied up in polar ice caps and glaciers. Freshwater lakes and rivers make up only 0.009 percent of water on earth, and groundwater makes up 0.28 percent.[5]

Clean, accessible drinking water is such a small percentage of the overall water on, above, and below the surface of the earth. It truly is precious. The very same molecules of hydrogen and oxygen have been watering the land and quenching the thirst of human beings for millennia. Yet today, as the population of the earth is rapidly increasing, water pollution remains an environmental and social issue all over the world. More and more people and regions are facing the not-so-new realities of water shortages and scarcities. We can draw a few conclusions from the Torah about the religious, ethical, and moral obligations to promote awareness for the need to conserve water and advocate for the millions, if not billions of the world's poorest, who day in and day out do not know whether or not they will have adequate water supplies for their families.

Water is a basic human right. The mitzvah of providing water should go hand in hand with the commandment to feed the hungry. The responsibility for human beings to be *shomrei adamah*, "guardians or stewards of the earth" (based on Genesis 2:15), means taking care of the earth's waterways in addition to land and the animals who live on land and in the sea. Water should not be wasted. It should be treated as the precious resource that it is. To this end, we must advocate from a social justice standpoint for clean and fresh drinking water for all earth's citizens. And we can advocate from an environmental justice viewpoint on the importance of quick and efficient cleanup efforts when there are catastrophic spills and accidents that pollute earth's major waterways. When I am thirsty I drink. Don't all earth's citizens deserve the same opportunity?

Notes

1. "Water Cooperation: Facts and Figures," UN Water World Water Day 2013, http://www.unwater.org/water-cooperation-2013/water-cooperation/facts-and-figures/en/.

2. "Making Water a Human Right," United Nations Regional Information Centre for Western Europe, http://www.unric.org/en/water/27360-making-water-a-human-right.

3. "New Study Finds Oceans Arrived Early to Earth," Woods Hole Oceanographic Institution, October 30, 2014, https://www.whoi.edu/news-release/OriginEarthWater.

4. Ibid.

5. Matt Murphy, "Global Water Cycle and Supplies," Water Is Life, http://academic.evergreen.edu/g/grossmaz/murphymw/, citing http://www.bbc.co.uk/science/earth/atmosphere_and_climate/climate.

12

What If?

The Sacred Potential of Water

SHAINA HERRING AND
RABBI SARA LURIA

*God then said, "Let the waters beneath the sky be collected
[gathered] in one place, so that the dry ground may be seen!"*

Genesis 1:9

On the first day of Creation, the world was swirling, uncontained, dark, deep water; on the second day, God pushed an expanse through the waters, like a version of the parting of the sea in Exodus, but horizontal. About a decade ago, I bought a beautiful print in an outdoor market in Tel Aviv of a picture of a Torah scroll open to the words *Y'hi rakia b'toch hamayim* ("Let there be an expanse in the midst of the waters"; Genesis 1:6), with the image of a droplet of water overlaid on it. The image hung in my Jerusalem kitchen and I considered it an inspiration—if, on only the second day of the world's existence, God could separate the waters of Creation into the heavens and the seas, then surely I could throw something together for dinner most nights.

As the story of Creation progresses, the elemental chaos prior to Creation is made more organized with each passing day. Water plays a fundamental role in this process. On day one, water is everywhere. Day two, water is separated by the sky. Day three, water is further gathered to make space for land. In Hebrew, the collecting or gathering of waters is called *mikveh hamayim*. The root *k-v-h* is repeated during the description of the third day, emphasizing the importance of the action of gathering.

The *mikveh hamayim*, the "gathered waters" of our Creation story, speak to the origin and primal power of what mikveh is today: a gathering of water for the purpose of sacred transformation.

Gathering of Water

A mikveh is a Jewish ritual bath historically used at specified times and filled with *mayim chayim*, "living waters." In Leviticus 11:36, we read, *Ach mayan u'vor mikveh mayim yih'yeh tahor*, "Only a naturally occurring spring or a person-made pit that gathers waters will be fit." Thus, the waters of a mikveh must come from natural sources such as the ocean, a natural spring, or rainwater. Many modern *mikvaot* (plural of *mikveh*) use rainwater that is collected in a cistern. This *mayim chayim*, this idea of "living water" or water that comes straight from heaven without undergoing any processing or channeling, connects the mikveh back to the original waters of Creation and the waters in Eden. Genesis 2:10 describes a river that begins in Eden and then divides into four branches. Rabbi Aryeh Kaplan argues in his book *Waters of Eden* that all of the waters in the world today come from these four branches, which originally stemmed from Eden.[1] In *Taking the Plunge: A Practical and Spiritual Guide to the Mikveh*, Miriam Berkowitz explains that while we had to leave Eden, the use of mikveh allows for a degree of return to our original source: "When we step into the natural waters of a lake, river, ocean, or *mikveh*, we are trying to reconnect with the waters of these four ancient rivers, with our Source, with Eden, with our truest selves, with God."[2]

Sacred Transformation

Mikveh immersion is an ancient practice that honors the sanctity of our bodies and our experiences. This ritual has been used for conversions and women's monthly immersions following menstruation (*nidah*) for millennia. Prior to immersing, it is customary for the one immersing to shower or bathe and to remove anything that could come between one's body and the water. This includes clothing, makeup, and jewelry. Doing so requires the person immersing to approach the water as his or her most basic self, with no additional adornments, and to be fully embraced by the water. Traditionally, there are specific blessings to say during the immersion, and many find it meaningful to incorporate other personal touches such as poems or songs into their immersion.

A mikveh looks like a small pool, but immersion in a mikveh is not the same as swimming in a pool or taking a bath. The Rambam, a prominent medieval scholar, explains that one must immerse with the specific intention of having a transformative experience. He writes:

> If a person immersed and had special intention, the person becomes ritually [ready] even though there is no physical bodily change; [because] the person immersed with the intention of purifying their soul.[3]

Rambam highlights the idea that mikveh is a gathering of water with a specific purpose. It is not enough to just jump into a pool of water; rather we must also imbue the water with our own intention for transformation to occur.

At ImmerseNYC, our community mikveh project in New York City, we have guided immersions meant to mark a wide range of important life-cycle moments, including *b'nei mitzvah*, finalizing a divorce, completing chemotherapy, coming out, and giving birth to a child. Just as the waters in the Creation story are vast and endless, so too are the possibilities for using mikveh in our lives today.

The waters of the mikveh create a safe space for honoring the wide range of lived experiences that often go unacknowledged in Jewish communal life or are honored in a public way with little space for personal reflection. For example, life-cycle events such as the birth of a child or a bar/bat mitzvah are celebrated with much fanfare, but there is rarely time or space set aside for personal reflection upon reaching these milestones. Just as the water in the Creation story ends the *tohu vavohu*, the primordial chaos, mikveh allows for a break from the chaos that often accompanies these very public celebrations. Mikveh provides a safe and quiet space to reflect on an experience and to mark it in a personal and meaningful way. One bride describes:

> My immersion experience completely changed the pace of my wedding weekend. It gave me a chance to be still, reflect, and welcome in this new chapter without distraction. In this special moment I stopped to think about where I am going and to be thankful for the journey I've had so far. . . . [This immersion] helped me to become more mindful and present on my wedding day.

Further, there are many transitional experiences for which there is no traditional Jewish ritual. Becoming an empty-nester, reaching a milestone birthday, experiencing a miscarriage, or getting a promotion at work are just a few examples. I once worked with a person who immersed who explained, "I felt supported, guided, and understood. This immersion was a great way for me to mark transitions that unfortunately have gone unmarked."

On the second day of Creation the literal *mayim* (water) was divided into two, with limitless potential for what could happen next. The word *mayim* itself hints at this potential, containing within it two words: *mah*, "what," and *im*, "if." We can ask ourselves this question when examining the endless possibilities of mikveh use today. Clergy might ask: What if I suggested a mikveh immersion to a congregant experiencing a life transition? What if a group from my synagogue immersed before the High Holy Days to symbolically renew ourselves for the New Year? What if I immersed in the mikveh after a personal challenge? Community members can ask themselves: What if mikveh was an option for marking an experience in my life? What if I turned off all of the background noise and immersed in the mikveh completely present and focused? What if there was a ritual within Jewish tradition that could simultaneously hold me in the present moment while connecting me with the distant past? When we look into the *mayim*, the water, of the mikveh, we ask ourselves, *Mah im?* There are so many possibilities for honoring our lived experiences in a Jewish way. Perhaps just as God took a second look on day two of Creation and separated the waters, we can take another look at the rich possibilities of how mikveh can enhance and bring new levels of meaning to significant moments in our lives.

Notes

1. Aryeh Kaplan, Waters of Eden: An Explanation of the Concept of Mikvah, (New York: NCSY, 1976), pgs 30–36.

2. Miriam Berkowitz, *Taking the Plunge: A Practical and Spiritual Guide to the Mikveh*, ed. David Golinkin (Jerusalem: Schechter Institute of Jewish Studies, 2007), 4–5.

3. Maimonides, *Mishneh Torah, Hilchot Mikvaot* 11:12.

Day Three

✦

LAND AND VEGETATION

God then said, "Let the waters beneath the sky be collected in one place, so that the dry ground may be seen!"—and so it was. And God called the dry ground Earth, and called the collected waters Seas. And when God saw how good it was, God said, "Let the earth grow vegetation, seed-bearing plants, fruit trees on the earth that bear fruit, each true to its type, with its seed in it!"—and so it was. The earth brought forth vegetation, seed-bearing plants, each true to its type, and trees bearing fruit, each true to its type, with its seed in it. And God saw how good it was, and there was evening and there was morning, a third day.

Genesis 1:9–13

Plant breeding?

13

The Holiness of Wild Places

RABBI JAMIE KORNGOLD

God then said, "Let the waters beneath the sky be collected in
one place, so that the dry ground may be seen!"

(Genesis 1:9)

My mind feels like a pile of rocks, heavy, weighted, constrained.
The demands of the day, of the week, overwhelm me. There is too
much to do, at least too much to do well. I need to be at the top of
my game, lively, agile, and attentive. But my mind feels tight. I cannot
mold a thought; I cannot create creativity.

I turn off my laptop, leave my phone on my desk, pull on my hiking
boots, and head up the trail behind our house. I enter into the freedom of
ponderosas and Douglas firs who do not tax themselves with to-do lists and
carpool schedules; who stand, strong and rooted, yet flexible and yielding.

I try to turn my mind away from the stress of my life, to consciously turn off the chatter and tune in—like on an old-fashioned radio—to the frequency of the trail. It's staticky at first, hard to get a fix.

I have physically arrived, putting one foot in front of the other on
a piece of Creation's dry ground, but mentally, emotionally, that takes
longer. "Be here now!" I remind myself.

The old Chasidic tale rises in me: "What was the most important thing to the great rabbi? Was it Torah or Talmud? Values? *Tikkun olam*? The most important thing to the great rabbi was whatever he happened to be doing at the moment."

"Be here now!" I command myself. The elixir is here. Deuteronomy teaches, "The thing is very close to you, in your mouth and in your heart" (Deuteronomy 30:14). It is not in a book. It is not online. It is here in these rocks, in these plants, on this trail. Now.

I've hiked a half mile and have hardly noticed the trees except as monolithic stretches of green on brown trunks. Slowly, slowly I awaken to my surroundings.

Now, what at first seemed green becomes many greens: the green of the ponderosa needles is different from the green of the Douglas fir needles, and the green of the Douglas fir needles that grew this year is different from the green of last year's needles.

Some greens are almost not green when I look more closely. The poison ivy, so lush and ironically inviting in the summer, begins to redden with autumn. The sumac too slowly transitions to orange-red. I too am beginning to change, to relax. My shoulders soften, loosen just a little. The Rabbis have blessings for everything because they understand the power of pausing, of slowing down enough to notice. Blessings are speed bumps commanding, "Stop! Notice what you are doing/seeing/tasting/feeling." For me, a switchback in the trail or a precariously balanced rock works the same way.

Wild places feel holy. They urge us to pause, to notice, because if we don't notice, then danger awaits us. Too quick a descent can twist an ankle; a careless brush against a noxious plant can bring on an itchy, red rash.

But when we do notice the details of the woods, our reward is an entrance into something far greater than tree or rock or mountain. With each step on the trail, with each deep inhalation of breath, we are reminded that we are not a single untethered soul, but rather are part of something larger than ourselves, part of something grander, bolder, calmer than our own individual whirlwinds. We are one with the power that animates all.

Oneness is the magic of the woods, the wisdom of the wilderness.

Our holy books speak often of the power of the wilderness. Ironically, we often study them in our air-conditioned sanctuaries or heated study rooms, where we miss out on their essence. Why does the Torah begin with the story of the creation of the earth? To remind us of our elemental connection to the land.

Wilderness feeds our spiritual selves, something we often forget. Just as our bodies need good food to eat and clean water to drink, just as our muscles and bones need exercise and rest, so too our souls need nourishment. It is not accidental that Moses first encountered God in the wilderness.

Wilderness nourishes us in many ways. The vistas we greet in nature cleanse us down to our souls. The great open expanses wash over us, cleansing off the detritus of our days in civilization. A hot shower after a mountain bike ride washes off the mud caked to our legs; a hot bath after a demanding day at the desk relaxes our taut muscles and achy shoulders. As these pleasures refresh our bodies, wide-open spaces and uninterrupted landscapes refresh our souls.

Wilderness gives us perspective. Out there we realize our smallness. Suddenly our problems seem less significant and more surmountable. Or even if our challenges still loom large, there is something comforting in knowing that the flowers still bloom and the moon still rises. Even as we face our personal challenges, the world goes on.

In the wilderness, even as we feel small, we also feel part of something larger than ourselves. The Hebrew word *midbar*, "wilderness," can be read as *m'dabeir*, "speaking." The wilderness thus becomes a space of meeting, of speaking, of connecting. We feel connected to the rivers and the trees, to the mountains and the breeze. We realize we are part of something so much larger than ourselves. And through this connection we are comforted.

The comforting power of nature is part of the ancient wisdom of Judaism, as we see in Psalm 23:

> The Eternal is my shepherd: I shall not want.
> I am laid down in green pastures.
> I am led beside still waters.
> My soul is restored.
> I am guided in the paths of righteousness for the Eternal's name's sake.
> Even though I walk through the valley of the shadow of death, I will fear no evil, for You are with me.
> Your rod and Your staff, they comfort me.
> You prepare a table before me in the presence of my enemies.
> You anoint my head with oil.
> My cup runs over.
> Surely goodness and loving-kindness shall follow me all the days of my life,
> And I shall dwell in the Eternal's house forever.

This psalm is part of the shared Jewish and Christian heritage, and for hundreds of years it has given comfort to mourners and those going through difficult times when it is read at funerals and shivah houses.

What does the psalm say to do in times of grief? It does not say join a support group or go talk to your rabbi. It does not say read psalms, although those are both good ideas. What it says is go outside! Sit by a lake, walk through a meadow. Experience the wonder of Creation. When we listen to this inside a funeral chapel, we often think it speaks in metaphor but the psalm is actually telling us to go outside! Why? What is it about the outdoors that is so comforting?

Physicists tell us that when the universe began, there was a singularity. One. In religious terms we might choose to call this God. But whatever you call this oneness, so it was. One. And then something happened! Bang! A bang of such tremendously big proportions, it became known as the big bang. Scientists don't know what caused the big bang, but suddenly that singularity, that oneness, divided into many—from one to light! Heavens! Planets! Water! Air! Trees! Mountains! Fish! Plants! Creepy-crawly things! Animals! You! Me! This book!

In other words, the one (*echad*) had become many.

The words of the *Sh'ma*, taken from the Torah, are about that oneness:

Sh'ma Yisrael: Adonai Eloheinu, Adonai Echad.
Hear, O Israel: *Adonai* is our God, *Adonai* is One.

(Deuteronomy 6:4)

Although I love these words and sing them with my children before I tuck them in at night, this prayer always puzzled me until a physicist described the big bang to me. Then suddenly, it made sense. One! Everything is one! Everything began as one and so remains connected in some primal way. Suddenly the idea of monotheism, one God, made absolute sense to me on an entirely richer level.

I'm not talking about the God people talk to and the God who makes things happen in their lives. I'm talking about a concept of God as the ultimate connection between all beings, who has been there since the beginning of time. This God does not necessarily have a consciousness or interact in our lives, yet it connects us all.

What are the consequences of such a ubiquitous connection? When we realize that we are connected to everything, that we are part of a greater whole, what does that mean?

For each of us, the meaning is different. For some, it's the soothing reassurance that the earth abides, that life continues beyond our singular lives. For others, it's the powerful reassurance that we are not alone. For others, it's a call to action to look out for the vulnerable and less fortunate.

We live in a world that conspires to separate us. Not only are we separated by technology and distance, but we are divided and subdivided by groups and subgroups. Many of us live close to neighbors we hardly know. We collect hundred of friends on Facebook but have few friends that we actually make time to have a coffee with. Our culture divides us into wealthy and poor, Republicans and Democrats, college-educated and not, believers and atheists, and so on.

In contrast, when we are in the wilderness, we are reminded of our interdependency. Eventually we come to realize that in matters of planetary wellness, each of us affects one another, even when far away.

One of my favorite ancient Jewish texts addresses our responsibility to care for the earth.

> When God created the first human beings,
> God led them around the Garden of Eden and said:
> "Look at My works!
> See how beautiful they are—how excellent!
> For your sake I created them all.
> See to it that you do not spoil My world:
> For if you do, there will be no one else to repair it."
>
> *Kohelet Rabbah* 1 on Ecclesiastes 7:13, ca. 800 CE

Even in antiquity, our people were wise enough to know that nature is a sacred space that must be treated with care.

Back on my hike, my breathing is now deep and full, my shoulders are relaxed, and my thoughts finally roam freely. All around me, the foliage is ripe with berries and seeds. The lupine, the wild rose—all the plants are heavy with pods. So too, I am ready to create. The words and phrases of my next writing project begin to coalesce in my mind. The wilderness has again worked its magic. As I make my way down off the mountain, I am calm yet inspired.

14

The Jewish Imperative of Healing the Land

ALEX CICELSKY

God then said, "Let the waters beneath the sky be collected in one place, so that the dry ground may be seen!"—and so it was. And God called the dry ground Earth, and called the collected waters Seas. And when God saw how good it was, God said, "Let the earth grow vegetation, seed-bearing plants, fruit trees on the earth that bear fruit, each true to its type, and with its seed in in it!"—and so it was. The earth brought forth vegetation, seed-bearing plants, each true to its type, and trees bearing fruit, each true to its type, with its seed in it. And God saw how good it was, and there was evening and there was morning, a third day.

Genesis 1:9–13

When I *listen* to the stories in Genesis, I imagine myself in ancient times, sitting with my tribe under the stars, around a campfire, grateful for a successful hunt, baskets filled with berries, bodies sated and healthy.

When I *read* the Genesis stories, I imagine myself as a scribe, tasked to record my civilization's oral mythologies on papyrus. There are many versions and varieties of stories. I'm curious as to why certain stories were selected to be written down and why others were left out.

Today though I *saw* a spectacular "Genesis moment" and posted the Creation pictures on Facebook. They were photographs of baby lettuce growing out of the ultimate "dry lands" that God created: the arid sands of the Aravah desert. I can describe the baby green's surroundings by quoting straight from the story of Creation. The baby greens were growing under some "tree[s] bearing fruit": sweet figs, green olives, and juicy dates. They were surrounded by "herb[s] yielding seed": basil, mint, sage, and rosemary. There were flowers all around, and as I watched it all from under the shade of a grape vine, I ate from the ripe fruit. If God had been standing next to me, She'd certainly comment on how good it was!

I can easily relate to the story of Creation on the third day because I have personally experienced creating something from nothing. At the age of twenty-two, I wandered through the desert wilderness to seed, nurture, and harvest the first fruits ever in history from the sands that would become Kibbutz Lotan in 1983. I had studied agriculture at Cornell University with an intent to use my knowledge to play a part in ending famine in the world. The founders of Kibbutz Lotan, all ideological pioneers like me, became experts in ultramodern farming. We harvested bumper crops from the sands. To do this we used the best technologies available, including using drip irrigation to utilize every drop of brackish water in our quota mixed with industrial fertilizers. Our fields of crops, which we sprayed to protect from pests and weeds, reached the border with Jordan. It was a postcard vista of green framed by the Edom mountains.

Is Environmentalism a Jewish Ethic?

In 1962 Rachel Carson published the book *Silent Spring*, which opened the public's eyes to the connection between the chemicals that protect our food supply and dwindling bird populations. Her observations in-spired the new environmental movement, creating a new "Torah"[1] of how to care for land, soil, air, and animals. Her research was consid-ered a catalyst to the creation of the U.S. Environmental Protection Agency. The EPA regulations that ensued, including the banning of DDT, saved the lives of farmers who had been exposed to excessive poisons and reversed the road to extinction of many species, including the bald eagle. On Lotan we came to learn the lessons of *Silent Spring*, using pesticides responsibly and only when needed to stop insects from ravaging our vegetables.

As our only income, the tons of tomatoes, onions, and melons we harvested were our "bread and butter." To bake bread one needs to grow wheat and mill flour. As *Pirkei Avot* teaches, "When there's no flour, there's no Torah. When there's no Torah, there's no flour" (*Pirkei Avot* 3:17).

This adage from *Pirkei Avot* described our work on the kibbutz perfectly. Being a religious and agrarian community, we were proud of the balance we achieved between the physical and spiritual re-sources needed to sustain life. We were literally growing our own "flour" (income and food) that allowed us to sustain ourselves spiri-tually by living out our egalitarian/Reform interpretation of Judaism and the Zionist ideology of our people's need to return to our *eretz*—our land. We thought we had it all right. Then the bird-watchers arrived.

The bird-watchers complained of the "new" desert we had created. They castigated us for killing off the insects that millions of migratory birds could be feeding on as they crossed through our valley between Africa, Europe, and Asia. The green fields that the birds saw as a rest-ing and feeding stop was now, at best, a "food desert" with no life in it. They were also incredibly concerned that the birds would ingest pesticide-laden insects—maybe we weren't heeding all of the lessons from *Silent Spring*.

In the early 1990s a handful of Lotan members decided to intentionally address these issues. What would it mean to face this dilemma and weigh the environmental costs of our actions against our need to make the income needed to sustain our community? Is caring for the environment even an inherently Jewish value? It seemed more magical than serendipitous that even from the hinterlands of the Aravah we were able to connect with friends, rabbis, and scholars who were, like us, wrestling with the latter question—is environmentalism inherently Jewish? We reread the Torah, analyzed Jewish texts, and were inspired by the writings of Rabbi Abraham Joshua Heschel. We discovered that our Jewish bookshelf and practices resonated with environmental intentions.

Rav Heschel, for example, framed Shabbat as an opportunity to step out of a mechanized and consumer society and into nature—to allow oneself to be awestruck. Other evidence for the Jewish argument for the environment came from the Jewish practice of saying blessings before eating to show appreciation for the gifts the natural earth gives us. Further, contemporary interpretations of the stories that gave us the concepts *bal tashchit* (not wasting) and *tzaar baalei chayim* (animal protection) are Jewish mirrors of common environmental ethics and practices. We even investigated if there were biblical stories that demonstrated the specific directive to protect nature. We weren't the first to recognize that there are two distinct stories of Creation in Genesis and that both related to food supply. Reading the stories, now as farmers, we recognized how our lives paralleled those of our ancestors working to build successful settlements and how it seemed to have posed a cultural, perhaps even theological dilemma between contradictory worldviews reaching back thousands of years.

An interpretation of the second Creation story in Genesis (Genesis 2:4–25) argues that the world was barren and there was no reason for life to be set in motion until there was a human being who would tend the garden God planted in Eden.

So God Eternal took the man, placing him in the Garden of
Eden to work it and keep it. (Genesis 2:15)

Once the first farmer was trained, then all the animals could be
created and fed. This egotistical tale has humans being given the job
to "work it and keep it" (Genesis 2:15, "it" being the Garden of Eden)
for the purpose of self-preservation by securing sources of food. It is
anthropocentric by creating a hierarchy where plants and animals exist
essentially as a service to humans. Farming is the most important job.
But it wasn't the first way that humans were fed.

In Genesis 1, the first Creation story, on the sixth day the first
male and female are told to hunt animals, gather seeds and fruits, and
reproduce:

God then blessed them, and God said to them, "Be fruitful
and multiply; fill the earth and tame it; hold sway over the fish
of the sea and the birds of the sky, and over every animal that
creeps on the earth." And God said, "Look, I have given you
all the seed-bearing plants on the face of the earth, and every
tree that has in it seed-bearing fruit—these are yours to eat."
(Genesis 1:28–29)

There are many interpretations of the intentions of the instructions that include "tame it" and "hold sway over [the earth]." Some
interpretations have fired provocative discussions about the historical
role of religious interpretation of the Bible in colonialism, "manifest destiny," and destructive global development (this is addressed
in other chapters of this book). My interpretation is that these terms
subscribe to the inherent right of humans to survive, just as animals
and plants are created with the ability to survive and reproduce. Survival for our ancient hunting and gathering ancestors was a daily
challenge. Humans and animals alike eat and reproduce to survive.

Unlike the animals, however, humans tell stories about the world around the fire at night.

What fascinates me about this particular part of the Creation story is that it is a remnant of our ancestors' understanding of two fundamental things about the world. One is that plants are the foundation for life. On the third day of Creation, when dry land became earth, plants came forth. Plants preceded, perhaps because they require it, the natural cycles of sun and moon and seasons created on the fourth day. The second fundamental point is that there was no Garden of Eden.

This revelation astounded me. As a child, I melded the first and second chapters of Genesis together into one Creation story. Tomes have been written about the derivations of these distinct stories and their complementary and contradictory aspects. It took me time to realize that *haaretz* (the earth), from which plants grew, was not a confined land. On the third day there is no distinction between inside and outside a garden. The earth is the garden. Here was a fundamental view of the world from *my* heritage that resounded and connected between my most basic comprehension of Judaism and my comprehension of nature. Judaism is founded on "Listen! *Sh'ma . . .* God . . . is One." God and Creation are a unified whole of many parts. Here, a Jewish ethic parallels and complements a universal tenet of the environmental movement and the ethical behavior that it dictates. *Haaretz*, the land, is much more than a mineral medium for supporting plants. Aldo Leopold, the twentieth-century conservationist and early developer of environmental ethics, explains this concept in his essay "A Land Ethic":

> The land ethic simply enlarges the boundaries of the community to include soils, waters, plants, and animals, or collectively: the land. . . . In short, a land ethic changes the role of *Homo sapiens* from conqueror of the land-community to plain member

and citizen of it. It implies respect for his fellow-members, and also respect for the community as such."[2]

Leopold's land ethic combines an astute observation and a dictum. Land is an inclusive ecological system of mineral, plant, and animal components, and this association demands mutual respect and protection from all of its members (double entendre intended). We're blessed with the opportunity to survive and thrive, fully dependent on the sustenance this world provides. For that we give thanks. *L'ovdah ulshomrah*, "to work it and keep it" (Genesis 2:15)—respect, honor, and till the garden plot and guard both the soil and the harvest. Combining the two stories of Creation: agriculture developed together with growing human populations who were dependent on concentrated and predictable food production. We on Lotan depended on this relationship completely. So, how could our Israeli farming initiative be at odds with nature?

Disregarding conventional wisdom and our own experience in desert farming, we decided to grandly experiment in organic farming. We moved the little organic vegetable patch we tended with our children onto a large plot of sand. Imagine the challenge of planting vegetables on the beach. Authors of organic gardening books are emphatic about the critical importance of healthy, insect- and microbe-filled soil, but none instructed us how to turn sand into soil. We found the answer in the Torah and by emptying out our garbage.

God said, "Let the earth grow vegetation. . . ." (Genesis 1:11)

The emphasis is on developing an earth that can successfully put forth plants. Instead of planting seeds and then adding nutrients to the sand as we did with our conventional plants, we started creating soil. We separated the organic waste from the garbage in our communal kitchen and dining hall, and we composted it. Composting in the

Aravah takes work, time, water, and attention. It will not happen on its own. Today composting seems trivial, but in 1996 it was revolutionary. The evolution of the garden was as slow as the growth of the trees. It was a period of failures and discoveries as we searched for varieties of vegetables and herbs from around the world that would thrive in a previously untested combination of the climate of the Aravah desert, the salty irrigation water, the local predators, and the lack of inputs of industrial fertilizers or protection from insecticides or herbicides. Some vegetables died. Others survived. Each year another layer of compost protected by mulch was spread on the fields. Eventually we collected seeds for the coming year and were joyful when the herbs and some vegetables seeded themselves. Just like on the third day of Creation.

I'm amazed while photographing the baby greens poking out of the soil. A desert oasis is an amazing place and this garden, tended with lots of hours of love and hard work, is exceptionally beautiful. The sand has now become soil, and digging up a handful, I watch the "creature[s] that creep on the ground" (Genesis 1:25). It has the fragrance of a forest after the rain. This soil, unlike the sand, retains water and nutrients to share with young plants. Sitting under a grape vine, I am surrounded by fig trees, mulberry, guava, olives, figs, dates, kale, chard, and lettuces; orange, yellow, and red tomatoes; eggplant, broccoli, and cauliflower. Nestled inside the soil are blue, white, and sweet potatoes, onions, and garlic. Butterflies and bees alight on edible flowers, sage, rosemary, basil, sweet and Sinai mint. When we arrived at this site there were no bees. Now I'm looking at numerous varieties vying for access to the flowers. There are enough for all. This garden was an experiment that the regional agricultural advisers considered science fiction. If you were thrilled by the recent movie about an astronaut stuck on Mars who survives by growing potatoes in sand and anthropogenic organic matter (human waste), come experience a real-life version of sand turning into soil full of potatoes in our Garden of Eden at Kibbutz Lotan.

Gardens Supply More Than Food

All four of the elements of life on earth come together for the first time on day three of Creation: water, air, earth, and sun. The plants trap the sun's energy that will power the explosion of simple and complex creatures. Today we can explain the relationship, the process and evolution of photosynthetic plants, whose waste product (from sequestering carbon from the primordial atmosphere) is the oxygen we breathe today. Sit in a field, garden, or forest and take a long, slow, deep breath. We're inhaling the third day of Creation. Eat any food you love slowly and intentionally. Consider that food, in its entirety, is a combination of the four elements of Creation. Our life cycle is dependent on the transfer of nutrients from the soil, air, and water, with encapsulated sunlight, that will break apart into your body and allow you another bite and breath.

Consideration of the third day extends further than appreciating the benefits from nature's inherent ability to grow food from seed and seed from fruits. The experience I have sitting in our green oasis is spellbinding. It's nothing short of a miracle, considering the climate and environment. I feel that the miracle I see, smell, touch, hear, and taste is beyond my common senses. When we are deep in the forest, surrounded by prairies, gazing at the sunset on the beach, immersed in nature—the sight, sounds, and smells—something stirs deep inside our bodies. This is a physical description of the paradigm shift in our appreciation of our environment that Rabbi Abraham Joshua Heschel called "radical amazement":

Wonder or radical amazement is the chief characteristic of the religious man's attitude toward history and nature. One attitude is alien to his spirit: taking things for granted, regarding events as a natural course of things. To find an approximate cause of a phenomenon is no answer to his ultimate wonder. He knows that there are laws that regulate the course of natural processes; he is aware of the regularity and pattern of things. However, such knowledge fails to mitigate his sense of perpetual surprise at the fact that there are facts at all. Looking at the world he would say, "This is the Lord's doing, it is marvelous in our eyes" (Psalm 118:23).[3]

I sit in the garden in absolute amazement of what is growing around me. Visitors have the same experience, and together we talk about our deep desire to share this experience with everyone, in particular people living in urban landscapes. I love to kvell about the graduates of our Green Apprenticeship in Permaculture,[4] who grasp both the utility of the garden and the wonder experienced in small patches of nature. They are responsible for bringing nature into cities and organic food to schools around the world. They lead youth to build garden beds raised above polluted inner-city dirt. Together their hands dig into soil to plant seedlings and learn to protect nature, protest waste, and support change. The outcome of the simple act of putting their bare hands into the soil, the earth, is an intimate bond with nature. Both Creation stories, a borderless world of food and the small garden tended by humans, have relevant morals for us. We can learn to limit our intake because we see the garden as a limited resource that must be shared with all. To do so we must redefine what it means to feel satisfied and recognize when we have enough. The third-day metaphor envisions a healthy world of luxurious growth; unharmed by wars and unscarred by commodification of resources associated with mining and oil extractions; with unpolluted water, soil, and air. Physical contact with the earth develops this intellectual comprehension.

Heschel's thoughts preceded the coining of the term "ecopsychology,"[5] the study of the impact of "nature deficit" on human behavior. Heschel warned of the effects disconnecting from nature might have on the soul:

As civilization advances, the sense of wonder declines. Such decline is an alarming symptom of our state of mind. Mankind will not perish for want of information; but only for want of appreciation. The beginning of our happiness lies in the understanding that life without wonder is not worth living. What we lack is not a will to believe but a will to wonder.[6]

That disconnection grows when people spend all their day in classrooms and offices and all night in houses. The disconnection is manifested in our insatiable extraction of resources, resulting in the ravages of air and water pollution and the wanton disposal of waste. The path to understanding that this is unhealthy for us and our world seems to elude many people in our communities. Legislators who believe that God created the world for their personal entertainment or as a utility to provide financial profit don't support laws that ensure environmental protection and conservation. What is missing? Heschel thinks that the task of religion is to create in us an intelligence to sense, beyond merely following prescriptive practices:

> Awareness of the divine begins with wonder. It is the result of what man does with his higher incomprehension. The greatest hindrance to such awareness is our adjustment to conventional notions, to mental clichés. Wonder or radical amazement, the state of maladjustment to words and notions, is therefore a prerequisite for an authentic awareness of that which is.[7]

I love the concept "higher incomprehension." I think I first began to grasp it when stargazing and attempting to comprehend an infinite universe. I remember our amazement in sixth grade when we realized that the carbon in our skin, the carbon in the apple, and the carbon dioxide in the air were created in the big bang and are shared over and over. We could be breathing oxygen that a plant "exhaled" a few billion years ago or yesterday. The "vegetation, seed-bearing plants, fruit trees on earth that bear fruit" (Genesis 1:11) grow with the carbon dioxide we exhale. All creatures are products of this continual recycling. We know that it happens, we have terms to describe it, and we can manipulate it, but we can't make life. Life is pretty incomprehensible. Amazing.

Today, in peace-building work I'm involved with between Israelis and our Arab neighbors, we say, "Nature knows no boundaries," as a metaphor for the way that we need to model our relationships in conservation, resource protection, managing pollution, and protecting the rights of migratory species as citizens of the land—citizens of the earth. Leopold, Heschel, and Carson were reacting to what they observed: centuries of disregarding our impact on the environment because of the inherent policy of destruction of nature (and indigenous societies) built into modern cultures. We may not have centuries to change and bring our cultures into an era of sharing and caring, but I am optimistic.

I am heartened because I have experienced the restorative power of the earth, the *eretz*, when people make contact with it. It's not magic, but it is intentional. I see more and more people, businesses, and communities that make the connection between being kind to each other and being good to the earth. I've seen a change happen in children planting tomatoes in our garden and in adults building a raised bed for tomatoes in Baltimore. I grew up next to a poisoned lake in upstate New York that now teems with edible fish. All of manufacturing and energy production needs to change. Agricultural policy and methods need to reflect the goals of a healthy diet for humans and increasing fertility of the soil.[8] For many, the will to address these challenges has its roots in a child who had an intimate relationship with nature. We can all do our small part in re-extending the third-day breadth of fertile and productive land that nurtures all the plants, that supplies every living thing that grows from her, moves through her, and walks on her with life itself.

On the sixth day, the day when humans and animals were created together, the text of the third day of Creation is implanted, and
God informs us of the purpose of the third day of Creation's world-
encompassing greenery. Simply, to eat. To survive:

And God said, "Look, I have given you all the seed-bearing
plants on the face of the earth, and every tree that has in it
seed-bearing fruit—these are yours to eat. And to every land
animal, and to every bird of the sky, and to all that creeps on
the earth in which is the breath of life, I [give] all green vegetation for food."—And so it was.

Through objective appreciation, radical amazement, and collective intelligence, we will learn to protect and sustain the entirety
of this food-bearing, species-filled planet as if it is (and it is) our
only resource. A shared resource for all of earth's citizens. A world-
encompassing shared garden we call earth, *haaretz*.

Notes

1. "Torah" in Modern Hebrew has three meanings: the physical parchment, hand-
written scrolls of the Five Books of Moses; the collection of written and oral holy
books and commentaries; an ideology or set of ethics. *Torat haadamah* is literally
"the Torah of the earth/soil" and descriptively "environmental ethics."

2. Aldo Leopold, *A Sand County Almanac, and Sketches Here and There* (New York:
Oxford University Press, 1949), 204. It is possible to translate "a land ethic" as *derech
eretz* (literally "the way of the land"). This adds another layer to the term that already has a plethora of meanings, all stemming from an understanding of what is
inherent in nature and its projection on the nature of people's behavior. Leopold
flips it back to how people should behave toward nature.

3. Rabbi Abraham Joshua Heschel, *Between God and Man* (New York: Simon &
Shuster, 1959), 41.

4. Permaculture is a set of ethics and strategies derived from the diversity, stability, and resilience of natural ecosystems in order to sustain healthy human settlements and the earth. Bill Mollison and David Holmgren coined the term in 1976
and started a worldwide movement.

5. Theodore Roszak is credited with coining the term in his 1992 book *The Voice of the Earth*. He later expanded the idea in the 1995 anthology *Ecopsychology* with coeditors Mary Gomes and Allen Kanner.

6. Heschel, *Between God and Man*, 41.

7. Ibid.

8. There is a direct correlation between increasing the fertility and organic matter in the soil and decreasing carbon dioxide in the atmosphere.

15
—

Why We Must Teach Our Children to Care for All Living Creatures

RABBI RAYNA GEVURTZ

God then said, "Let the earth bring forth living creatures of every type: domestic animals and creeping things and wild animals, each true to its type!"—and so it was.

Genesis 1:24

Treatment of Animals within Our Sacred Tradition

Once a calf en route to slaughter passed before Rabbi Y'hudah HaNasi. It broke away, hid its head under the rabbi's skirt, and lowed pitifully, as though pleading, "Save me." "Go," said Rabbi Y'hudah HaNasi. "What can I do for you? For this you were created." At that moment it was declared in heaven, "Since he showed no pity upon this calf, let us bring suffering upon him." The rabbi was afflicted with a stone in his urinary tract and with thrush for thirteen years.

One day his maidservant was sweeping the house. Seeing some weasel pups lying there, she was about to sweep them away. The rabbi said to her, "Let them be, as it is written: 'God's compassion is over all God's creatures'" (Psalm 145:9). At that moment, it was said in heaven, "Since he is now compassionate, let us be compassionate to him," and he was cured. (Babylonian Talmud, *Bava M'tzia* 85a)

This ancient tale told in our Rabbinic literature illustrates the centrality of the mitzvah of *tzaar baalei chayim*, the prevention of animals' suffering, in our sacred tradition. Even the great Rabbi Y'hudah Ha-Nasi, the wise sage credited with compiling the Mishnah, had to be reminded that the care and protection of all of God's creatures is in our hands. This mitzvah is woven into the very fabric of our people's understanding of how God created the world as well as our role within it.

The deliberate choice of language used to describe the first living creatures in the world is striking. As we read, "God then said, 'Let the waters bring forth swarms of *nefesh chayah* [living creatures]'" (Genesis 1:20), and further on in the Creation narrative we read, "Let the earth bring forth *nefesh chayah* [living creatures]" (Genesis 1:24). The phrase *nefesh chayah* is literally translated as "living souls." From the waters to the land, the earth is filled with beings that are described in this way. Moreover, it is this exact phrase that is used to describe the creation of the first human being: "Then God Eternal fashioned the man—dust from the soil—and breathed into his nostrils the breath of life, so that man became a *nefesh chayah* [living being]" (Genesis 2:7). Through the specific language chosen to describe God's new creatures, we glean that humankind, at our essence, is tied to the other beings of God's world.

As we move forward in the *Tanach*, we read of the important role of animals in the lives of our ancestors and the various laws guiding *tzaar baalei chayim*, the prevention of animals' suffering. While the ancient

Israelites relied heavily on animals in their agricultural work, they were also given laws to treat them in a compassionate manner. From the ruling, "You shall not plow with an ox and an ass together" (Deuteronomy 22:10), reminding an owner that one animal might cause injury to another, to the law that reminds us that an animal must be able to find nourishment as it works, "You shall not muzzle an ox while it is threshing" (Deuteronomy 25:4), over and again we are shown that the animals used by the Israelites were more than merely tools of the field. They were seen as God's creatures, upon whom humanity must have compassion.

Perhaps the most striking law in our Torah pertaining to animal welfare is found within the mitzvah of Shabbat, "The seventh day is a Sabbath of the Eternal your God: you shall not do any work—you, your son or daughter, your male or female slave, or your cattle" (Exodus 20:10). At a time when our people's livelihood depended on the physical work of their animals, it is remarkable that the Torah focuses on even the animals' need for rest. Once again we are reminded that the animals in our midst are God's creatures, beings endowed with a *nefesh chayah*, a "living soul," for whom we are obligated to provide care. This is brought home once again in the words of the Proverbs, "A righteous man knows the needs of his animal" (Proverbs 12:10).

While the *Tanach* and later Rabbinic literature overflow with passages illustrating the importance of compassion in our treatment of animals, it is within the Talmud that we find the description of the actual mitzvah of *tzaar baalei chayim*, preventing animals' suffering, as a religious obligation rooted in Torah, and therefore considered directly from God. Based on the interpretation of the biblical command to unload a pack animal ("When you see the ass of your enemy lying under its burden and would refrain from raising it, you must nevertheless help raise it" [Exodus 23:5]), the Rabbis conclude, "We have learned that *tzaar baalei chayim* is a biblical obligation" (Babylonian Talmud, *Bava M'tzia* 32a–b). This majority opinion is later supported throughout history in the Jewish legal commentaries and codes.[1] Moreover, the Rabbis teach that *tzaar baalei chayim* is of such importance that we are permitted to break other basic commandments in order to prevent suffering to animals, including the laws governing Shabbat and *Yom Tov* (holidays).[2] It is from this, the core of our legal literature concerning this mitzvah, that the use of the term *tzaar baalei chayim* has been expanded in recent years to express the more general value that our tradition places upon the compassionate treatment of animals.

The Realities of Animal Cruelty in Our World Today

It is clear throughout the Jewish textual and legal tradition that Judaism places an extremely high value on the compassionate treatment of animals. Therefore, when we learn the reality of how billions of animals in this world actually spend their lives on this planet, we are struck by the multitude of human practices currently in place that clearly violate this central Jewish tenet. Throughout the world today, our fellow creatures live lives of unspeakable pain and fear caused by the callous way some humans make use of them in many industries. Among the many trades that cause this suffering are the entertainment industry, including circuses, horse racing, and dog racing; captive animal displays, such as zoos and aquariums that do not give animals adequate space and social opportunities; the millions of animals used for drug, food, and cosmetic experimentation and testing; as well as the animals that suffer in the name of fashion, at the hands of the wool, fur, and leather industries. While every one of these issues demand our active and immediate attention, it is to yet another horrific violation of the principle of *tzaar baalei chayim* that we turn our attention: that of the factory farming industry, which produces the majority of our animal-based food products.

Factory farming, which is also known as "agribusiness," is the system of agriculture today by which the majority of the meat, milk, and eggs are produced in the cheapest and quickest manner possible. In the United States alone, it is estimated that approximately ten billion animals are raised under the least humane conditions possible for the sake of our food industry.[3] On today's farms, laying hens are raised in overcrowded cages and de-beaked with hot searing knives. Most male chicks are deemed useless and are therefore thrown live into garbage bags to suffocate or into shredding machines to be turned into food for other chickens. Calves that are raised for veal are taken from their mothers a day or two after birth and placed in tiny dark cages with their heads chained in place to prevent licking the bars, which may add iron, and therefore color, to an animal that humans prefer to be pale. Cattle that are raised for beef are overfed, then castrated, dehorned, and branded without anesthetics, and finally shipped in overcrowded trucks to be slaughtered. And this is just scratching the surface.

The idyllic image of the animals of this world living a life on "Old Macdonald's Farm" has given way to dollar-driven mega-farms in which the animals' quality of life is suffering enormously. Furthermore, we must remember that animals that are eventually slaughtered for kosher meat or are farmed for products that will be later declared kosher are raised in the same system as all other factory-farmed animals. The distinction between a kosher and nonkosher animal-based food product only occurs at the slaughterhouse.

While the impact upon the lives of billions of animals should be enough reason for us to work for an end to current factory farming practices, the effect of this cruel industry reaches even beyond God's creatures to the very earth we live on. Our Torah teaches us, "God called the dry ground Earth, and called the collected waters Seas. And . . . God saw how good it was" (Genesis 1:9–10). The goodness of the land and sea that were formed on the third day of Creation is currently under direct attack by the realities of modern agribusiness. The Food and Agricultural Organization of the United Nations describes the consequences of factory farming to our world: "This expansion of the livestock sector is exerting mounting pressure on the world's natural resources: grazing land is threatened by degradation; deforestation is occurring to grow animal feed, water resources are becoming scarce; air, soil, and water pollution are increasing."[4]

Farm animal production also contributes heavily to climate change. The industry accounts for an estimated 18 percent of the world's greenhouse gas emissions, including 9 percent of the carbon dioxide, nearly 40 percent of the methane (a greenhouse gas 25 times more potent than carbon dioxide), and 65 percent of the nitrous oxide (300 times more potent than carbon dioxide).[5] The good earth and seas formed on the third day of Creation are rapidly being destroyed by the massive factory farming industry.

Just as we must study and teach our children the traditional Jewish sources that guide the mitzvah of *tzaar baalei chayim*, so too is it our sacred obligation to stay informed about the current status of all animal cruelty issues. Our Jewish obligations to care for our fellow creatures as well as the world that God has created require us to make informed lifestyle choices while also actively working to change the broken realities of our world. There are many ways we can take part in fulfilling these Jewish obligations, such as boycotting food products that come from factory farms, supporting the small but growing industry of cruelty-free farms, choosing to limit or eliminate our consumption of animal-based food products, and working to advocate for improved animal protection legislation. As we learn and are inspired by the story of Creation, we must each do our part to recommit ourselves to the sacred value of *tzaar baalei chayim*.

Notes

1. *Rosh* on BT *Bava M'tzia* 32 a-b (3:28); *Nimukei Yosef* on BT *Bava M'tzia* 32 (17b); *Tur, Choshen Mishpat* 272:10–14; *Rema* on *Shulchan Aruch, Choshen Mishpat* 272:9; *Aruch HaShulchan, Choshen Mishpat* 272:2.

2. Babylonian Talmud, *Shabbat* 128b; *Rosh* on BT *Bava M'tzia* 32 a-b (3:28); *Mishneh Torah, Hilchot Shabbat* 25:26; *Shulchan Aruch, Orach Chayim* 305:19; *Mishnah B'rurah, Orach Chayim* 305 (68, 69).

3. Farm Sanctuary, "How We Treat Animals We Eat," www.farmsanctuary.org.

4. Food and Agriculture Organization of the United Nations, "Livestock and Environment," www.fao.org.

5. Worldwatch Institute, "Rising Number of Farm Animals Poses Environmental and Public Health Risks," www.worldwatch.org.

16

Bal Tashchit

God's First
and Most General Call

RABBI FRED SCHERLINDER DOBB, DMIN

God then said, "Let the waters beneath the sky be collected in one place, so that the dry ground may be seen!"—and so it was. And God called the dry ground Earth, and called the collected waters Seas. And when God saw how good it was, God said, "Let the earth grow vegetation, seed-bearing plants, fruit trees on the earth that bear fruit, each true to its type, and with its seed in in it!"—and so it was. The earth brought forth vegetation, seed-bearing plants, each true to its type, and trees bearing fruit, each true to its type, with its seed in it. And God saw how good it was, and there was evening and there was morning, a third day.

Genesis 1:9–13

"Do not destroy/waste anything!" is the first and most general call of God.

Rabbi Samson Raphael Hirsch[1]

From rocks and water and light: life. This is the great innovation at the end of the third day of the Creation story and a key turning point in the *seder b'reishit*, or "order of beginning-ness."

Our religious and scientific myths serve distinct functions in our lives. Both can matter, and each can be relevant in its own way without fully aligning—yet here, they converge. The universe knew only cosmology in its first nine billion years or so; as our solar system formed, geological bodies followed. Then biological life burst forth, an entirely new realm of existence. Though science can roughly explain it, the emergence of life bears all the hallmarks of a miracle.

Life begins within a closed-loop system. Barring the occasional meteor strike from above or upwelling from within, the biosphere is a giant sealed terrarium, constantly recycling its key elements. Our "spaceship Earth" receives a steady supply of sunlight, the energy behind generation after generation of life. Nothing is wasted, and nothing is subtracted from the system; vibrancy ensues. Our job is to assiduously emulate this (cosmic or divine) creativity.

Analogies between nature and ethics are challenging, since nature is inherently amoral[2]—religion addresses what ought to be beyond nature's rich presentation of what is. But at the center of the Creation story, as in the heart of life, conservation is not just a good idea; it's the law (whether articulated by God or by physicists).[3] Zero waste. Closed loops. Sustainable systems.

Judaism offers many great principles that might be the *k'lal gadol*, our great central notion.[4] Rabbi Samson Raphael Hirsch (1808–88) does not assign priority to that which comes first in the narrative, the mitzvah of *p'ru ur'vu* (be fruitful and multiply), a challenging instruction in our overpopulated world. Nor does he choose Shabbat, kashrut, monotheism, or any of the other cause célèbres of German Orthodoxy. Rather, he considers as "the first and most general call of God" what others deem a tertiary commandment, number 529 out of the complete 613 mitzvot: the mitzvah of *bal tashchit*, or "thou shalt not waste."[5]

From a prohibition on cutting down an enemy's fruit trees in war-time (Deuteronomy 20:19–20), tradition expands *bal tashchit* to cover everything from anger management ("do not rend garments or destroy vessels in anger")[6] to energy efficiency ("one who errantly covers an oil lamp, or uncovers a naphtha lamp, violates the law").[7] "Waste not, want not" becomes a Torah ethic, as important as any mandate from our Creation narratives, even if not stated overtly in those narratives. Medieval pietists make of this a yardstick of righteousness, by which good folks "prevent wanton waste with everything they've got," whereas the wicked "delight in destroying the world as they destroy themselves."[8] This mitzvah's (debatable) centrality in Jewish environmental ethics is well outlined by scholar-activists Eilon Schwartz and Jeremy Benstein.[8]

So should we consider "do not waste" law number 529 or law number 1? Will we accept this mitzvah's priority only after consequences of our short-term thinking mount? Must we wait until the ill effects of disposability, planned obsolescence, and fossil fuel addiction become yet deadlier and clearer? Or can we take this message to heart, today?

Here, through fanciful divine diary entries on Creation's day three, we might come to join Rav Hirsch and lift up *bal tashchit* as God's "first and most general call."

✦

Year One. Week One. Day Two. (Wait, no—day three already!
I'm so used to eternity, this "time" thing will take a while . . .)

Monday evening, 7:43 p.m.:
Really liked the "lightset" tonight, second one (ever!). It just ended—great colors in the western heavens. Hmm, what if I concentrate the *or* into an orb (note to Self: Wednesday, maybe)?

I'm so glad I started to *recycle* the dark and the light, alternating them. Keep the best stuff moving; throw nothing away—those are ideas I can carry through Creation.

These light shows are sweet scenes to the Eternal and worth savoring.[10] Why'd I let primordial darkness go unabated 'til just a couple of nights ago! Glad I decided to start creating—this process is *good*.

Will think and plan tonight, and by first light, let the Creation continue . . .

Monday night, 9:20 p.m.:

Enjoying jotting down thoughts every so often—it's divinely clarifying.

"Creating heaven and earth" (Genesis 1:1) looks to be a multiday endeavor—six, maybe seven? To figure out next steps, a quick look back: waters were there from the beginning (1:2), along with My spirit—then light (1:3), darkness (1:4), and day and night (1:5). Then yesterday, firmament (1:6), aka heaven (1:8). Sunday was busier; I'd best pick up the pace.

Decision: do more with the waters, the lower ones for now, going forward. And since heaven is Mine, let whatever I'm making space for be earthy ("heaven and earth" implies separation) and also wet ("waters beneath the heavens").

Tuesday, wee hours, 2:21 a.m.:

Decision: *cycles* are where it's at. Having seen how well light-and-dark went, Creation should be full of 'em. Cycles everywhere. Cycles within cycles.[11]

For this, edges seem promising—where earth and heaven meet could be a lively space. Edges or boundaries between two things enable ebb and flow; I'll enliven surfaces, more than depths, to capture cyclicality.

And with this focus on cycles maybe I can make "not wasting," the conservation of stuff, not just scientific reality, but a moral litmus test.[12]

It can be at the center of how the world *does* work, and how it *should* work.

Will noodle on what else can cycle, and how . . .

Tuesday morning, 4:37 a.m.:

Spent most of the morning getting My feet wet, literally. Water is cool!

And talk about cycles—what I did with water is so elaborate, so awesome—evaporation-transpiration-condensation-precipitation. For the record, it's all "water," but I love how the same thing acts so differently when it's vapory or freezy.

And the cold form *floats* above the wet stuff! I'm toying with "life" starting in the water. On background, setting up physics, I made solids denser than liquids. Cold hard water should sink. But these "life" forms would smother—so, for water-ice, an exception.[13] Trying to plan ahead here: "the end of the doing comes first in the thinking."[14]

And the water is *conserved*. It cycles; it changes form; it goes up, and comes down, and flows around; it returns. Nothing is wasted! The water cycle—My proudest creation yet.

Tuesday morning, 6:13 a.m.:

Strains of light appearing. Getting cracking. Contemplating the rest of the day, I feel *edgy*. Really liked the heaven-earth boundary; thought of another *edge* that can be long, and shifting, home to a whole mess of cycles (can even be fractal!). My real over-third-night insight: the "earth" (as in "heaven and earth") can mean both the *whole* realm, and just the *non-water* part. Land, I'll call it. Land above the water? (True in altitude terms, but heaven lies straight over water.) Unwet? Unmoist? Ah, got it: dry.

Dry land, coming up. So this I'll say right now: "Let the waters under the heaven be gathered together, into one place, so dry land can appear. Done" (Genesis 1:9)! The land all in one place, and contiguous waters, but with a long and winding shore where they meet. Waves, surf, intertidal ecosystems—endless possibilities here.

For the record, since Who knows when this story's outline will get told—the dry land is "earth," and the big pools of water are "seas." I see now: this is gonna be *good* (1:10)!

Tuesday morning, 7:02 a.m.:

Lightrise! Gorgeous. It's the third one, and I've loved them all. But now seeing it from land, over water, it's even better. Land, water, light—maybe something that covers the land, or lives on it—something's gelling . . .

Tuesday morning, 11:36 a.m.:

Admiring Creation so far. Could call it quits after one big separation (like yesterday); but there's still plenty of daylight. And if there's to be such a thing as Shabbat (note to Self, day seven?), I'd best keep it moving. Life is coming, for sure; just need the right form first . . .

Tuesday afternoon, 2:57 p.m.:

Whatever comes next should be an organic development, an expansion of the best ideas and processes so far that also opens new doors. Idea: make more separations (but I like unity and want to build up "oneness" some more). Or idea: develop heaven / the waters above (nah, let those stay inscrutable a while).

I know! I'll get specific on light and dark. Still think that fits tomorrow better, though, so Creation can spiral—the current week-plan, if I can wrap it up in six, is that day four follows day one; five'll expand two; Friday builds on today's efforts. But how does today set up what'll happen later this week? Wait—idea—I've got sub-cycles within those cycles I'm so into, like waves at the shore—the best processes so far *are* the cycles themselves! The water cycle was awesome; parlay that into something even bigger, something lively, alive . . . Back to work . . .

Tuesday afternoon, 4:57 p.m.:

It's coming together. But how to make something from nothing, at the base of a chain? How to do this "life" thing, making it scalable? And sustainable? Need a mechanism for replicability.

Tuesday afternoon, 6:06 p.m.:

Just had a very happy hour, sketching this out: Waters came first, then light—now, synthesize the two! Call it "photo-hydro-change"—"hydro-photo-synthesis"—something like that. Truly creative, if the Creator may say so Godself. I'm the producer, but with this, things can *re*produce on their own, after their own kind—from light and water will come plants, to sustain "life."

With that, I realize three fundamental truths, at the exact same time:

1. Need someone to lighten the load. I can make earth a *partner*, giving it generative power.
2. Let a big thing make a little thing, which grows into another big thing! A mini—a distillation—a seed.
3. The real miracle: When big things die, they'll decompose and add to the land—they'll become nutritious soil, in which even bigger things can grow! A closed system; a perfect cycle. *Nothing will be wasted*, in nature.[15] As long as no one creation gets too greedy, it can just go on and on, "after its kind" (Genesis 1:11). May the circle be unbroken, by and by . . .

So I'll "tell the earth to sprout forth sprouting things—plant, bearing its own seed; fruit tree, making fruit, after its own kind—whose seeds are in it. Upon the earth. Not My clearest expression, but heck, it's tons of new stuff all at once. It'll do" (1:11).

Tuesday afternoon, 6:53 p.m.

By the fading light of day three, I saw those sproutings—grass, herb, tree—each with seed, some with fruit too—earth did good (1:12)!

We're onto something here. Man, this is fun. (Man? Hmm . . . note to Self: play with "seed" idea, follow it to more complex life forms . . . see if one organism replicates itself or two must tango—and if so, how can the "sexes" evolve differently, yet be fundamentally equal? Tricky stuff here . . .)

What a night and day I had, this third time around (1:13)—*we* had, actually, now that earth's generating alongside Me. Can't wait to see what comes next . . .

Year One. Month One. Day Eight.

Saturday night, 10:00 p.m.

Meant to write, but things changed nonstop since day four, 'til sundown yesterday—then I crashed. The animals seem to enjoy eating the plants and seeds and fruits—including that last pair of big apes I made. (What to call them? Naked apes? Humanoids? They seem smart enough; let them figure out their family name.) Proud of their opposable thumbs and extra front cortex. There's a million things they haven't done, but just you wait!

"Everything is foreseen, though permission is granted,"[16] by Me. The humanoids will experience each moment as if they had free will (ha!). Thus, they can mess up. Should I have been more specific, telling future shapers of the earth to respect and emulate My beloved closed systems? (Note to Self—make that a commandment some day.) For sure, that late-day-three innovation—"don't waste anything"—was the turning point. Will that be clear, though, to whoever reads the executive summary of the Creation story?

I can foresee the descendants of Chavah v'Adam thinking too much of themselves—focusing more on being *apart* from, rather than *a part* of, creation.[17] Will their *t'shuvah*, their turning around, come in time? Can they reclaim the wisdom of day three and return to the path of justice and sustainability?

God knows . . . and hopes . . .

Notes

1. Samson Raphael Hirsch, Horeb: *A Philosophy of Jewish Laws and Obervances*, trans. I. Grunfeld (New York: Soncino Press, 1962), p. 279.

2. Theologically, I stand here in the shadow of Mordecai Kaplan and Arthur Green (see in particular Green's *Radical Judaism: Rethinking God and Tradition* [New Haven, CT: Yale University Press, 2010]). Regarding the limits and risks of analogies between nature and ethics, consider: when we posit with Dr. King that the long moral arc of the universe bends toward justice, we affirm a great spiritual truth but ignore the law of entropy; a proper reading of Darwin does suggest more cooperation than competition, yet large parts of nature are indeed "red in tooth and claw."

3. In science, this is the law of conservation of mass (first outlined in 1748 by Mikhail Lomonosov, critical to the budding fields of chemistry and physics). In the spiritual and moral realm, this is the bedrock principle that we should not waste anything. This connection of science with spirit is well modeled in biomimicry, where we look to nature to design sustainable human systems; see the "zero waste" movement, as well as such important works as William McDonough and Michael Braungart, *Cradle to Cradle: Remaking the Way We Make Things* (New York: North Point Press, 2002).

4. In the Jerusalem Talmud (*N'darim* 9:4), Rabbi Akiva famously deems *v'ahavta l'rei-acha kamocha*, "Love your neighbor as yourself," the great principle; Ben Azzai prefers *zeh sefer tol'dot adam* "This is the book of the generations of humanity (when collectively created in the divine image)." The introduction to the *Ein Yaakov* (a medieval compilation of Talmudic aggadah) has Ben Zoma advocating *Sh'ma Yisrael Adonai Eloheinu Adonai Echad* "Hear, O Israel, *Adonai* is our God, *Adonai* is One"— and Ben Nanas citing "Love your neighbor as yourself"—along with Shimon ben Pazi privileging constancy by offering Exodus 29:39, "You shall offer one lamb in the morning [as a sacrifice], and you shall offer the other lamb at twilight." (*et hakeves haechad taaseh baboker, v'et hakeves hasheni taaseh bein haarbayim*)

5. S. R. Hirsch wrote *Horeb* in 1838, including this, from chapter 56: "Yea, 'Do not destroy anything!' [*bal tashchit*] is the first and most general call of God, which comes to you . . . when you realize yourself as master of the earth. . . . [God calls:] 'The things around you. I lent them to you for wise use only; never forget that I lent them to you. As soon as you use them unwisely, be it the greatest or the smallest, you commit treachery against My world, you commit murder and robbery against My property, you sin against Me!' This is what God calls unto you."

6. Maimonides, *Mishneh Torah, Hilkhot M'lakhim* 6:10.

7. Energy efficiency is indeed a Talmudic mandate. Rav Zutra taught (Babylonian Talmud, *Shabbat* 67b) that "whoever covers an oil lamp or uncovers a naphtha lamp"—i.e., who fails to take note of their use of fuel, and does not apply the best available technology for minimizing the amount that must be burned—"transgresses the law of *bal tashchit*."

8. *Sefer HaChinuch* 529 (in some editions, 530). This medieval pietistic German text explicates and offers rationales for each mitzvah and is the epitome of the Rabbinic expansion of *bal tashchit* from a limitation on war tactics into an entire way of relating to the world.

9. Eilon Schwartz literally wrote the article on *bal tashchit*, initially in "*Bal Tashchit*: A Jewish Environmental Precept," *Environmental Ethics* 19, no. 4 (Winter 1997): 355–74; then accessibly in "Is the Tree Human?" in *Trees, Earth and Torah: Tu B'Shvat Anthology*, ed. Ari Elon, Naomi Mara Hyman, and Arthur Waskow (Philadelphia: Jewish Publication Society, 1999), and "*Bal Tashchit*: A Jewish Environmental Precept," in *Judaism and Environmental Ethics: A Reader*, ed. Martin Yaffe (Lanham, MD: Lexington Books, 2001). Schwartz digs up numerous commentaries on Deuteronomy 20:19–20 and highlights Judaism's tension between appreciation of nature for its own sake and an instrumental utilitarian approach to nature (in which the value of the fruit tree is monetized without regard to its intrinsic importance, its aesthetic or spiritual value, or the ecosystem services it renders). His then-colleague at Israel's Heschel Center, Jeremy Benstein, offers a greener view of *bal tashchit* in his *The Way into Judaism and the Environment* (Woodstock, VT: Jewish Lights, 2006).

10. Leviticus anthropomorphizes God as appreciating burnt flesh's "sweet-smelling savor, unto the Eternal." With sight as the recurrent human sense attributed to God in the opening chapter of Torah, the metaphor gets recycled.

11. Genesis 1 and Ezekiel 1 were the chapters of *Tanach* that attracted the earliest kabbalistic speculation, leading respectively to the *heichalot* and *merkavah* literature. Ezekiel saw not just the wheel, but "wheels within wheels"; with wheels being so connected to cycles, the metaphor fit.

12. As outlined above, here the law of conservation of mass meets the moral law. The moral litmus test here is also *Sefer HaChinuch*'s "mustard seed test": if something is even as large as that seed, we must work hard to avoid wasting it, if we are to be righteous individuals.

13. This "miracle," this counterintuitive reality of ice floating, truly enabled life. It's one of a number of low-odds scenarios—like a stable orbit around a stable star, just the right amount of volcanic activity, and good magnetic field and ozone layer—upon which our existence is dependent. The "anthropic principle" makes theological and philosophical hay out of these phenomena.

14. *Sof maaseh b'machshavah t'chilah* (from *L'cha Dodi*, sixteenth-century Tzfat composition based on passages from Deutero-Isaiah).

15. "Nothing is wasted in nature or in love" is the conclusion of Linda Pastan's remarkable poem "Life After Death," which in some communities is read at funerals, shivah gatherings, and *Yizkor* remembrances. (See *Kol Haneshama: Shabbat VeHagim*, the 1994 Reconstructionist siddur, page 790). Pastan beautifully encapsulates how the natural and interpersonal realms intersect and bear interlocking insights.

16. Rabbi Akiva—*hakol tzafui, v'har'shut n'tunah* (*Mishnah Avot* 3:15). cf. "Tractate Avot" (p. 67) and "Pirkei Avot" (p. 93).

17. This elegant formulation—that in Genesis, *adam* is "both a part [of] and apart [from] the rest of creation"—is from Phyllis Trible, *God and the Rhetoric of Sexuality* (Philadelphia: Fortress, 1978), p. 90, reiterated in her "The Dilemma of Dominion," in *Faith and Feminism: Ecumenical Essays*, ed. Phyllis Trible and B. Diane Lipsett (Louisville: Westminster John Knox Press, 2014), 29.

17

The Third Day and Our Oceans

LIYA RECHTMAN

God then said, "Let the waters beneath the sky be collected in one place, so that the dry ground may be seen!"—and so it was. And God called the dry ground Earth, and called the collected waters Seas. And . . . God saw how good it was.

Genesis 1:9–10

W e are not told that we hold sway over the sea.

We are told that we hold sway over the animals. When God creates humankind, God grants dominion over the "fish of the sea, the birds of the sky, and over every animal that creeps on the earth" (Genesis 1:28).

We are told that we may do what we like with the plants. "These are yours to eat," God says on the sixth day (Genesis 1:29).

Later, this relationship between human beings and vegetation is modified with the additional command *l'ovdah ulshomrah,* translated literally as "to work it and keep it," and commonly known today as "to till and tend" (Genesis 2:15). In the first contract with humankind, God establishes certain responsibilities for God's day six of Creation.

Humankind is intended to take care of and partake in all animals and all plants.

Day three of the Creation story has two components. Before God established plants, God first collected the chaotic waters of the earth and designated these as "seas," an area differentiated from "dry ground" (Genesis 1:9–10). The creation of each is concluded with a repetition of the central trope of Creation, "God saw how good it was" (Genesis 1:10).

These two acts of creation on one day create two parallel tracks for God's contract with humankind as a partner in Creation. We are told that we hold sway over the animals. We are told that we may do what we like with the plants.

We are not told that we hold sway over the sea.

The word *kivshuha*, translated by Rabbi Chaim Stern in *The Torah: A Modern Commentary* as "hold sway," is alternatively translated as "occupy," "flatten," or "rule over" the land. In Modern Hebrew, *kibush*, of the same root, is the word used for "occupation." Our text gives environmental theologians a tough word to chew on in processing our relationship to the animals and plants. If we are to be rulers over the world, what are the implications for our relationship with our environment? Are plants and animals good only insofar as they are good *for us*, human society? Then the case could be made that the natural world is only good so far as it has value in our ecosystem, our global economy.

This line of thinking is known as "dominion theology" and has been widely criticized by environmental theologians. The most famous recent critique of dominion theology comes from Pope Francis in his 2015 papal encyclical "Praised Be." On the problem of Genesis 1:28, Pope Francis writes that "we must forcefully reject the notion that our being created in God's image and given dominion over the earth justifies absolute domination over other creatures" (paragraph 67). Pope Francis goes on to argue that *kivshuha* must be taken in its broader context, which repeatedly calls for care of the earth. Further, he notes that "we are not

God" and should remember that we are created *b'tzelem Elohim*, in the image of the Divine, and are not ourselves divine. The land is on loan to us to *l'ovdah ulshomrah*, "to till and to tend" (Genesis 2:15), but it is never fully or rightfully ours. In this light we can see that even to occupy, flatten, or hold sway is not to own. Our dominance over vegetation and animals is incomplete and impermanent.

Given that non-ownership, what does it mean that we are not told that we hold sway over the sea? Where we are told to eat of the vegetation on earth and name the animals, God makes no requirement of humankind to rule the sea. This explicit lack of responsibility creates an implicit alternative directive. God says *natati*, "I have given," seed-bearing plants and trees so that humankind and animals may eat (Genesis 1:29). Literally, vegetation is bestowed as a gift from God to humankind. It is the right of humankind, then, to use vegetation as we will. On the same day as God makes these gifts, God also collects the seas. The sea, in opposition to seed-bearing fruits, is not a gift. The sea is not given to humankind, and therefore humankind may not do what we choose with the sea. In short, the sea is expressly not ours, according to this passage.

This lack of responsibility is its own obligation. According to day three, we must abstain from using the sea for our own purposes and refrain from incorporating the sea into our domain. Abstinence is itself an act, a requirement in God's contract with humankind apparent only in its absence.

And yet, humankind *has* ruled over the seas. We have disrupted the boundary lines distinguishing sea from land. Today in Miami, residents in low-lying areas experience sunny-day flooding that infiltrates the very concrete of their sidewalks and sweeps over their beaches. Low-lying nations like the Marshall Islands and the Maldives will likely disappear in the next fifty to one hundred years as sea levels rise globally. Whole populations will be displaced. Cities and states will be pulled underwater as the sea becomes entangled with dry ground. Further, rising sea levels are causing drinking water contamination and disruptions in agriculture, coastal plant life, and wildlife populations. In impacting the seas, we have also adversely affected life on dry land for humans, animals, and plants.

According to the Environmental Protection Agency, sea levels have risen approximately seven inches globally since 1900. We have added greenhouse gases like carbon dioxide and methane to our atmosphere through our use of fossil fuel energies to power our cars and homes. These greenhouse gases have caused an increase in global temperatures, which has led to the melting of glaciers across the globe. That melt-off water has led to the swelling of our oceans. Our industrial output of greenhouse gases has initiated global climate change and sea-level rise; we have failed to stay within the means of our God-given responsibilities.

How do we give up the sway that we now hold over the seas? How do we un-occupy territory that we have wrongly claimed and relinquish our rule? Or rather, if we should not hold sway over the oceans, what should our relationship to them be?

Climate change caused by human activity presents problems of an immense global scale with potentially infinite disruptive power. Currently, the vast majority of the energy used to heat our homes and fuel our cars comes from oil and gas. These sources require extraction processes that destabilize our environment and pollute our air and our water. Further, when we use oil and gas energy for fuel, we emit dangerous greenhouse gases into the air that cause global temperature rise. Rising global atmospheric temperatures in turn cause sea-level rise, disrupt ecosystems, limit crop viability, and lead to drought and extreme weather events. Many of our current international security and poverty crises can be traced back to these adverse climate change impacts.

These challenges have hopeful and plausible remedies. We can mitigate sea-level rise by investing in and advocating for the production and dissemination of clean energy technologies. Clean energy is one possible answer to the question of indistinct boundaries between dry land and the collected waters of the world depicted in Genesis. Instead of using nonrenewable energy sources such as oil and gas, we must make use of the clean energy alternatives, which we have had the technological knowledge to use since the late twentieth century. Clean energy harnesses power from preexisting and nonfinite sources, such as the sun and wind. Unlike clean energy's fossil fuel counterparts, the mechanisms for extraction (solar panels and windmills) are not disruptive. While we cannot turn back the clock on climate change, it is within our power to ensure that the current impacts of sea-level rise are not dramatically worsened as we continue to use nonrenewable sources. We need only shift from greenhouse-gas-producing technologies to renewable energy in order to minimize our negative impact on the oceans.

The shift to clean alternative sources of energy is incumbent upon us, both politically and textually. Clean energy solutions are within the bounds of the first, Edenic contract between God and humankind as well. Our influence on the seas has been an indirect consequence of our impact on the wider environment with our energy industries. Our reframing of energy consumption would be similarly indirect. By living up to our responsibilities on land, we can restore our seas. We can give back to them their autonomy as a space distinct from the dry ground. We must not hold sway over the seas.

On day three of Genesis, we read, "Let the waters beneath the sky be collected in one place, so that the dry ground may be seen!"—and so it was. And God called the dry ground Earth, and called the collected waters Seas. And . . . God saw how good it was" (Genesis 1:9–10). As Jews, we can look at this passage, in both its description of separation and, later, our absence of active human obligation, to make the case for a Jewish response to climate change through renewable energy.

We are at a crossroads in human history where we have gained rule over nature and have the responsibility and capacity to surrender that power. We have scientific evidence that we have created a problem. We have the global willpower to make the change. We are not told that we hold sway over the sea. We are told that God saw how it was.

Now, we just need our energy industry and our policy-makers to catch up.

18
—

From the Third Day to the Song of Songs

The Eco-Torah of an Indigenous People

RABBI ARTHUR WASKOW

God said, "Let the Earth grow vegetation, seed-bearing plants, fruit trees on the earth that bear fruit, each true to its type, with its seed in it!"—and so it was.

(Genesis 1:11)

On the third day, plants spring up all around the earth (Genesis 1:11–12). As befits an indigenous community of farmers and shepherds dependent on meadow grass, wheat, barley, olives, and other fruit, the vegetation of this day becomes the seed of the second story of Creation—the story of Eden.

Indeed, we can trace the crucial ecological outlook of Torah through a thread that begins with Eden and continues through Pharaoh's plagues, the parable of manna and Shabbat, the *Sh'mitah*/Sabbatical year, and the Song of Songs.

Just before Eden, the Torah says, "No shrub of the field was yet on the earth . . . *because* there was no human to till the soil" (Genesis 2:5). This suggests that the reason for the Creator to birth the human race is the need for shrubs and grasses to have the loving touch of human presence—an early wisdom about the intertwining of what we would now call an ecosystem. The shrubs need us; we need them.

The intertwining goes so deep that there is indeed a birthing. From the *adamah* (earth) comes forth *adam* (the human earthling). First this newborn loses the -*ah*, the Hebrew *hei* that is the sound of breathing. Then the Creator Breath of Life (*YyyyHhhhWwwwHhhh Elohim*) "blew into the newborn's nostrils the breath of life, and the human became a living, breathing person" (Genesis 2:5–7).

This tale of birthing was itself born from the birthing of an individual human being. While the fetus is still in the mother's womb, it has no independent breath. The mother's breathing sustains it, through the placenta. When the newborn loses this organic, suffused breath—this -*ah*, represented by the Hebrew letter *hei*—it must take its first independent breath. Perhaps someone taps the newborn's *tush*—and the child begins to breathe.

This biological process is the very model for the Torah's story of how *adam* is born from *adamah*—from Mother Earth. Since the mother here is not a mammal but the earth itself, which sprouts the shrubs and trees as the soil sprouts humankind, we see another artful teaching reinforcing that vegetation and humanity are family.

The human species is born into the Garden of Delight. One of the myriad ways to understand the parable of Eden is that the Breath of Life speaks to the human race: "On this earth there is wonderful abundance. Eat of it in joy. But you must restrain yourselves just a little: Of this one tree, don't eat" (Genesis 2:15–17). Notice that the focus of the story is vegetation from the third day of Creation: a tree. Indeed, the description of abundance is focused on many forms of vegetation—not on killing or eating animals.

The human species then refuses to restrain itself, eats from the forbidden tree, and as a result the abundance disappears. Only by toiling every day of our lives with the sweat pouring down our faces, the story warns us, will we find enough to eat from an earth that gives forth mostly thorns and thistles (Genesis 2:17–19).

In our own lives, we relived this disaster in the Gulf of Mexico during the summer of 2010. BP would not restrain itself, and the result was the death of its own workers, animals, and others living in the region, as well as disastrous damage to the overflowing abundance of the Gulf. If we reconceptualize God not as a wrathful King but as the Interbreathing that brings consequences, fruitful or destructive, that result from our behavior, then we can see this disaster in the Gulf (and in the Garden) not as wrathful punishment but as predictable result.

The BP oil spill was not a moment unique in human history. The cautionary tale of the ruined Garden of Delight has been ignored by many human cultures that have despoiled some sacred patch of earth. Perhaps it was indeed the "original," or at least the ever-recurring, sin. Today we are faced with the prospect that if we cannot learn to restrain ourselves in pouring carbon dioxide and methane into the atmosphere of earth, that sacred source and venue for the Interbreathing of all life, we will ruin the abundance of the planet as a whole.

Meanwhile, we remember that besides the disappearance of abundance, there is a second disaster that emerges from trying to gobble up the Garden, trying to dominate our Mother Earth instead of loving her abundance. Just as the humans have intruded domination into their relationship with the earth, hierarchy and domination will come into human society. Men will rule over women (Genesis 3:16). If the human species insists on tyrannizing its own Mother Earth, then male human beings are likely to insist on tyrannizing their mothers, daughters, sisters, and wives.

In the story of Pharaoh and the plagues, the Torah points to the centralization of unfettered, unaccountable, arrogant, and stubborn power as the most dangerous threat to earth's abundance. Pharaoh oppresses human beings, and his arrogance afflicts the earth itself. Most of the famous Ten Plagues strike at the vegetation that arises from the fertile Nile. When each plague comes, at first Pharaoh is frightened. When it subsides, he evidently decides it was an accident, not a consequence of his behavior (Exodus 8:11, 8:28, 9:12, 9:34–35, 10:20). We can almost hear him saying, "Stuff happens."

Moses, Aaron, and Miriam know that it is no accident. They know this because they have learned from the Voice at the Burning Bush (Exodus 3:15) and then again in Egypt (Exodus 6:2–3) that the Divine Name that can only be pronounced by simply breathing names, indeed, that which is most sacred: the Interbreathing of all life that is aroused and infused with the *Ruach Hakodesh*, the Holy Breathing Spirit of the world.

The second time the Voice reminds Moses that *YHWH* is the sacred name, the Voice also acknowledges that Moses's forebears had known the One by a different name. But now that ancient name is no longer adequate. If humans are to undertake a transformation in the world, then humankind must learn to transform its deepest understanding of the world, of God. God's interactions with Pharaoh through the Ten Plagues plant the seeds of this transformative understanding.

The Plagues are brought on not by a Super-Pharaoh in the sky but by this Interbreathing that connects all life in Unity. They are the complex consequence of tyranny, which is itself the form of idolatry that tries to set itself up as a god who can triumph over the One who breathes all life (Exodus 7:13–11:9).

This story too is echoed by the man-made disaster in the Gulf of Mexico. In our own day, carbon pharaohs tyrannize both human communities and the earth itself. Both *adam* and *adamah* are equally oppressed, for in Hebrew the words themselves betoken the intertwining of ourselves and Mother Earth.

Then the Torah teaches that, of course, the Breath of Life, the Wind of Change, blows away the seeming power of the tyrant who thinks himself a god. His power dissolves into the Sea of Reeds— another form of the plant life created on the third day (Exodus 14:21–22, 15:8–10). Just as the *adamah* roused into life both the "shrubs of the earth" and the *adam* that was necessary to their nurture, as their food was necessary to *adam*, so too will these reeds outlive the tyranny of those facets of *adam* that have run amok.

Then the Torah provides us another parable on this same theme, a story that points toward the healing of the disaster at the end of Eden. This is the parable of manna and Shabbat (Exodus 16). For in this story, as in Eden, the Great Provider showers *adam* again with almost free abundance. The only work the Israelites need to do is to walk forth every morning and gather the manna—a strange "vegetation" that is like coriander seed but far more nourishing.

No sweat, no toil, no thorns or thistles. Self-restraint is built-in: anyone who tries to gather more than enough to eat for a day finds that the extra rots and stinks. On the sixth day, enough manna falls to feed the people for another day, and it does not rot. It will meet their needs for the seventh day. On the seventh day, Shabbat, no manna falls. Self-restraint is again built-in.

But this is a different kind of self-restraint. In Eden, self-restraint meant giving up a portion of delight. The Tree of Knowledge of Good and Evil was beautiful; its aroma beckoned toward a delicious taste. Who could embrace asceticism in the face of such a tree?

Shabbat is a kind of self-restraint that itself is filled with joy and celebration. This is a new invention, and it beckons toward a way of relating with the earth that is filled with love, not domination, and gives a fuller life to both *adam* and *adamah*.

How do we turn this parable into an active practice when we cross the river into becoming farmers? The Torah answers this question with the teaching of *Sh'mitah* (Leviticus 25:1–7). We shift from the wistful "vegetation" of the manna to the real vegetation of the Land. We can celebrate a yearlong Shabbat when we restrain ourselves from organizing the sowing and the reaping that are the necessities of ordinary agriculture. We can remember the need for shrubs and grasses to have the loving touch of human presence through our self-restraint.

Instead of subjecting the plants to our will and our work, we are to practice *tzimtzum*, the act of personal self-restraint in the face of another being's need to freely grow. The Torah voices the concern of some who fear that there will not be enough to eat. And then the Torah soothes us: if we will allow the earth to rest as the Breath of Life demands, there will be even more abundance (Leviticus 25:18–22, 26:3–13).

Then the Torah warns us yet again: if we refuse to let the earth rest for the *Sh'mitah* year, if we prevent the earth from resting for its yearlong Shabbat, the earth will rest anyway—on our heads. Through drought and famine, pestilence and plague, through an exile that today we would call a flood of refugees, our Mother Earth will turn away from us because we have oppressed her (Leviticus 26:14–46, especially verses 34–35 and 43; II Chronicles 36:20–21).

The disasters listed in Leviticus 26 are echoed today in the predictions of climate scientists who warn us of the consequences of overworking earth by choking its air, its breath, by burning fossil fuels. What we call the climate crisis is indeed a crisis in the sacred name of the God who is *YyyyHhhhWwwwHhhh*. As our prayer book teaches, *Nishmat kol chai t'vareich et shimcha, YHWH Eloheinu*, "The breath of all life praises Your name, Yahhh our God"—for the name is itself the breathing of all life, and "our" God is the deepest God not of Jews alone, not of humans alone, but of all life. That is why *YHWH* is *Echad*, "One."

Sh'mitah is the Torah's effort to teach us a path of practical peace in the human community and between the earth—especially its crops, its vegetation—and human earthlings. And then our sacred writings reach once more beyond the practical to lift up a vision of that peace made whole. In the Song of Songs, we see and hear and smell and taste the Garden for grown-ups. Eden for a grown-up human race. Earth is playful, joyful, freely giving forth the nuts and fruits of the third day. Apples and apricots, almonds and raisins, the wine that flows from grapes and the spices that grow in our gardens—these forms of vegetation permeate the Garden of the Song.

We notice that in this poem of maturity, the Song does not mention eating animals. The fruits and nuts, the wine and spices, seem to be enough. This is the diet of the Tu BiSh'vat seder in its celebration of the ultimate vegetation, the Tree of Life. It is the recipe for *charoset*, the innermost kashrut of the specially liberating kosher foods of liberated Pesach. These fruits and nuts are the diet of the Garden, where no life—not even a carrot or a horseradish, ripped from the earth—needs to be killed in order to be eaten.

In the Song, we humans have learned to love the earth, not dominate it; and in turn, the earth loves us. The disaster that came from trying to tyrannize the Garden has been assuaged.

And the second disaster that emerges from the human effort to dominate our Mother Earth has in the Song been cured as well. No longer do men rule over women. The Song beyond all Songs shows us the free and loving interplay of men and women, shows us a poetry led and probably written by a woman, shows us a sexuality that is free and bold and joyful—not shameful, as it came to be in Eden. A sexuality that is not severed from the Spirit but united with It—so that we do not have to choose between seeing the Song as an allegory of love between God and humankind or as a celebration of love between human beings, but can see the Song as both, and One. We can hear its entire text as the name of God, which would be disrupted if a lesser name intruded.

The story of Eden is a tale of children growing into rebellious adolescence, eating what they please and as much as they please, rejecting the sage advice of Parents in order to grow into adulthood—but an adulthood of drudgery and hierarchy.

Torah teaches us that we have still more space and time to grow. The Song of Songs beckons us to becoming a fully grown-up human race. In Eden, Papa-Mama God commands us. In the Song of Songs, the name of God nowhere appears. Like grown-ups, we have absorbed the wisest teachings of our parents and have grown an ethic of our own. An ethic of love.

In this ethic, the spiritual, the edible, and the erotic are interwoven. Even the yearnings of Isaiah are transcended.

Kein y'hi ratzon! May we and the Interbreathing of all life conspire to make it so. May we who bear the Spirit, who breathe the Breath, who bless the fruit of the trees and the fruit of the earth as we taste them, make it so.

Day Four

✦

TIMES AND SEASONS

God then said, "Let there be lights in the expanse of the sky, to separate day from night, to be markers for sacred seasons, for days and years, and to be lights in the expanse of the sky, spilling light upon the earth!"—and so it was. Thus God made the two great lights: the greater light to govern the day, and the lesser light to govern the night and the stars. God set them in the sky's expanse to spill light upon the earth, to govern the day and the night, to separate the light from the darkness; and God saw how good it was. And there was evening and there was morning, a fourth day.

Genesis 1:14–19

19

If Not Now, Why?

Celebrating Festivals at Their Set Times

RABBI JILL L. MADERER

God then said, "Let there be lights in the expanse of the sky, to separate day from night, to be markers for sacred seasons, for days and years."

Genesis 1:14

In a letter I recently received, an advocate for Jewish convicts requested that the seder held at the state prison be arranged for the actual evening of Pesach. Currently, there is a seder scheduled for a few days later, but nothing for the first night of Pesach. Apparently, the prison officials did not believe the precise timing was critical, so they chose a date they deemed more convenient. I received this request in my role as co-president of the Board of Rabbis of Greater Philadelphia; after some consultation, my co-president and I agreed to respond. We explained to the prison that there is nothing wrong with a seder held a few days after Pesach begins. However, such a rescheduled experience ought to be understood as an educational initiative, rather than as a replacement for the ritual of seder. The actual seder should be observed on the first night, which is, after all, supposed to be different from all other nights.

The celebrations of our festivals are scheduled for set times. One does not need to be at the state prison to know well the potential inconveniences of the set times! And today's is not the first generation to consider alternate time for holiday observance. The early Reformers in Europe introduced a Sunday Sabbath service as a pragmatic response to the six-day workweek. The clergy of the foundational Reform rabbinical conference in Pittsburgh in 1885 followed this model, suggesting that a Sunday service might serve more Jews. Although a portion of congregations went on to offer Sunday services, most did so as a supplement, maintaining worship on Shabbat as well.

Only a few American congregations maintain the Sunday service today. Yet, the observance of our festivals remains a challenge for many contemporary Jewish communities, because our everyday lives are so bound to the secular calendar. A portion of congregations today observe some or most holidays on the closest pragmatic time, such as a weekend day, in order to make it accessible to more people and increase participation. For instance, some congregations observe Purim on the nearest Saturday evening. The practice applies in the home as well; some families observe seder on the closest Friday evening to the actual date. Scheduling conflicts are real, and if the challenge to bring together more people can be more easily achieved on a different day, I understand the appeal. But something vital is lost when our set times are reset to an alternative day.

What is so important about accurate timing for set times? My eight-year-old daughter just participated in a performance of a short children's musical, "Eden."[1] The show began with an extended instrumental number in which all of the actors depicted the days of Creation through props and dance. The separation of the ground from the waters was powerful, the formation of the sea animals was captivating, and the arrangement of the enormous planets orbiting the sun was moving (and not only because my daughter played Pluto).

In attributing creation of our universe to God, our text makes everything of the natural world divine. And as we witness changes that come with the cycles of nature, our tradition helps us to understand that we are bound to these other components of Creation. A seasonal festival, as all of our festivals inherently are, celebrated a few days late misses out on a rootedness in the physical world. A festival observed at its set time magnifies the beauty of nature's cycles and our connection to them through sacred time.

So vital is our connection to the seasons that Jewish tradition adjusted its annual calendar. Despite roots in a lunar calendar, our sages determined a way to heed the instruction "Observe the month of Aviv and offer a passover sacrifice to the Eternal your God, for it was in the month of Aviv, at night, that the Eternal your God freed you from Egypt" (Deuteronomy 16:1).

The organization of our Hebrew calendar remains based on the lunar months, something we share in common with Muslims, who follow a purely lunar calendar. But because the days of the year of Hebrew months total only 354, a purely lunar system would shift Jewish festivals around the solar year, and the holidays would not line up with the seasons. Therefore, by the time of the fourth century, the Jewish sages inserted what in English we call a leap year and in Hebrew we call *shanah m'uberet* (pregnant year), adding a second month of Adar, called Adar II. This leap year, added about every three years, allows the Hebrew calendar to catch up with the Gregorian and remain aligned with the sun's seasons.

Medieval commentator Rashi's interpretation of Genesis 1.14 is inspired by our hybrid calendar model. Rashi interprets that when the text says "for days," it indicates not only the sunlit hours of each day but also the moonlit hours of each twenty-four-hour period. He specifies, "The sun's service is for half a day, and the moon's service is for half of it. [With both together] a day is complete." Rashi's commentary offers a perspective not only on each day but also symbolically on the yearly calendar. With both sun and moon, the day is complete; with both solar and lunar, the year is complete. Rashi's words offer symbolism for our hybrid model that continues today.

Yet, our tradition's emphasis on connection with the natural world through the seasons, critical as it is to our festival traditions, cannot be the whole purpose of a close attachment to the set times. There has to be something more. A recent Facebook post highlighted the reason why our commitment to set times can't only be the seasons. About a week before Pesach, I noticed a Facebook friend's post with a photo of his family on the airplane getting ready to attend a seder with their extended family in Australia, where it would be autumn. I was reminded that for him, Pesach was never about spring, and that for some, Chanukah is a summer holiday!

Should our Jewish brothers and sisters in Australia celebrate Pesach in October, so that they can taste *karpas* as the leaves are turning green? Of course not. In Australia for Pesach just as in Philadelphia for Tu BiSh'vat, the connection is to the season "in the Land of Israel." A rabbinic colleague who once served a pulpit in Australia recalls the impact of off-season festivals. For each holiday, they would remark on the season "in the Land of Israel," and that mention would further bind the community to Israel. He partially credits his community's strong Zionist commitment to the seasonal reality that triggered those mentions.[2] A connection to the season in Israel promotes an important devotion to our homeland and to the natural world there. Yet, its significance extends beyond our attachment to Israel.

There is another force that I believe completes our experiences of the Jewish holidays. That force is our bond with the Jewish people. Even more critical than the climate we see out of our window is the shared experience of Jews from the United States to Paris to Argentina to India to Melbourne to Tel Aviv. When we connect to the season in the Land of Israel, we have a common season for the entire Jewish people. By all doing the same thing at the same time across borders, no matter where we are in the world, our sacred times bind us together.

Certainly, one can individually draw inspiration from the message of self-improvement on Yom Kippur, the fragility of life on Sukkot, the meaning of liberation on Pesach, the revelation of purpose on Shavuot, and the impact of mindfulness on Shabbat. But to stop there, to only experience profound personal meaning on our holidays, would highlight the individual experience while losing the fullness of a communal aspect of our holidays. Only with a connection to the ultimate Jewish community—the Jewish people—can our holidays root us to something larger than ourselves: the values, the history, the future of the Jewish people, and the sense that we are connected to a world outside of ourselves—a sense that some of us would call God.

Always striving for a groundedness in the natural world, our festivals ought to root us in the seasons. Yet, generations beyond the universal Creation story of the Torah, our festivals serve as a connective tissue between disparate communities.

So why do I love to see Jewish communities celebrate our set times, on the prescribed date when possible? Because our times we call *kadosh*—sacred and separate—are a part of what makes us as a people *kadosh*; those common celebrations connect us through time and space. For generations, and in sometimes challenging circumstances, Jews have found ways to observe our sacred times. And today, that's what Shlomo in Jerusalem is doing, and that's what Hannah in South Africa is doing. That's what Moshe in Argentina is doing, and that's what Sarah in Chicago is doing. And Yonatan and Shira and Carlos and Yevgeny and Pierre and Priya. That's what our Jewish brothers and sisters are doing all over the world.

Notes

1. John Rea, "Eden" composer and director, MacGuffin Theater and Congregation Rodeph Shalom partnership.

2. Thank you to Rabbi Michael Torop for an exchange in which he shared the perspective of Australian Jewish communities.

20

A Light for the Nations

RABBI DENISE L. EGER

God then said, "Let there be lights in the expanse of the sky, to separate day from night, to be markers for sacred seasons, for days and years, and to be lights in the expanse of the sky, spilling light upon the earth!"—and so it was. Thus God made the two great lights: the greater light to govern the day, and the lesser light to govern the night and the stars. God set them in the sky's expanse to spill light upon the earth, to govern the day and the night, to separate the light from the darkness; and God saw how good it was. And there was evening and there was morning, a fourth day.

Genesis 1:14–19

The heavens above light our way. The sun rises and sets each day. The moon glows and stars twinkle at night. On day four of Creation, God created these heavenly lights, including the sun and the moon. The verses in Genesis 1 teach that the greater light (the sun) is to shine by day and the lesser one (the moon) is to shine by night. Our Torah teaches us that the heavenly lights, the sun, the moon, and the stars, provided for the earth and its inhabitants a heavenly guidance to navigate the world. These heavenly, natural lights lit up the earth out of the darkness and chaos of Creation and have continued throughout the ages.

They are a constant in our lives. The heavenly lights shining upon the earth have critical functionality. The sunlight literally provides nourishment for plants, triggering their mechanisms that produce everything from oxygen to fruit. The sunlight and moonlight initiate systems in nature, including in human beings for our bodies, such as sleep cycles and responses when we get overexposed to excessive amounts of sunlight or darkness. Our bodies are tied to the light of the sun and moon and stars and the pull of gravity upon them.

The sun and moon mark the passage of time. The position of the sun in the sky marks the seasons. The waning and waxing of the moon mark the passage of the month. Night and day are distinguished by what appears in the heavens above. Even the opening lines of the Torah emphasize that the first day began because of a light that emanated from God. "Let there be light!" says God (Genesis 1:3). That primordial light was then harnessed to be the heavenly lights we know today to be planets, galaxies, stars, and other heavenly bodies. According to the mystics of our tradition, that early light of the first day of Creation helped to form the lights of the firmament on the fourth day.

In the ancient world, the sun, moon, and stars were worshiped as if they were gods and goddesses. Their importance to ancient civilization in marking the time of calendars and seasons, as well as recognizing the critical importance of sunshine for crops and animals, is well documented in many cultures. But the Torah teaches us that the sun, moon, and stars are not gods. The Book of Deuteronomy specifically warns the Israelites not to worship them (Deuteronomy 4:19, 17:3). The sun and moon are not independent actors in the universe, but are rather created by and products of the primordial light of God. These heavenly spheres are part of the creation of the entire universe, created by God with purpose for all the people and plants and animals of the earth. And that purpose is to shed light on and illuminate our world.

Enlightenment and illumination are not only brought about by the sun's rays shining upon us by day and the moonlight glowing by night. When we hear the words "to illuminate the world," we also think about the ways we can reflect and shine the spiritual light that God created. We think about knowledge and opening our eyes to see the world in new ways. We seek to understand God's mission to illuminate the world and to find how, through our endeavors, that mission becomes reality.

One way we illuminate the world is through the justice we pursue and the justice we bring about by shining light on the ugliness and the inequities that are sometimes the result of human interactions. The world can be a cold and dangerous place even with the heavenly lights above. There are many dark corners of the world where human beings are brutalized and oppressed by others. When we work to create a society where human dignity is upheld, where all are treated as being made *b'tzelem Elohim*, "in the image of God" (Genesis 1:27), we bring enlightenment to our world. We help shine God's light and thus bring freedom to those who are captive and compassion to those whose lives are held together by tenuous strings. The responsibilities of being Jewish that we call mitzvot teach us to be fair to the worker, to provide for the poor, to lift up the fallen, to clothe the naked, and to study morning, noon, and night. The pursuit of justice alongside knowledge and learning of Jewish texts and traditions shapes the kind of light we bring to our families, our communities, and the whole world. This idea surges through our prayers and our teachings. *Mishnah Pei-ah* 1:1 teaches:

These are things that are limitless, of which a person enjoys the fruit of the world, while the principal remains in the world to come. They are:

honoring one's father and mother,
engaging in deeds of compassion,
arriving early for study, morning and evening,
dealing graciously with guests, visiting the sick,
providing for the wedding couple,
accompanying the dead for burial,
being devoted in prayer,
and making peace among people.
But the study of Torah encompasses them all.[1]

This list from the Mishnah is part of our daily morning worship. It is a way to remind us of the Jewish responsibilities that shape our interaction with the world and bring God's enlightenment to daily living. Enlightenment comes from our embracing of Jewish knowledge as deeply as we embrace science, psychology, economics, law, medicine, and other contemporary bodies of knowledge. And enlightenment comes when we build sacred relationships with our family and friends through acts of *chesed*, "loving-kindness."

One of the greatest challenges for progressive Jews is that the divine light brought forth through Jewish knowledge is diminished when we do not understand our texts. Jewish illiteracy in our time continues to distance our people from our teachings and our Torah and dims the Jewish light that we can reflect into the world. This is why the ancient wisdom of our sages reflected in *Mishnah Pei-ah* includes study as a core responsibility. The creation of knowledge, and the sharing of knowledge, matters. And when we study morning, noon, and night, when we embrace the study of Torah, we know that our worldview will be expanded and our strengthened heart space will bring a new kind of light into focus.

We live in a global environment. Today, through modern technology and multicultural societies, we can cast our eyes around the world with little effort. Beyond the shtetl and villages of our grandparents and great-grandparents, we live in a world where we interact with many different kinds of people. Our particular Jewish way of life and our mitzvot, the Jewish obligations that are a part of our covenant with God, bring light to each of us. This light helps us refine our relationships with others, even our non-Jewish family members and neighbors. This light brings with it an ethical challenge to harness the power of God's light within us and, as Reform Judaism has long taught, "be a light unto the nations."

Reform Judaism has actualized this value "of being a light to the nations" throughout the years (Isaiah 42:9). Our long-held commitment to social justice, whether marching for civil rights with African Americans or standing shoulder to shoulder with farmworkers or working to end discrimination against LGBTQ people around the world, is a clear example of living out this mission. Our interfaith work engages our brothers and sisters in other faith traditions, inviting them to share in this holy work with us. This spreads the divine light to yet further corners of our worlds.

Reform Judaism has long stressed deep commitments to ethical mitzvot over the ritual mitzvot, in order to bring this sacred enlightenment into daily life. This emphasis has made social justice and the commitment to ethical living pillars of Reform Jewish spirituality. Sometimes more than belief in God as a separate being, Reform Jews' dedication to healing the world, *tikkun olam*, and ethical behavior becomes synonymous with a faith in the Divine. Being a light to the nations is an example of our faithfulness and righteousness and one of the ways we help to heal the world of its injustices. When we engage in *tikkun olam*, social justice, and ethical living, we bring this light to the world. We can be the light when we bring these Jewish values to the forefront and when we structure our days and nights with Jewish learning and enlightenment.

The kabbalists of our tradition prayed for divine *shefa* to flow down from the heavens. *Shefa* is the divine emanation of God.[2] The kabbalists understood that strength, beauty, wisdom, endurance, justice, and other divine attributes flow from God into our world. They understood then that it was our duty, our responsibility, to utilize these divine attributes carefully in our world to heal it of its brokenness, and in turn, by our effort we would draw closer to God. It is no accident that the medieval kabbalists of our Jewish tradition associated the divine *shefa* with light. Just as light beams forth from the heavenly luminary bodies, moon, stars, planets, and the sun, so do these divine attributes beam forth into our world and ultimately into each and every one of us. The kabbalists also believed that it was our sacred duty and responsibility as Jews to then take that divine light and reflect it back into the world by holy living. Thus the divine light that beams from God's world to our world, from the heavenly abode to the earthly realm and into each one of us as a sacred vessel, beams forth from within us through our holy and sacred acts of living that we Jews call mitzvot.

In the Book of Exodus, just as the Children of Israel are about to embark on their journey to freedom and the Promised Land of Israel, they are given the mitzvah of blessing the new month and establishing a calendar based on the moon. By blessing the moon, the lesser light, and by marking the months by the lunar calendar, the Jewish people start their journey to freedom as the full moon lights their way to the Promised Land. At their darkest hour of slavery to Pharaoh, the light of the full moon illuminates their journey from the horrors of slavery toward the bright light of freedom. And fifty days later the Children of Israel stand at Mount Sinai to receive the greatest enlightenment the world has known since the creation of the sun and moon and stars: the Torah given on Mount Sinai. The prophet Isaiah teaches that the Jewish nation left Egypt with a purpose, a mission that would begin by receiving the Torah, and through the Torah the Jewish people would become "a light unto nations." "I, *Adonai*, have called unto you in righteousness, and have taken hold of your hand, and submitted you as the people's covenant, as a light unto the nations" (Isaiah 42:6). The early

Reform rabbis rightly identified this ideal as the Reform Jewish emphasis on the ethical. They taught that the revelation at Sinai, and the covenant that was made with the Jewish people there, was the mission to spread the moral imperatives of the Torah throughout the world.

Rabbi David Saperstein said in a conversation at the 2010 Faith Angle Forum of the Ethics and Public Policy Center:

> We believe that we're called to be God's partners in creating a better and more hopeful world for all God's children. That is part of our religious mandate—to be a light to and of the nations, to be bearers of the flames of justice and weavers of dreams of freedom for all humankind. To be a light to the nations, to really work and not stop until that day when justice shall well up like waters, righteousness like a mighty stream and we'll have created the world our ancestors dreamed about and our children so richly deserve. That is the Jewish religious task in the world at its deepest level. It is one shared by Jews across the spectrum today.[3]

The Reform Jewish emphasis on social justice, on healing the world of its ills as a core Jewish value, recognizes this aspect of divine emanation. The creation of the heavenly lights calls us to reflect that divine light into the world through holy relationships with other human beings and the rest of Creation. We bring enlightenment and hope, healing and purpose when Torah guides our decision-making and our efforts to heal the ills of the world for all of society. We bring to the forefront efforts on ethical and moral living, ensuring that society around us is also shaped by an ethical-, moral- and justice-filled way of life.

The formation of the heavenly lights out of the light of the first day reminds us of the teaching of the Psalmist, "In Your light, do we see light" (Psalm 36:10). And when we see God's light in the heavens, it should remind us to reflect that light and enlightenment back into our world through our Torah, our holy relationships, and our focus on *tikkun olam*.

Notes

1. *Mishkan T'filah: A Reform Siddur* (New York: CCAR Press, 2007), 206.

2. Matt, Daniel, *The Zohar: Pritzker Edition*, Vol. 1, (Stanford: Stanford University Press, 2004, p. LXXI.

3. "Dr. David Galernter and Rabbi David Saperstein at the March 2010 Faith Angle Forum," Ethics and Public Policy Center, http://eppc.org/publications/gelernter-and-saperstein/.

21

The Physics of Jewish Time and the Fourth Day of Creation

LOUI DOBIN

God then said, "Let there be lights in the expanse of the sky, to separate day from night, to be markers for sacred seasons, for days and years."

Genesis 1:14

There is Newtonian time, which along with space, matter, and motion is a fundamental structure of the universe. There is relativistic time, Einstein's concept of the "space-time continuum," holding that an event must have both a "where" it takes place and a "when" it takes place; space and time are aspects of each other.

There is also "Jewish time," which, as the *Urban Dictionary* says, is "often relaxed about punctuality."

According to author Thomas Cahill, Jewish time has specific properties that can be described but is also more than the sum of its properties.[1] Jewish time is "the gift of the Jews"—our gift to the rest of the world. Cahill, in his book *The Gifts of the Jews*, wasn't talking about tardiness, but about just one of many specific properties of Jewish time.

From the very first verse of Genesis, the Torah looks at time as unidirectional. Genesis 1:1 begins, "When God was about to create heaven and earth," a clear starting point to the story of our world. In the ancient world, the idea that time ran in only one direction was radical. This is the "gift" that Torah brought the world. While Jews adopted rules and rituals of other ancient cultures, their reality was new. Rather than an endless cycle of reincarnation and rebirth, the common belief of many ancient faiths, our ancient ancestors developed the concept that time has a specific historical starting point. The story of Creation begins with the formation of the heavens and earth—there was evening and there was morning on that first day, a kind of "Yom Big Bang." From there, time keeps marching forward, each day building toward Shabbat.

While there is a cycle of night and day, the story never moves in reverse. Day follows night, which turns to day: "There was evening and there was morning." Though "the seasons they go 'round and 'round," time itself marches forward. Arthur Eddington, a British astronomer of the twentieth century, captured this aspect of Jewish thought and described the "asymmetrical" or "one-way direction" of time as an "arrow of time."[2]

Amazingly enough, the one-directional nature of time as described in the Torah continues to be our modern understanding of the way our natural universe works. Indeed, modern culture is built on the very premise of forward motion. Cycles of time may revolve around each other and may be embedded within each other, but they are all moving ever forward through time. Hours revolve around days, which revolve around years that move into the future. This seems to be parallel to the way in which our moon circles our planet, and the planets in the solar system circle our sun, and the suns circle inside our galaxies that travel around an ever-outward-expanding universe.

Therefore, the first property of Jewish Time is *unidirectionality*.

As much as we value memory and Judaism emphasizes the importance of our sacred past, there is no reverse and no going back in time. We will never pass this way again, and that leads to certain wonderful imperatives that force us to embrace the notion of *carpe diem*, to behave as though time matters and our lives make a difference. We return to the past for inspiration, not reincarnation.

Jewish time also has the property of *symmetry*.

On the fourth day, when God created the sun, moon, and stars, God didn't simply create lights in the sky. God delineated and made the first divisions of time. Not only that, but in a beautiful use of symmetry, God put the day that created divisions of time in the direct middle of the week, the pivotal point, dividing the week in half. Jewish thought tells us that every moment has an equal and opposite moment in time, a kind of law of "conservation of time." "A time to be born, a time to die. A time to plant, a time to reap" (Ecclesiastes 3:2).

Another property of Jewish time is a certain *ambiguity*.

While Einstein's theory of relativity has made time travel impossible, Jews have always had a respectful, but creative relationship with linear time and a very real interaction with the collective past. Were we all really standing together at Sinai, Jews from the then-present along with all of us from the then-future? Even the (challenging) biblical idea of punishing someone for generations upon generations into the future seems to indicate that we are all on a path forward. And some of our early predecessors took a very long time to leave the stage, with our patriarchs routinely reaching three-figure ages that even modern medicine cannot yet duplicate. Forty days and nights of flooding? And seven days of Creation?

Jewish time is *scalable* throughout history.

Our ancestors lived from generation to generation. Our grandparents lived from year to year, our parents lived from day to day. I live from hour to hour. My kids live from minute to minute. Revolutions in agriculture, then industry, then information have accelerated the pace and perception of time. With what measure of granularity will my grandchildren slice their time? How will the way we experience time inform the way we learn patience? This is not only perception— external things do move faster now than ever before. Our "internal processes" are trying to evolve and keep up. When Judaism was born, information transmission was measured in months. When time is measured in seconds, as it is now, what does that do to our expectations of each other? We have greater access to information about our past than our parents ever did, but will we use that to seek greater wisdom?

There is an interesting conceptual parallel between the sequence above and Moore's Law. Gordon Moore, founder of Intel, famously said that the speed and power of microprocessors (the brains that drive our computers) doubles every eighteen months. The beauty of Judaism is its ability to pass back and forth through these scales. In every place in time that Jews have called home, they have re-formed their Judaism to adapt.

In 586 BCE, many Israelites were exiled from their agrarian-based lifestyles and homes in the Land of Israel. They soon adapted to new lives in an urban civilization far away from home and in a completely different environment, under the control of a foreign culture. Not being able to duplicate their sacrificial culture from home, they replicated its calendar. In doing so they tamed time and continued to live the rhythms, if not the realities, of their former lives.

This ability to view time metaphorically gives Jewish time the ability to contextualize itself historically, while also giving individual Jews the opportunity to engage with and appreciate their own Judaism on that same historical scale. At the same time, we watch as history played out on a human scale through the narratives of individual lives. We call on those individuals to connect to our past. As we chant in the *Amidah*, "Blessed are You, God of our fathers and mothers."

Jewish time is *gravitational*.

Jews "gravitate" to each other. This is particularly true during periods of time that have been designated as holidays. The ability to raise up certain slices of time, to celebrate them and make them holy, made time as well as space a builder of Jewish community. These holidays are so important to fix accurately in time that equations, calendars, and star charts govern their placement. Some Jews even add an extra day to some holidays to make sure they get at least one of the dates right (e.g., Rosh HaShanah, Passover).

From early on as a people and from a young age as individual people, Jewish time is *perceptual*.

Many of the memories that we associate with the gravitational holiday moments above we also associate with special sights, smells, sounds, and especially tastes. They are the most primal ways in which we connect to our history and people.

Since we view the external world through our senses, every event in time and space that is precious to us is linked to the sensations of those moments. In Judaism, we are encouraged to mark certain times through prayer—to make holy even the most mundane times in which our senses experience something new or remarkable.

Physicists have long discussed the subjectivity of time, trying to decide whether we feel time as an actual sensation or whether the passage of time is a judgment based on a reading of the clock or the setting of the sun. Jewish time is set up to operate under the assumption that both possibilities are true. Shabbat can end when it's dark enough to see three stars. Shabbat can also end when the newspaper says so. Anyone who has been to a Jewish summer camp knows that the days last forever and the summer ends in the blink of an eye. Like quantum state, time can be perceived simultaneously as both never-ending and too short.

Some periods of time seem to end too quickly, and others can't end quickly enough. Both measure the same on your clock but differently in your head. We are admonished to make the beauty of

Shabbat last for as long as possible. Likewise, we are taught to make our seders last.

Jewish time is instructive and *predictive*.

Regarding the seder, one cannot find a better example of the final property of Jewish time. Jews are all about passing Jewish values along to the next generation. Jews are also about taking lessons for the future from stories of the past. When the seder states that "in every age, foes have risen to destroy us," it is being predictive, though hopefully wrong. But the real point is that the seder is not simply a retelling of history. Time itself is treated as a topic of the seder.

The seder is doubly important because it also highlights examples of every other property of Jewish time. Working backward through this essay, like "Chad Gadya," our time spent at the seder is as follows:

- Predictive: Time moves forward but with recurring themes.
- Perceptual: Moments are made special by connecting them with our physical nature.
- Gravitational: We need to tell the story to each other as a group, communally.
- Scalable: This time can be spent in big and small groups, young and old, Jew and non-Jew.
- Ambiguous: We know that the story is in progress. We don't know how it ends.
- Symmetrical: There is a "gematria" to the seder that lives in the recurrence of the number four, in the qualities of the seder plate, and in the expected balance between pre- and post-meal observance.
- Unidirectional: The arrow of time moves forward from Creation through redemption into the future.

Many of these properties of Jewish time have spread their cultural DNA throughout today's world. The true gift of the Jews was to see time as a one-way journey into tomorrow. Others have put their spin on the big bang, but it's been in our story for thousands of years.

Notes

1. Thomas Cahill, *The Gifts of the Jews: How a Tribe of Desert Nomads Changed the Way Everyone Thinks and Feels* (New York: Doubleday, 1998).

2. Laura Mersini-Houghton and Rüdiger Vaas, *The Arrows of Time: A Debate in Cosmology* (New York: Springer, 2012), 7.

22

Diaspora Time

RABBI MICHAEL G. HOLZMAN

God then said, "Let there be lights in the expanse of the sky, to separate day from night, to be markers for sacred seasons, for days and years."

Genesis 1:14

In his divine comedy *Mr g*, Alan Lightman identifies the instant when God begins to act as the moment time begins. Lightman also notes that time has no structure until the physical laws of the universe result in matter, in his case atoms whose vibrations Mr g counts. The same design is true for the biblical beginning of time. The words "In the beginning" establish a start point, but the structure appears on the fourth day, with day and night. From this bifurcation of each day and the patterns of the heavenly bodies that symbolize them flow all of our measures and systems for marking time: day, week, month, year, hour, minute, and second. Also emerging from these patterns is the possibility of storytelling: beginning, middle, and end. The stories that mark cycles of day and night, sun and moon, waxing and waning, summer and winter, all contribute to our sense of purpose in the world. As Creation shapes time, it also shapes us.

As a people, we use narrative to discover our identity and purpose. Cultural critic Neil Postman explains it clearly:

> I mean by "narrative" a story. But not any kind of story. I refer to big stories—stories that are sufficiently profound and complex to offer explanations of the origins and future of a people; stories that construct ideals, prescribe rules of conduct, specify sources of authority, and in doing all this, provide a sense of continuity and purpose. Joseph Campbell and Rollo May, among others, called such stories "myths." Marx had such stories in mind in referring to "ideologies." And Freud called them "illusions." No matter. What is important about narratives is that human beings cannot live without them. We are burdened with a consciousness that insists on our having a purpose.[1]

With this definition in mind, by looking at the rituals and narratives shared by a group, we uncover the national direction that shapes a people.

Groups mark cycles and stories with rituals, a distinctly human way to give meaning to the structures of time. Jewish rituals transform morning into daily miracles, Saturday into Shabbat, and the lengthening day (and its resultant crops) into the three harvest festivals. We can speculate that Jews, like all human beings, first celebrated natural changes in the seasons and then later grafted collective stories to existing folk traditions. That is how the three festivals also gained historical meaning: Pesach begins the spring harvest and also the release from Egypt; Shavuot is the early summer harvest and the revelation of Torah at Sinai; and Sukkot celebrates the late summer harvest and the wandering in the desert. It also explains the Shabbat *Kiddush*, which includes reminders for awe at the gift of Creation, as well as the memory of the Exodus from Egypt. Over time, the grafting becomes ever more

complicated. Layers of narratives and rituals become like a *tel*, an ar-
chaeological site, of Jewish narrative.

For Jews this is especially important because most nations build
their narratives and rituals around geography, not time. For the vast
majority of Jewish history, even during the monarchy period, our narrative as a people does not depend on the motherland. Abraham barely
arrives before departing for Egypt. Jacob comes and goes, as do his
children. The rest of the Torah is a journey to a land they never reach.
Joshua is supposed to conquer the land completely but gives up, allowing non-Israelites to remain. Eventually the Babylonian exile and
return (586–536 BCE) precipitates the canonization of large parts of
the *Tanach* itself. The same could be said of Mishnah and Talmud following the Roman exile (135 CE). As our texts emerge through our
displacement from the land, our narrative, rituals, and identity emerge
independent from geography.

Until the rise of modern Zionism, the land looms large but often
from offstage. We see this tension when the commentators ask why
the Torah begins with the Creation story and not Exodus 12:2, "This
month shall mark for you the beginning of months; it shall be the first
of the months of the year for you." In other words, does Jewish time
begin with the Creation narrative or with the Exodus narrative? Do we
mark time through our relationship to nature or through our journey
back to the Land of Israel? And this leads us to ask, do we define Jewish identity through how we spend our time or where we come from?

The answer to these questions, of course, is some combination of
both. We should not be surprised to find in our rituals and narratives—
the ways in which we regulate time—a dialogue about the Jewish relationship with our moments and our motherland. This is especially true
since the majority of our history as a people has been lived in countries
governed by non-Jews. By living in the Diaspora, we have negotiated
the ways in which Jewish time conflicts with government or sovereignty time, and as we have become more acculturated into non-Jewish

society, this has created more tension. Rather than see this tension between Jewish time and non-Jewish space as some kind of diminishing of Judaism, interrogation uncovers meaning in it.

The dialogue about time and space emerges through three entirely different mechanisms in our rituals. The most obvious markers of Jewish time are Shabbat and the holidays, whose themes overtly describe various central ideas of Judaism. Slightly subtler is the creation of the entire calendar, with its connection both to nature and the priorities of national cohesion. And even more covert is the way our rituals and stories explain the entire sweep of human existence. We live these three elements—special days, the structure of the year, and the scope of time writ large—and their messages shape the Jewish narrative, both consciously and subconsciously.

We see this most prominently in our holy days. By holding up particular moments in the annual calendar and imbuing them with special meanings, Judaism tells our narrative over the course of a year. The most obvious artifacts of our struggle between time and space are the remnants of agricultural time embedded in our holidays. If we can accept that each climate and locale demand variations in human activity—planting, harvesting, collecting rainwater, observing the presence of certain migratory species—then we can immediately see how the rituals for marking these activities will have to change based on locale. I have already mentioned the grafting of freedom from Egypt, Sinai, and desert wandering onto Pesach, Shavuot, and Sukkot. In addition, expulsion ended the sovereignty that allows for economic management of the land through taxation and offerings in the Temple. We find these artifacts on our calendar as well.

This transformation results in moments of confusion and creativity in our rituals. The most obvious example of this is the holiday of Tu BiSh'vat. Originally it was essentially a tax day marking the date after which new crops had to be counted as "first fruits" for the new year and thus taxed by the Temple. Expulsion ended that purpose. So the

fifteenth of Sh'vat was transformed in the Middle Ages into a mystical contemplation of God's emanation and the possibility of human
transformation. The economic relationship to the land was obliterated
in the ritual and replaced by a spiritual relationship to fruits, flowers,
trees, and rising sap. By the modern period, this same holiday became
synonymous with Jewish activism, whether it was through planting
trees in Israel or by advocating for enlightened environmental practices and policies.

All of these changes explain the absurd sight of American synagogues promoting tree planting while children trudge through ice and
snow on the way to religious school. Sometimes the Diaspora confusion over which theme to emphasize—the ancient celebration of
first fruits, the medieval mystical exploration of God, or the modern
progressive push for activism—leaves us floundering for a narrative.
Those of us who live in cold climes find the same dissonance, albeit less
jarringly, in the second paragraph of the *Amidah*, which in the winter
prays for rain and wind but makes no mention of snow and ice.

These problems become even more complicated when we compare
Diaspora and Israeli attitudes toward the rituals. Early Zionism was an
explicit rejection of the Diaspora, so we find labor socialists stripping
away non-agricultural meanings in the holidays. But contemporary
non-Orthodox Israelis would find a kibbutz celebration of Tu BiSh'vat
as quaint at best or obscure at worst. Rather, most Jewish holidays in
Israel have become opportunities for family gatherings driven not by
religious obligation, but rather by tradition and the shutting down of
businesses, schools, and government. A secular Israeli Rosh HaShanah
has far less religious content than in even the most liberal American
synagogue. In some ways Jews in Denver and Ramat Aviv share the
same confusion on certain holidays. Do any of us feel the importance
of the *etrog*, willow, myrtle, and palm on Sukkot? Sometimes our solutions converge, as when Purim becomes the central children's holiday on
the Jewish calendar. Other times we diverge, as when Diaspora Jewry

elevates the commercial side of the minor Chanukah miracle out of jealousy for Christmas, while classical Zionists emphasized the military victory, and today's Israelis celebrate with a focus on *sufganiyot*.

Each holiday is a case study in the dialogue between Jewish time and place. By adapting and explaining how we mark Jewish time in a Jewish or non-Jewish land, a meta-narrative of Judaism emerges. Where we converge with other strands of Judaism—traditionalism or secular Israeli religion being the most notable—we can produce a unified Jewish narrative, and the places of divergence best highlight what is particular about American progressive Judaism. Each holiday is a strand in our narrative fabric. In the Diaspora, Tu BiSh'vat holds up activism; Chanukah, Jewish pride; Purim, continuity. The stories we tell on these days and the rituals we sustain or create will produce the American Jewish future.

We also see that narrative emerge dramatically in the formation of the calendar itself. Since the Jewish holiday cycle is almost entirely based on observation of the moon, it requires far more active management than the secular, Gregorian, solar calendar. In ancient Israel the system depended on the observation of the new moon each month, the certification of two witnesses by the rabbinical court, and a network of communication by messengers. Even when communication shifted to hilltop pyres (as in *The Lord of the Rings*), distant communities still could not be certain they received word of the new month on the correct date. Therefore, to ensure that Jews did not accidentally transgress on a holiday, Diaspora rabbis added an additional day of holiday observance at the beginning and end of Sukkot and Pesach and an extra day of Rosh HaShanah and Shavuot. This frequently results in shifts of the Torah reading calendar as well. Despite highly accurate ways of measuring time and astronomical calculations, many Diaspora rabbis continue to hold onto these doubled holidays and the calendar they create.

The Reform Movement appeared on the stage of Jewish history as modernity sweeps across the Diaspora. As early Reformers applied modern rationalism to the Rabbinic and medieval calendar, one of their first innovations was to eliminate these additional days. That is why today one might see a Reform synagogue celebrate Simchat Torah the night before their Conservative or Orthodox neighbors, or observant Reform Jews happily eating pizza and pasta on the eighth evening of Pesach. It also explains how Reform synagogues will be reading different Torah portions than Conservative and Orthodox congregations on the same week.

The Reform Movement relies on two arguments for their reversion to a preexilic calendar. First, our tradition of rationalism screams at traditions that ignore modern science, like the atomic clock. When every person on the planet can sync their phones simultaneously, how can Jews not know which day a holiday begins or ends? Second, as a sign of Zionist solidarity we point to Israelis, who follow the calendar as we do.

Both of these choices reflect different narratives about Jewish life. In this case the tension becomes about adherence to a Diaspora traditionalism or the embrace of modern, scientific advancement and the reality of the modern State of Israel. The way we regulate time on the annual calendar forces communities and individuals to choose a path and which source of authority—tradition or science—will govern identity. If the modern Jewish narrative emerges from the storytelling around holidays, it emerges from our systems of authority around the calendar. Modern Judaism in the eighteenth and nineteenth centuries elevated science and rationalism as primary sources of authority, and thus our calendar promotes those values in our Jewish narrative.

My third topic brings us to the way we treat time writ large. In the course of structuring time with ritual and story, Judaism has a long tradition of predicting national and even global redemption through messianic narrative. We find the most obvious example at the end of the Pesach seder, which includes a cup for Elijah and the phrase reading, "Next year in Jerusalem." We also see this ideology in the singing of *"Eliyahu HaNavi"* (which prays to God to send Elijah the prophet speedily in our day with *Mashiach ben David*, "the Messiah, son of David") at the seder and also at the end of *Havdalah* each week. The narrative emerges also at every wedding, where the breaking of the glass serves as a reminder of the Temple's destruction and our pre-messianic state of brokenness.

Traditionally these rituals point toward a hope in the Messiah's appearance and the coming of the *olam haba*, "the world-to-come." A huge element of this narrative is the return of all Jews to the Land of Israel. There is a strand of Jewish belief that the messianic age will bring the resurrection of the dead starting in the Land of Israel, which explains the preponderance of graves on the Mount of Olives. In this way, time itself becomes a vector pointing back to the land.

More broadly, these rituals place time on a trajectory toward redemption. They help Jews feel a sense of development. For nationalists, this points us toward Jewish freedom and security (and for some dominance) in an unfriendly world. For universalists, development is an outgrowth of the human project toward bettering the world. One narrative elevates our struggle with enemies and, for some, the primacy of preserving our hold on as much land as possible. The other narrative elevates *tikkun olam* and our purpose as partners in God's Creation. When we include messianic elements in our rituals, we connect our current moment to our overarching purpose as Jews. So while holidays and calendar rely on storytelling and authority to influence narrative, the messianic belief in the world-to-come uses our national purpose.

On all three levels we see the tension that Diaspora causes in our structuring of time. Storytelling, authority, and national purpose, communicated through ritual, create narrative and thus Jewish meaning. This has been a part of our tradition since the beginning of Jewish history. We continue it today.

As we pass the year, the holidays, the calendar, and the messianic themes may do little to unify the Jewish people and crystallize our relationship to the Land of Israel. But they open up fertile opportunities for conversation. The dissonances we see on the calendar compel us to examine how we see nature, economics, social justice, power, and military force. For each holiday, the themes we choose to emphasize reflect our attitudes about the Jewish narrative. As we follow the Jewish calendar, we face choices each month, with the Torah portion, and on some holidays about our embrace of modernity. And when we sing the words of "*Eliyahu HaNavi*," we ask ourselves if we pray for a national redemption for Jews against enemies or for a universal time of peace and prosperity. A staunch Zionist will emphasize different rituals and stories than a liberal spiritualist. A traditionalist Orthodox Jew will adhere to rituals that a modernist Reform Jew will abandon or adapt. These rituals and the time they regulate thus become the pens with which we write our narrative about the land, our people, and our personal spiritual path.

As time begins with Creation and achieves structure with day and night, so too do we see time both as a source of awe at the universe and a way to structure our purpose in the universe.

Note

1. Neil Postman, *Building a Bridge to the Eighteenth Century: How the Past Can Improve Our Future* (New York: Vintage, 1999), 101.

23

—

Separate, Mark, and Season— Just Don't Yawn

The Lesson of the Fourth Day of Creation

RABBI EDWIN COLE GOLDBERG, DHL

God then said, "Let there be lights in the expanse of the sky, to separate day from night, to be markers for sacred seasons, for days and years, and to be lights in the expanse of the sky, spilling light upon the earth!"—and so it was. Thus God made the two great lights: the greater light to govern the day, and the lesser light to govern the night and the stars. God set them in the sky's expanse to spill light upon the earth, to govern the day and the night, to separate the light from the darkness; and God saw how good it was. And there was evening and there was morning, a fourth day.

Genesis 1:14–19

In an age when the rich get richer and the poor grow poorer, one remaining democratizing factor is the so-called "168 rule." Simply put, rich or poor, we all have the same 168 hours a week allotted to us. "Time is money," they say, but you can always make more money. You cannot make more time. It is the ultimate limited resource. In economic terms, it is more valuable than gold, oil, or even diamonds. Or it should be, anyway. Like anything precious and limited, we should treat it with respect. In religious terms, we should make time sacred.

A twenty-first-century American observation: we are not very good at this task. We waste time. We kill time. We spend it on meaningless pursuits. Even those among us of the more intellectual classes are easily seduced by the attractions of the Internet, popular entertainment, and temporal pleasures. A little bit of guilty television is good, but not a lot. We don't budget our time in a meaningful way. People who desire immortal life are often terrified at the thought of an eventless weekend. Clearly our priorities are not always reflected in the calendar choices we make. Not only that but often we feel compelled to multitask during our time and not be fully present. In recent times a new term has arisen: "mono-tasking." It grieves me that we need a word to describe what was once a usual practice.

Imagine if we devoted time each week, if not each day, to reflect on how we use our time. Imagine if we made it a priority to grasp the limit of our 168 hours! We would see that it behooves us to have a plan—to understand that we can only do so much with the time allotted to us—not to mention taking the present as an opportunity for being more present.

Fortunately, the Creation story in the Torah provides us with a timely corrective. In it we find a perspective for treating time with the respect it deserves. We read in verse 14 of chapter 1:

God then said, "Let there be lights in the expanse of the sky, to separate day from night, to be markers for sacred seasons, for days and years.

When I ponder this verse, three key words jump out at me: "separate," "mark," and "seasons." Let's consider the import of these central terms.

Separate

These lights—the sun, moon (as a reflector), and stars—teach us *that time is divided into discrete units*. Time is not limitless for us, nor is it monolithic. Some moments are more special than others. We don't want to waste time, but we should recognize that not all time is the same. After all, if every day is special, then no day is special. If every day is Shabbat, then no day is Shabbat. As individuals, we mark what is personally significant. As a religious people, we share a communal identification of special, or sacred, time.

As a Reform Jew I do not consider our times sacred simply because God commanded that they be so. Rather, I believe that we ourselves make our times sacred. We human beings have a need to join together in delineating a division between the sacred and the ordinary. To do so is healthy. It is therapeutic. Most of all, it creates patterns of meaning.

I would posit that life has meaning only when we make divisions in time. Having one day a week as a Sabbath is important not only for purposes of rest. It also creates meaning through repetition and order. In contrast to Ecclesiastes, everything is not vanity. We can create a meaningful life through our ordering of time. Doing the same basic thing every Shabbat may seem the opposite of spiritually exciting, but the older I get the more I appreciate the anchor that comes from a consistent spiritual practice. Whether this be worship, meditation, Torah study, or even physical activity, the repetition is part of the meaning.

Modern scholars of Bible have convincingly argued that chapter 1 of Genesis was composed fairly late in the scheme of biblical writings. These scholars attribute it to the Israelite priests who lived in Babylonian exile. The myth's focus on clarity, division, and categorization would have been a tonic to these priests who had lost their vocation of sacrificial offerings when the First Temple in Jerusalem was destroyed by the Babylonians.

Personally, I prefer the narrative parts of the Torah. In a perfect world, Genesis 1 would be consigned to the back of the Book. After all, it sets up a contradiction. God, who brings the universe into being through speaking in chapter 1, quickly becomes the prototypical frustrated Creator in ensuing chapters. God does not enjoy any type of orderly behavior by the humans that are created. The early humans mate with semi-divines, and then Noah's generation are violent and evil. Following the Flood, the Tower of Babel symbolizes the bad choices and poor use of resources that God's creations continue to pursue. There is anything but order.

While lacking narrative drama, the first chapter of Genesis nevertheless teaches us an important lesson concerning the power of order in times of uncertainty. Ritual is based on disciplined, regular behavior. A worship service works for most people not when it is unpredictable, but rather when within a predictable ritual framework we are allowed to find creative expression. Growing up as a Reform Jew I never understood the freeing power of ritual until I prayed regularly at the Brandeis-Bardin Institute in California with mostly Conservative Jews. Every Shabbat service was exactly the same, except for the Torah reading. At first I was bored. But after a few weeks I found the routine paradoxically to be liberating.

Why is ritual so liberating? The simple answer is it helps us unlock the right side of the brain. Doing the same thing every week gives us the chance to leave the linear behind for a while. My daily practice is to arise early and read the newspapers. After my reading I usually feel fairly stressed (i.e., it is a scary world), and so I follow my newspaper reading with ten or twenty minutes of stillness, or mindfulness meditation. This practice is not at all boring for me, although I am in effect doing nothing. Through it I am then able to meet the day with energy and focus.

To divide our time into meaningful and discrete units, with much forethought, may seem like work, because it is. But it is very important work. Division is our way of creating meaning. And the very act of ritualizing this division opens us up to creative, spiritual expression.

Mark

What are the markings associated with the sky? Perhaps this is a reference to astrology. The ancient Rabbis did not completely discount reading the stars for insights into the future. For instance, when astrologers tell Rabbi Akiva that his daughter will die on her wedding night, the great sage does not rush to warn his daughter, since he knows what the Talmud will teach: Jews don't depend on the stars for meaning (Babylonian Talmud *Shabbat* 156a). And yet the rabbi also does not discount the warning completely. Human brains have not changed much in two thousand years. Even the most rational among us struggle with uncertainty. The pull of the stars as signifiers of meaning is inescapable. Even the Jewish phrase for "good luck" or "congratulations," *mazal tov*, literally means "may you have a lucky star." The ancient Rabbis may have condemned those who worship stars, but they too could not help but ponder their fate in light of the mysterious constellations.

And what of us? We may not read the daily horoscope, but the stars continue to serve as signs of God's Creation, the mysteries we still cannot comprehend, and the natural course of the universe. We no longer steer our ships by the stars or depend on natural sources for our light. I am grateful for more sophisticated navigational equipment and electric light, but I do miss the natural rhythm of sunrise and sundown. Or even the opportunity to see the stars.

There is an old Jewish tradition of greeting the new moon with a special sanctification (*Kiddush L'vanah*).[1] The community would go out into nature to greet the new moon together. Because of the lack of moonlight, the print for this prayer was very large. (In most countries, the largest headline font size in the newspaper is "Second

Coming type." In Israel, it is called *"Kiddush L'vanah* type." That says a lot about the division between Jews and Christians.) In our super-technical age, one wonders if some of these ancient traditions should be revisited.

Seasons

The seasons reflect the holidays contained within them. Classic Rabbinic commentary associates the seasons with the Jewish festivals and their inherent meaning. For example, Sukkot is a time for thanksgiving, Chanukah an occasion for finding light within the darkness of winter, and Passover celebrates redemption from Egypt (and the return of spring). Having lived twenty years of my adult life in places with no real discernible seasons (i.e., Southern California and South Florida), it is refreshing to be in a place once again with true seasons (i.e., Chicago). There is something comforting about the ritual of changing one's wardrobe, if no longer one's storm windows or snow tires.

But there is something more. *Allowing ourselves to be sublimated in a ritual of weekly and yearly observance, for that matter, enables a diminishment of our ego.* We become more communal, less tied to our own desires. Instead of planning our activities based on our own desires, we enlarge our experience by joining with others in community. Part of the reason Jews are supposed to pray with at least nine others is so we don't restrict our spiritual time and focus to our own needs. We expand our consciousness through joining community.

The notion of allowing our individual egos to be diminished in light of the vast work of Creation is spiritually potent. Consider another verse from the fourth day of Creation: "Thus God made the two great lights: the greater light to govern the day, and the lesser [smaller] light to govern the night and the stars" (Genesis 1:16). There seems to be a contradiction here. If God made two great lights, then how can one be large and one be small? Many commentators address this apparent irregularity. One comment from an ancient midrash sees a moral lesson within the disparity. The moon complained to God that it did not like being the same size as the sun, so God "rewarded" the moon's complaint by making it smaller.[2]

A more favorable treatment of the moon is found in the midrash:

> Rabbi Acha said: Imagine a king who had two governors, one ruling in the city and the other in a province. Said the king: Since the former has humbled himself to rule in the city only, I decree that whenever he goes out, the city council and the people shall go out with him, and whenever he enters, the city council and the people shall enter with him. Thus did the Holy One, blessed be God, say: Since the moon humbled itself to rule by night, I decree that when she comes forth, the stars shall come forth with her, and when she goes in [disappears], the stars shall go in with her. (B'reishit Rabbah 6:4)

This teaching reflects an ancient Rabbinic support for humility in our leaders. As another sage (Hillel) once observed, "When I exalt myself I am humbled, but when I humble myself I am exalted."[3] It is only when we create space for the world that we are able to find our genuine selves. The power of having time ritualized is, in part, that we can subsume our reality into something larger than ourselves. The medieval mystical notion of *tzimtzum*, or contraction, by which God could create the world only by contracting God's Self, teaches us the spiritual power of creating space within our own egos for the world around us. By letting go of some of the ego needs that distract us, we open space for enjoying the present and being more present for others.[4]

The great twentieth-century writer E. B. White once observed, "I arise in the morning torn between a desire to improve the world and a desire to enjoy the world. This makes it hard to plan the day." Our 168 hours a week afford no leeway. They are finite. But we can decide how to *divide* our time. We can use rituals to *signify* what matters most. And we can *season* our lives with a healthy dose of humility.

Ultimately, when we consider the creation of the fourth day, the sun, moon, and stars, we should be humbled but also inspired. Mostly, we should revel in our rituals that seek not to bore us with rote observance, but rather awaken in us a profound simplicity, an awareness of the majestic around us.

Recently I served on the faculty of a summer camp, and the tenth graders were planning a Friday night service. Their Israeli counselor was frustrated that the group had not come up with some amazing way to impress the camp with their service. I told her that, in my opinion, Shabbat itself is special and we need not push or market it too hard. In essence, our job was to remove the outside impediments and let Shabbat and the liturgy be what they were meant to be. The creative "wow" need not come from some radical idea, but from allowing the community to revel in an ancient and time-tested practice. The real goal of the service was not to make the campers feel special, but to allow them to feel the natural joys of community, rest, and sanctity. Our job was more to not get in the way.

Yiddish writer Aaron Zeitlin captures this sentiment with his well-known poem:

Praise me, says God, and I will know that you love me.
Curse me, says God, and I will know that you love me.
Praise me or curse me
And I will know that you love me.
Sing out my graces, says God,
Raise your fist against me and revile, says God.
Sing out graces or revile,
Reviling is also a kind of praise,
says God.
But if you sit fenced off in your apathy,

says God,

If you sit entrenched in: "I don't give a hang," says God,

If you look at the stars and yawn,

If you see suffering and don't cry out,

If you don't praise and you don't revile,

Then I created you in vain, says God.

In other words, let's *separate* the time in our days wisely, allow certain *markers* to remind us of life's natural gifts, and *season* our lives with insights from our collective Jewish practice. And perhaps just as important, when you look at the stars, *don't yawn.*

Notes

1. The source of the *Kiddush L'vanah* is in the Babylonian Talmud, *Sanhedrin* 42a: Rabbi Yochanan taught that one who blesses the new moon, in its proper time, is regarded like one who greets the *Shechinah* (Divine Presence), as it is written in Exodus 12:2, "This month [shall mark for you the beginning of the months]."

2. For more on this comment, see Louis Ginzberg, *Legends of the Jews* (Philadelphia: Jewish Publication Society of America, 1968), Vol. 1, pp. 23–26; *Pirkei D'Rabbi Eliezer* 6; Babylonian Talmud, *Chulin* 60b.

3. *Vayikra Rabbah* 1:5. We find a similar sentiment in Matthew 23:12.

4. Borowitz, Eugene B., "Tzimtzum: A Mystical Model for Contemporary Leadership," in *Religious Education*: The official journal of the Religious Education Association, Volume 69, Issue 6, 1974, pp. 687–700.

24
—

Music and the
Punctuation of Time

CANTOR ELLEN DRESKIN

*God then said, "Let there be lights in the expanse of the sky, to
separate day from night, to be markers for sacred seasons, for
days and years, and to be lights in the expanse of the sky, spilling light upon the earth!"—and so it was. Thus God made the
two great lights: the greater light to govern the day, and the
lesser light to govern the night and the stars. . . . And God saw
how good it was.*

Genesis 1:14–18

This is the story of a fourth day. From the mystery emerge patterns,
cycles, the measuring of time as we know it. Years, seasons, nights and
days, all with their own series of markers and movements in the sky.
Day four is all about patterns, the dependability of cycles of time in
which we live. These patterns are the foundation upon which we build
our lives.

And because of the innate capacity for patterns to quickly progress
from lovely routine to painfully boring rut, it is in reference to time,

178

and specifically Shabbat, the seventh day, that we first engage with the word "holy" (*kadosh*) in *Tanach*. In recognition and appreciation of both the patterns and the passage of time, we realize the desire to make distinctions. In order to make and take meaning from the random events of our lives, to vary the endless patterns, we must somehow mark one moment from the next, and also connect one moment to the next, in a way that makes sense over seasons, over years, over generations.

Music and time are inexorably intertwined. Music that we see on a page is only a hard-copy representation of something that cannot exist without the passage of time. Music must move forward within the context of the passage of time, as must the planets and stars in their revolutions in the sky. In the same way that the patterns of the solar system and the constellations of the night sky exist only because of the relationship between all of the heavenly bodies involved, music also has no meaning except that which is found in the relationships between its elements. The balance and relationship between notes and rests, varying tempos, intervals, patterns, and flow help us make sense out of our time, much like a connect-the-dots children's game. The single notes, much like single stars, mean nothing unless connected to others in a way that can be noticed and appreciated in the universe.

Music both decorates and commemorates time. It can (and often does) tell us how we are supposed to feel at any given moment. Imagine your favorite movie without the soundtrack: the passionate love scenes; the tension-filled chases; the suspenseful anticipation of something unexpected (a bit of an oxymoron); the mournful accompaniment of a good-bye kiss or a longing gaze. Most of it would be dreadfully boring without the musical enhancement of what our eyes behold. By the same token, every culture has its own melodies that mark birthdays and other life events, seasons of the year, and ritual practice. The patterns that make up our own cultural *nusach* (distinctive melodies) ground us in our communities, both religious and secular.

Country music composer Trisha Yearwood has a tune called "The Song Remembers When." It is a beautiful piece expressing the power of a single melody to send one hurtling back in time and to take others along. That's the real meaning of the word "commemoration": remembering together. With a single melody, I can be transported, along with innumerable others, to another space and energy and emotional state. Trisha Yearwood writes, "Even if the whole world has forgotten, the song remembers when."[1] In this way, music clothes our lives with personal and/or communal significance. It helps us to both awaken to and immerse ourselves in special set times of celebration and commemoration, as well as to the *k'doshim b'chol yom*, the holiness inherent in every moment of every day.

In their book *Filling Words with Light: Hasidic and Mystical Reflections on Jewish Prayer*, Rabbis Lawrence Kushner and Nehemiah Polen remind us that there were two splittings of seas in *Tanach*.[2] The Sea of Reeds story is one that we know quite well. The second occurs in Joshua 3:15–17. Few, if any of us remember this second miraculous occurrence of Israelites crossing a sea on dry land, when "*Adonai* your God dried up the waters of the Jordan before you until you crossed, just as the *Adonai* your God did to the Sea of Reeds, which God dried up before us until we crossed" (Joshua 4:23).[3]

Rabbis Kushner and Polen share with us, from the teachings of *Itturei Torah*,[4] that the reason that one story is paramount in our people's faith formation and the other has fallen by the wayside is because of song. Our crossing of the Sea of Reeds has a soundtrack—Moses and all the people sang the experience! And when we sing *Mi Chamochah* we are taken back, each time, to when we emerged from the sea, from slavery to freedom. With a melody, we co-remember that things can change in an instant through miraculous means. While the words themselves connect us to the story, the various musical settings that we choose convey everything from the ecstasy of the crossing to the sorrow at the death of the Egyptians; from being filled with the joy of freedom to being in awe of One who is capable of defying the laws of nature.

In their collaborative project *A Song to Sing, a Life to Live*, father and daughter Don (composer and church musician) and Emily (Indigo Girls) Saliers teach, "Our heartbeats, our breathing out and in, our cries of delight and pain, and our movements through space and time are already musical, gifted with pulse, pitch, pace, and rhythm."[5] In our individual, day-to-day lives do we not establish rhythms, fall into patterns, change our tone, exist in harmony, experience varying degrees of silence, of connection, of repetition of entire passages, and of variations on a theme? Connections between notes and rhythms help us to connect and glean significance from the moments of our lives. Just as a single note relies upon the ones surrounding it and must give itself up to the next note in the process, just as the difference between a major interval and a minor interval can transform energy, so too are we continually affecting each other according to various pitches, paces, and patterns.

Music is not only about what is there, but what is not there. Not only about the present and the past, but the future as well. Early on in our *Shacharit* (morning) worship, we encounter the blessing commonly known as *Yishtabach*. It signals the end of the introductory prayers and the transition to the body of the service. The *chatimah*, or concluding declaration of the prayer, expresses gratitude for One who chooses *shirei zimrah*, commonly translated as "melodious song." Both Hebrew words mean "song," and so this odd combination of synonyms leaves itself open to rabbinic interpretation. Early nineteenth-century rabbi Zev Wolf of Zhitomir encourages us to interpret *shirei* not as "melodious," but as a possessive form of a similar word, *shirayim*, that means "leftovers" or "crumbs."[6] It gives us permission to interpret the blessing as one of gratitude for what remains after the music has gone. The crumbs of the melodies of our lives. What remains after we are no longer here? The song that is my life, and the ways in which it reverberates and echoes in the universe will change everything that comes after. Rabbis Kushner and Polen liken this to the ways in which the silence after the symphony is different from the silence before.[7] The presence of the music, the ways in which it moves our spirits, has the ability to change us, as well as whatever comes after, either by connecting us to our deeper selves, giving us insight into our past, reaffirming our commitment to action or our connection to each other, or our deep emotions in the face of art and beauty and song.

And all of these blessings that music brings somehow coalesce in the function of music in our ritual lives.

All faith and secular cultures mark the passage of time with ritual: the annual seasons of harvest, rainfall, balance of darkness and light; the commemoration of historical or mythological events that form the foundation of our worldviews; and the universal benchmarks within each individual life—birth, learning, coming-of-age, various passages of adulthood, and death. The melodies that we associate with these events become our spiritual sun, moon, and stars. Music raises the level of discernment: it not only tells us that a particular time, based on patterns in the changing sky, has arrived, but also contextualizes moments within our own communities, connecting us to those who arrived at this very moment in ages past.

Can you imagine an important Jewish ritual or holiday celebration without music? Although they vary according to region and origin, the specific modes and melodies used at different times of the year have helped Jews over the centuries to celebrate the patterns of their lives. Our music connects us not only to our present-day communities, but to Jewish communities across the millennia. As older melodies are, over time, replaced by more contemporary sounds, we also merge our unique stories of the past with the story of the communities in which we presently live.

Rabbi Abraham Joshua Heschel, in *Man's Quest for God*, speaks of the importance of song in the act of prayer:

In no other act does man experience so often the disparity between the desire for expression and the means of expression as in prayer. The inadequacy of the means at our disposal appears so tangible, so tragic, that one feels it a grace to be able to give oneself up to music, to a tone, to a song, to a chant. The wave of a song carries the soul to heights which utterable meanings can never reach.[8]

Our *nigunim*, or wordless melodies, express our emotions beyond the limitations of language. Music understands and conveys our yearnings, our fears, our joy, and the various patterns of our daily lives. Whether we are active participants in the melodies with our own voices or instruments or we are participating simply by allowing the melodies to move our souls, we are affected nonetheless. The melodies enhance our access to emotions, spirituality, identity, and the way we perceive the world.

By paralleling and making us mindful of time—its patterns as well as its passage—music allows us to go far beyond the spoken word. By adorning and providing context for the ways in which we travel under the sun, moon, and stars created on the fourth day of Creation, music has the power to open our hearts to that which is "within our reach, but beyond our grasp," according to Heschel.[9] Music connects us to any human who has ever looked to the patterns in the skies and celebrated with instrument, rhythm, and voice; it allows us to reach upward and inward, simultaneously touching our individual souls, our shared stories, and our stars.

Notes

1. "The Song Remembers When Lyrics," Lyrics.com, STANDS4 LLC, 2016, http://www.lyrics.com/lyric/4371877.

2. Lawrence Kushner and Nehemia Polen, *Filling Words with Light: Hasidic and Mystical Reflections on Jewish Prayer* (Woodstock, VT: Jewish Lights Publishing, 2004), 42.

3. Adapted from *JPS Hebrew-English Tanakh*, 2nd ed. (Philadelphia: Jewish Publication Society, 1999), 464.

4. A. Chayn, *Itturei Torah*, ed. Aaron Jacob Greenberg (Jerusalem: Yavneh, 1987), 3:124.

5. Don Saliers and Amy Saliers, *A Song to Sing, a Life to Live: Reflections on Music as Spiritual Practice* (San Francisco: Jossey-Bass, 2005), 22.

6. Zev Wolf of Zhitomir, *Or Hameir* (*Yesod Haavodah*, 28), cited in Kushner and Polen, *Filling Words with Light*, 43.

7. Kushner and Polen, *Filling Words with Light*, 43–44.

8. Abraham Joshua Heschel, *Man's Quest for God: Studies in Prayer and Symbolism* (New York: Charles Scribner's Sons, 1954), 39.

9. Abraham Joshua Heschel, *The Vocation of the Cantor* (New York: American Conference of Cantors, 1966).

Day Five

✦

ANIMALS OF
LAND AND WATER

*God then said, "Let the waters bring forth swarms of living
creatures, and let the birds fly over the earth, across the face of
the expanse of the sky!" God then formed the great sea monsters, and every living creature that creeps, with which the
waters swarm, all true to their types, and every winged bird,
each true to its type; and God saw how good it was. God then
blessed them, saying, "Be fruitful and multiply, fill the waters
of the seas, and let the birds multiply in the earth!" And there
was evening and there was morning, a fifth day.*

Genesis 1:20–23

25

Global Swarming

Can We Become Worthy of Creation?

RABBI MATTHEW SOFFER

God said, "Let the waters bring forth swarms of living crea-
tures, and let the birds fly over the earth, across the face of the
expanse of the sky!"

Genesis 1:20

In *This Changes Everything*, Naomi Klein quips, "The only thing rising faster than our [carbon] emissions is the output of words pledging
to lower them."[1] What has yet to be said regarding the mandate to
respond to environmental destruction? Our natural world desperately
needs a geopolitical intensive care unit. The scientific data on global
warming (and other calamitous ecological conditions) now conclu-
sively incriminate human behavior. Denying this fact is worse than in-
correct; it is morally bankrupt.

So fragile is our condition on earth today; so precarious is the
promise of a humanity that will endure well beyond this century. The
mere facts are astounding. Countless studies elucidate the severity of
the damage, and Jewish social justice leaders have already made the

cases for why our tradition demands reparative action as a top priority. The Religious Action Center of Reform Judaism summarized the most alarming data pertaining to human health, gleaned from a 2016 World Health Organization report:[2]

- Nearly one-quarter of all deaths in 2012—12.6 million—can be attributed to environmental factors such as pollution, chemical exposures, and climate change.
- There has been a rise in deaths due to noncommunicable diseases, while deaths from infection diseases have decreased. Sixty-five percent of environmental-related deaths were due to noncommunicable diseases such as heart disease, cancers, and stroke. Many of the deaths due to these diseases, about 8.2 million, can be attributed to air pollution.
- Children under five years old are most impacted by environmental factors, which cause death in 26 percent, or 1.7 million, of these children annually.
- Low- and middle-income countries face the greatest burden of environmental disease.
- Disease and death as a result of environmental factors are preventable through efforts to reduce air, water, and soil pollution.

These facts account only for the impact on human beings. As Pope Francis writes, "The Bible has no place for a tyrannical anthropocentrism unconcerned for other creatures."[3] This haunting reality renders our current chapter of world history "unchartered territory." If Judaism is to remain a prophetic tradition in the twenty-first century, then Israel—not the country but the people whose namesake connotes wrestling with God—is responsible for the weighty task of repairing a world decaying in the pernicious hands of human greed, waste, and exploitation. Israel has always discerned its responsibility by embracing Torah and reading it through the prism of our conscientious minds and hearts. In this manner, the biblical account of Creation now deserves paramount attention.

In *B'reishit Rabbah*, the Rabbis guide us toward the core questions that humanity faces:

> Rabbi Shimon said: When the Holy One blessed be God was about to create the first human being, the ministering angels formed themselves into groups and parties, some of them saying, "Don't create!" while others urged, "Create!" Rav Huna the Elder of Sepphoris said: "While the ministering angels were discussing with each other and disputing with each other, the Holy One blessed be God created him. [God then] said to them: 'What are you debating? Humanity has already been made!'"[4]

This misanthropic Rabbinic story prompted premodern listeners to contemplate the purpose of humanity. *Why are we here? If God created us, how do we make sense of our "evil inclination"?* Today, however, the unthinkable devastation that humanity has wreaked on our natural world plunks the modern reader down alongside the ministering angels in the story, demanding we engage their conversation in ways even more urgent and acrimonious than the Rabbis ever could have fathomed.

We might imagine the perspective of the ministering angels by taking note of the work done thus far in Creation. Since the story is set when God was "about to create the first human being," we can suppose these angels are arguing during day five, when God says, "Let the waters bring forth swarms [*sheretz*] of living creatures, and let the birds fly over the earth, across the expanse of the sky!" (Genesis 1:20).

Biblical scholar Avivah Zornberg calls attention to the significance of the word *sheretz*, which repeats twice on this day of Creation. *Sheretz*, "swarming," is a distinctly horizontal, creeping movement. For this reason, she notes, Rashi comments that *sheretz* refers to "insects that are low, crawling on the ground, and look as though they are being dragged."[5] What distinguishes human beings, created on day six, is their predicament of being creatures that are both horizontal and vertical. Human beings are dwelling with insectile horizontality but also, through a unique relationship with their Creator, divine verticality.

Naturally the angels would have a problem with human beings, since angels, in the Rabbinic imagination, are vertical beings, "on high," not just *able* but *situated* to converse with God. The introduction of human beings to the universe blurs a critical boundary, with a creature in the divine image that, somehow, also swarms.

Swarming is what the Israelites do in the very beginning of the story of Exodus. While in Egypt, the Israelites "were fruitful, swarmed [*vayishr'tzu*], and multiplied" (Exodus 1:7). Human beings are commanded on day six only to "be fruitful and multiply" (Genesis 1:28). Swarming is what gets them in trouble. Swarming intimates the transformation from the verticality of Joseph—whose ascent saves Egyptian society—to the lowly depths of enslavement, under the torment of a new and unfamiliar Pharaoh. Just as the midrashic ministering angels ask the universal question "Are human beings worthy of Creation?" the imagery of swarming Israelites alludes to the very day before human creation, thus hinting at the question, "Is *this people* worthy of redemption?"

Later in the journey of the Israelites, their success rests on their will to move vertically. Entry into the land of Canaan is usually described as an *ascent*. The contrarian scout Caleb argues against the majority of faithless naysayers who complain that entry into the Promised Land is impossible, crying out: *Aloh naaleh . . . ki yachol nuchal lah!* "We can indeed ascend . . . yes, surely we can!" (Numbers 13:30).

The sacrificial cult, too, relies upon vertical movement in daily communication with God. On the altar the priests would set fire to offerings, watching the smoke rise (God loved the smell!). Of course, all of these instances of verticality led to the liturgical custom of calling the act of blessing the Torah an *aliyah*, "ascent."

The dialectic between vertical and horizontal, so core in the Torah, still figures into our contemporary connection to God and the fulfillment of our obligations today. However, in our natural world, the "offerings" that go upward to the atmosphere constitute overwhelming pollution. We might call this, in recollection of the tragic story of Aaron's sons, "strange fire." We have perverted the day six privilege of verticality, of showing ourselves worthy of dominion over other aspects of Creation.

Are human beings worthy of Creation? The Rabbis give the last word to God: "What are you debating? Humanity has already been made!" God does not tell the angels that they are asking the *wrong* question. God says, in essence, "This is not *your* debate." The end of the midrash plunges the question downward toward humanity. The Rabbis, in particular the redactors of the midrash, inscribe the question for future generations of Israel. This is now an enduring question for all of humanity to answer: *How can our actions make us worthy of Creation?*

As we read Genesis, we are reminded that this is only the beginning of the story. Just as Zornberg sees the swarming of day five as a necessary seed for subsequent actions in the beginning of the next book—actions that set up the very conditions for redemption—the state of the natural world today is not irrevocably doomed. The story has not been finished, and human action now, as in our text, plays the central role. Whether humanity acts like insects or angels, like Pharaoh or Moses, is undecided.

The Pharaonic forces in society are mighty. In the United States, power comes from organized money and organized people. Clearly, the money is on the wrong side. As the *Guardian* reported in 2013, between the years of 2002 and 2010 more than $100 billion dollars was spent funding efforts to undermine proof of climate change, influencing policymakers away from environmental stewardship.[6] The people, too, are not organized well enough for change. Research shows that Americans who care most passionately about the environment are among the least likely to vote.[7] In other words, given the realities of elections and campaigns, *our political leaders*—that is, those most well situated to make long-term impact on the environment, in a nation that is among those causing the most severe environmental destruction on earth—*are incentivized against environmental stewardship.*

Yet, powerful forces are not all corrupt; prophetic voices in our society are growing louder by the day. Pope Francis's recent encyclical on the environment reflects a movement of world leaders eager to respond, giving reason or reminder not to lose hope:

> The urgent challenge to protect our common home includes a concern to bring the whole human family together to seek a sustainable and integral development, for we know that things can change. . . . Humanity still has the ability to work together in building our common home. Here I want to recognize, encourage and thank all those striving in countless ways to guarantee the protection of the home which we share. Particular appreciation is owed to those who tirelessly seek to resolve the tragic effects of environmental degradation on the lives of the world's poorest. Young people demand change. They wonder how anyone can claim to be building a better future without thinking of the environmental crisis and the sufferings of the excluded.[8]

Exemplifying this movement of young activists making a difference on the ground are Nathaniel and Melanie Stinnett, two congregants of Temple Israel of Boston. Upon learning about the overwhelmingly low number of "super-environmentalist" voters, they founded the Environmental Voter Project, a nonprofit devoted to identifying inactive environmentalists and turning them into consistent voters and activists. Teaming up with Clarity Campaign Labs, a political data analytics company, the Environmental Voter Project has already taken significant strides toward sparking change within the populace of eligible voters. They are building power by organizing people.[9] This is merely one example, but it speaks to the power of organizing people to change the current system from one that corrupts to one that bends our polity toward environmental justice.

Rabbi Nachman of Bratzlav taught, "If you believe that you can destroy, believe that you can repair."[10] The biblical narrative creates human beings with the equivocation of agency for destruction or repair; we can dwell along a horizontal or a vertical plane of existence; we can swarm like insects, or we repair Creation, like symbols of God. The current condition of our precious planet is an opportunity to answer the age-old question, "Can we become worthy of Creation?" with the words of Caleb, "*Yachol nuchal lah*—Yes, we surely can!" We are human beings, created on day six, with the divine ability to repair.

Notes

1. Naomi Klein, *This Changes Everything: Capitalism vs. the Climate* (New York: Simon & Schuster, 2014), Kindle edition, 11.

2. Rachel Landman, "Impacts of Environmental Risks on Human Health," Religious Action Center of Reform Judaism, http://www.rac.org/blog/2016/04/07/impacts-environmental-risks-human-health#sthash.amTNbRE5.dpuf, summarizing the report of the World Health Organization Report, *Preventing Disease through Healthy Environments: A Global Assessment of the Burden of Disease from Environmental Risks*, http://www.who.int/quantifying_ehimpacts/publications/preventing-disease/en/.

3. Pope Francis, *Encyclical on Climate Change and Inequality: On Care for Our Common Home* (Brooklyn: Melville House, 2015), Kindle edition, 10.

4. *B'reishit Rabbah* 8:5.

5. Avivah Gottlieb Zornberg, *The Beginning of Desire: Reflections on Genesis* (New York: Knopf Doubleday, 2011), Kindle edition, 368–70.

6. Suzanne Goldenberg, "Secret Funding Helped Build Vast Network of Climate Denial Thinktanks," *Guardian*, February 14, 2013, http://www.theguardian.com/environment/2013/feb/14/funding-climate-change-denial-thinktanks-network.

7. Nathaniel Stinnet, "The Science Behind Turning Out Environmental Voters," *Campaigns and Elections*, April 26, 2016, https://www.campaignsandelections.com/campaign-insider/the-science-behind-turning-out-environmental-voters.

8. Pope Francis, *Encyclical on Climate Change and Inequality*, 10.

9. Environmental Voter Project, www.environmentalvoter.org.

10. *Likutei Moharan* II:112

26

Reading Sacred (Con)Texts Today: Historical Background, Modern Interpretations

RABBI RIFAT SONSINO, PHD

*God said, "Let the waters bring forth swarms of living crea-
tures, and birds that fly above the earth across the expanse of
the sky." God created the great sea monsters, and all the living
creatures of every kind that creep, which the waters brought
forth in swarms, and all the winged birds of every kind. And
God saw that this was good. God blessed them, saying, "Be
fertile and increase, fill the waters in the seas, and let the birds
increase on the earth." And there was evening and there was
morning, a fifth day.*

Genesis 1:20–23 (JPS, 1985)

In order to appreciate an ancient text, we need to follow two different
methodologies. The first would be to try to understand the historical

and religious context out of which the document has emerged, and the other is to interpret the material for our time using the contemporary categories and thinking patterns.

Genesis 1:20–23 describes the fifth day of Creation. This is a text edited by the priests during the Babylonian exile, about the sixth century BCE and thereafter. The priestly material was, in reality, based on an earlier collection, commonly referred to as Elohistic (where God is called *Elohim*), which was most likely put together in the Northern Kingdom of Israel in the tenth century BCE. In our paragraph, having created the primordial light (day one), the *rakia* ("dome"; see below) (day two), the land (day three), and the heavenly bodies (day four), God decides to create living creatures (*nefesh chayah*) who would dwell above the earth and in the seas.

In this section, each sentence plays a key role. Genesis 1:20 is an anticipated summary of what will happen. In the rest, only two main categories of creatures are mentioned: the inhabitants in the waters and the forming of the birds. The details, listed in verse 21, seem to follow a certain progression, from the largest animals to the smallest ones. First, the great sea-monsters (*hatanninim hag'dolim*) are formed. This is followed by the fashioning of "all the living creatures of every kind that creep, which the waters brought forth in swarms," and finally by the creation of the winged birds. The section concludes with God's satisfaction with God's deeds, the blessing of the animals by God, and a final statement identifying the entire process as having taken place within the fifth day.

There are a number of major features that are worthy of note in our text:

1. It is remarkable that in the Hebrew Bible plants, already formed on the third day, are not called *nefesh chayah* (living beings). Perhaps the reason is that vegetation depends primarily on water and sun to reproduce, whereas our text appears to concentrate

on those "living creatures" that multiply themselves through sexual intercourse.

2. On day five Creation is restricted to animals that inhabit the seas and the sky, whereas on day six, in addition to the first human being, different types of animals, such as cattle, creeping things, and wild beasts are formed. Two different types of animals are included on day five: those that "swarm" (*sh-r-tz*), namely, those that climb with hands and feet; and those that "creep" (*r-m-s*), namely those that crawl about (Genesis 1:21). Neither category is further identified. According to Rashi, a medieval Jewish commentator (d. 1105), the "swarming" animals include flies, ants, worms, and rodents. "Creeping" animals probably included lizards and reptiles. According to our biblical editor, they all have their origin in water.

3. According to our biblical text, the birds were created so that they may fly "above the earth across the expanse of the sky" (*r'kia hashamayim*; Genesis 1:20). It is based on the belief, popular in antiquity, that the land is flat, that above it there is a dome that holds the heavenly waters (also acting as the abode of the divine beings), and that the earth rests upon pillars sunk into subterranean waters at a place called *sheol*.

The combination of *rakia* and *shamayim*, already recorded in Genesis 1:14–15, is strange. The primary Hebrew word for "sky" is *rakia* (already mentioned in 1:6, "expanse," in day two). It is not known in other Semitic languages. Some scholars (see Gerhard von Rad's book on Genesis[1]) connect it to a Phoenician root meaning "that which is hammered" (cf. Job 37:18), and based on the Septuagint (Greek translation of the Bible, second century BCE) and the Vulgate (Latin translation of the Bible, fourth century CE), it is usually translated as "firmament."

In the ancient Near Eastern view of the universe, the *rakia* played an important role. It was primarily viewed as a canopy covering the earth, which was supported with pillars (Job 26:11; II Samuel 22:8) and carried openings/windows that allowed the rain to come through (Genesis 8:2; Isaiah 24:18). The *rakia* "separated the water which was below the expanse [*rakia*] from the water which was above the expanse" (Genesis 1:7). Birds flew across the *rakia* (Genesis 1:20), and the sun, moon, and the stars were set on it (1:14–18). Eventually *rakia* and *shamayim* were combined and considered as the abode of God (Isaiah 66:1).

4. The laudatory statement that "God saw that this was good" (Genesis 1:21) is included in day five, even though it is missing in days one and two. However, it is added to days three, four, and, in an extended form ("very good"), six. The words "God saw that this was good" basically mean that God was pleased with God's handiwork and considers the world a good place in which to live, and this promotes a positive attitude toward life in general.

5. During day five, in addition to fish and birds, God creates what the text calls *taninim*, in the plural. What are those? Most translations render the expression as "sea monsters" or "dragons." Everett Fox, in his Schocken Bible translation, calls them "sea-serpents."[2] The Septuagint as well as the Vulgate has "whales."

   In order to better understand the background of the *taninim*, it is necessary to turn to ancient Near Eastern texts where the word *tanin* (written as *tnn*) is found. There are many references to primordial monsters in ancient Babylonian as well as Ugaritic texts. We don't know which texts originally influenced the biblical editors. Many scholars believe that the influence came from the Canaanite (i.e., East Mediterranean shores, including present Israel, south Syria, Lebanon, and western Jordan) sources, which are closer to biblical Israel, rather than texts that originated in a faraway Babylonian milieu.

   Ugarit was a major Canaanite city in the second millennium BCE, which generated voluminous texts in the Ugaritic language, akin to Hebrew. The people of Ugarit (today Ras Shamra, Syria) had a popular myth called the "Baal Myth," which dealt with the ascendency of Baal, the god of storm and fertility, within the pantheon of all the gods. In this myth, the word *tanin* occurs a few times. In one of the episodes, though the sequence of the events is still debatable, it appears that during a conflagration of various gods, a *tanin*, a sea dragon-god, assisted Yam (the sea god) in a battle against Baal: "I have bound the dragon's [*tnn*] jaws, have destroyed it" (tablet 3). In Job 7:12, *tanin* appears to be identified with Yam.

In the Hebrew Bible, the word *tanin* has four different meanings: in some cases it means "dragon" in general (Jeremiah 51:34; Job 7:12); in other parts of the Bible the word refers to a "serpent" (Exodus 7:9–12; Deuteronomy 32:33); in Isaiah 13:22 it describes a "jackal"; and in our Genesis text it refers to a "sea monster." It is most likely that the image of a Canaanite primeval sea dragon influenced the biblical editors in using the term *taninim* as a general term for "dragons" or "sea monsters," not only in Genesis but also in other parts of the Hebrew Bible.

According to Rabbinic tradition the *tanin* refers to Leviathan, a monster serpent and its mate. It was believed that God originally created a male and a female Leviathan, but lest they mated with one another, God castrated the male and slew the female, reserving her flesh for the banquet that will be given to the righteous in the world-to-come (Babylonian Talmud, *Bava Batra* 74b). The *Meam Loez*, a Sephardic commentary of *Jacob Kulli* (eighteenth century Izmir, Turkey) says that the term *tanin* also refers to angels, who, some say, were created on the fifth day.

What can we learn from our text that would be special and noteworthy?

1. In ancient Near Eastern texts, monsters have mythological divine attributes, and are considered part of the pantheon of the gods. Similarly, the sea, in itself, was considered a divinity with generative powers of its own. In the Hebrew Bible, even though all life appears to start in water, the sea itself does not have a divine quality. It is God who creates the new beings. God is the only creator. From this we learn that God is the only God. The rest of existence is God's creation and is subservient to the Divine.

2. On the previous days of Creation, natural beings come into existence by the creative "word" of God. Thus, for example, in day three, God decrees that the dry land should appear, and it does. In day five, however, as in day four, God actually gets involved in the process of Creation, as it states, "God created" (Genesis 1:21), not with a divine decree but with God's personal involvement. From this we learn that whatever exists in the world contains the imprint of the Divine. Life and nature are set aside as precious—in other words, sacred—and we need to treat them as such.

3. After the creation of the birds, God "blesses them" (i.e., all creatures), saying, "Be fertile and increase" (Genesis 1:22). Here we probably have the original meaning of the word "blessing," and that is fertility. To bless someone means to wish the object of blessing a good life and a bright future through descendants. Isn't this also what we wish our loved ones when we invoke God's blessings upon them today?

Day five, in referring to the formation of the living creatures in the heavens and on the earth, highlights the personal involvement of the Divine in the process of Creation, reiterates God's happiness in the result of God's labors, includes a blessing of fertility, and provides a transition to day six, when not only domesticated and wild animals are created, but the first human being, the pinnacle of Creation, is formed.

Note
1. Gerhard von Rad, *Genesis* (Philadelphia: The Westminster Press, 1972).
2. Everett Fox, *The Five Books of Moses*, (New York: Schocken Books, 1995), p. 15.

27

The Animal Kingdom

RABBI DR. SHMULY YANKLOWITZ

God then said, "Let the earth bring forth living creatures of every type: domestic animals and creeping things and wild animals, each true to its type!"—and so it was.

Genesis 1:24

Living creatures possess a moving soul.

Nachmanides[1]

In all of Jewish tradition, the mitzvah of *shiluach hakein*—the commandment to send away the mother bird before taking the egg—is the most seemingly eccentric and confusing. What religious imperative could there be to send away a mother bird only to steal away its most prized resource? What pedagogical or ritual function can this possibly serve? To the enterprising mind, however, this supposedly ethical dilemma of *shiluach hakein* offers one of the most potent teachings about animal welfare in all of Jewish thought. Not only that, it underlies the divine enterprise that the Creation story presents to humanity.

On that point, the fifth day of Creation presents the Jewish people with an overarching moral quandary. The previous four days concerned themselves with God's elemental creations: the heavens, the winds, the earth below, and the waters. But on this antepenultimate day, living creatures are first introduced into the ethers. It's an unusual divine statement. Surely, the Creator could have skipped over the animal kingdom and only had humans dwell upon the earth? Would this not be a less complicated world to oversee? As we will discern, the universe would not be complete without the diversity of the fauna that roams upon the lands. The totality of Torah articulates a myriad of responsibilities that humans have for animals. These responsibilities are intertwined with opportunities for the cultivation of Jewish values. Perhaps the premier mechanism to cultivate reverence for the wondrous multiplicity of Creation is to avoid eating God's creatures altogether.

Indeed, vegetarianism/veganism—and Jewish awareness toward the overarching umbrella of animal welfare—is the most dynamic and growing trend in the American Jewish community and has been for the past few decades. As the Jewish community becomes more educated about the detrimental effects of using animals for food has upon human health, animal suffering,[2] the environment, and global hunger, the more clear the epistemological realities of the fifth day become.

Yet, immediately, the biblical text presents us with a conundrum. In the latter part of the Creation story, humans are told they "shall hold sway over the fish of the sea and the birds of the sky, over the beasts, over all the earth, over all that creeps upon the earth" (Genesis 1:26). In other words, humans have complete dominion over the animal world. This seems to be in contradiction to the human obligation to emulate God's ways and be "good to all" (Psalm 145:9). How could the consumption of God's creatures be commensurate with the duty to uphold mercy? Maimonides explained that animals contain within their divine existence a teleological purpose: they are a part of Creation for their own sake.[3]

How we take care of and interact with animals is an indicator of our moral fiber. Well before the advent of a theory of evolution, medieval French-Jewish philosopher Yosef Caspi explained that animals are akin to our forefathers, since they preceded us in procession of Creation.[4] To be certain, they are even closely related to humans in substance, with the same synapses having the ability to comprehend feelings and emotions. This presents us with another philosophical conflict. According to Jewish tradition, humans are imbued with a level of dignity not granted to animals. Elevating the human to an existence detached and designated with special rights does not preclude the possibility for some level of obligation that exists toward animals. Nor does it call into question humans as the pinnacle of existence; the welfare of *all* creatures is still valid. In our contemporary perception of the human-animal dyad, it is apparent that there is too much of a proclivity to not consider the concept of *tzaar baalei chayim*—the Torah prohibition against inflicting unnecessary pain upon animals—as a building block toward a more compassionate existence for all. The notion of vegetarianism in this broader context acts as a restoration of the ideal toward a cruelty-free world.

The biblical history of animal consumption experienced three distinct eras. In the Garden of Eden, which was presumably created concomitantly on the fifth day to house the recently formed beasts and creatures, humans did not consume animals. After the Great Deluge[5] and construction of the ark, God perceived the violent nature of humans and thus permitted meat consumption as a concession so they would channel their violent nature to kill animals instead of people. Finally, we come to learn that after meat was only permitted as a sacrifice to God, it later became permitted as a more regular staple of diets outside of the real sacrificial worship. These three eras mark the progression of an admittedly supernal ideal and evolution of a certain religious pragmatism. The protracted advent of mass production and corporations dedicated to mass-scale factory farming means we have entered a new era requiring a revised religious perspective on the consumption of meat. Are we in a fourth era?

Or, more potently, are we in the position to consider the well-being and rights of animals as comparable to the basic rights that humans are privileged to hold? Freedom to move, freedom from torture, freedom to live?

There is a Talmudic parable that frames the biblical desire for universal vegetarianism:

> Rav Y'hudah stated in the name of Rav, "Adam was not permitted meat for purposes of eating, as it is written, 'For you it shall be for food and to all animals of the earth,' but not animals of the earth for you. But when the children of Noah came [God] permitted them [the animals of the earth], as it is said, 'As the green grass I have given to you everything.'" (BT *Sanhedrin* 59b)

Following this reasoning, there are two medieval explicators of Jewish law who viewed vegetarianism as a Jewish and, more broadly, human ideal. Rabbis Yosef Albo and Yitzchak Abarbanel both suggested that promoting a diet without meat could serve as a moral lodestar because the slaughtering process has the ability to unlock traits that burrow into the negative nature of human beings.[6] Rabbi Abraham Isaac Kook,[7] perhaps the greatest figure of the modern Jewish vegetarian movement, argued for the ideal of vegetarianism as a means of preparing for the age of the Messiah, who will bring forth the utmost justice in the world. In Rav Kook's view, certain ideals would not be fully actualized until the era of the redemption, when Jewish theology instructs that the Jewish people act in spiritual and moral ways that attempt to bring messianic ideals to fruition.

These ideals are constantly in conversation with each other. To wit, a midrash explains that Moses was chosen as the leader and prophet for the Jewish people because of his consideration for animals.[8] It is not only the prophets and kings of Israel who are so often portrayed as compassionate shepherds; this is also a popular way of personifying God: "The Eternal is my shepherd, I shall not want" (Psalm 23:1). We may not treat an animal merely as property. Rather, we are told that we may not sell an animal to a non-virtuous person for fear of how they will treat that animal. One of the best-known instances of animal protection is that we may not eat until we have fed our animals (BT *B'rachot* 40a). Indeed, one measure of Judaism's virtuosity is its treatment of animal life.

It is important to note that while the Torah gives full permission *for* the consumption of meat, this allowance does not transmute into an *obligation* to consume meat. Rather it grants permission for those who desire it. The Torah states, "When . . . you say: 'I shall eat some meat,' for you have the urge to eat meat, you may eat meat whenever you wish" (Deuteronomy 12:20). Meat may be consumed on the basis of desire for meat. And certainly, if one finds the action physically, spiritually, or ethically repugnant, then one has the choice to abstain. A commentary in the Talmud goes even further, interpreting the verse from Deuteronomy to mean that "a person should not eat meat unless they have a special craving for it" (BT *Chulin* 84a).

Throughout the millennia, Jews have yearned to return to the Garden of Eden, a world where eating sentient creatures is not imaginable, and we are called upon to be a people of holy compassion. In fact, the great sages of the Talmud consider mercy and compassion to be essential characteristics of being Jewish (BT *Beitzah* 32b). By being compassionate to animals, we not only fulfill the mandate of the Torah, but we regain our humanity. Choosing not to eat meat for ethical reasons has the power to imprint the values of mercy and compassion deep within our souls. When we take a step back to consider the awe-inspiring enormity of the creation of animal life on the fifth day and the spiritual grandeur it is meant to cultivate, vegetarianism becomes more tangible and more visceral.

Further, animal welfare is not only a Jewish concern, but a human concern. The Creation story is not the story *of the Jews*, but of *every creature* that God found worthy to exist. From the lowliest microbe to the most complex being, all gain life from the same holy source. When we forget our divine origins, we also forget our core mission. To be a holy person means to consider the plights of those weaker than ourselves, to empathize and bring succor to the weak and vulnerable. Concerning ourselves with the welfare of animals helps us to enact our own holy mission on this earth. If the message of the fifth day is anything, it is that humans are not alone on this earth.

When we arrive at the insight that the world was not created for us alone[9]—that the mother bird and her egg are precious to God—and that we are not entitled to consume whatever we wish, we reach a powerful Torah ideal, one that may be the most spiritual ideal of all. We share this beautiful world with a remarkable diversity of life. We are only one aspect of this biosphere. And when we respect it for what it is, we venerate that which brought it forth from the far reaches of time and space.

Notes

1. Nachmanides, commentary on Genesis 1:29.

2. According to Farm USA, citing Department of Agriculture statistics, nearly 9.3 billion animals were slaughtered for consumption in 2010. Source: farmusa.org/statistics11.html.

3. Maimonides, *Guide for the Perplexed* 3:13. Also known by his acronym, Rambam, Maimonides was a twelfth-century scholar and physician whose contributions to Jewish thought and literature have been unparalleled in the field of biblical commentary.

4. Yosef Caspi, commentary on Deuteronomy 22:6.

5. Also known as the Flood, seen later in Genesis 6–9.

6. Albo, *Sefer HaIkkarim*, vol. 3, chap. 15; Abarbanel, commentary on Leviticus 11:3.

7. The first chief rabbi (Ashkenazi) of pre-state Israel (1865–1935).

8. *Sh'mot Rabbah* 2:2.

9. Maimonides, *Guide for the Perplexed* 3:13.

28

Creation as Intimate Partner

RABBI MIKE COMINS

God then said, "Let the waters bring forth swarms of living creatures, and let the birds fly over the earth, across the face of the expanse of the sky!"

Genesis 1:20

The creation of the biosphere that sustains, nurtures, and houses us humans culminates on the fifth day of creation. On the sixth day, right before God makes humankind, the text narrates the introduction of birds, sea creatures, and land animals into the world. The table is set for us; our intimate partners await.

I am a Jew who feels closest to God in wilderness, who loves to practice Judaism in the natural world. But my experience in nature places me outside the mainstream. Judaism's major practices—Shabbat and holiday observance, study, communal prayer—generally take place indoors. In the face of declining synagogue membership and environmental degradation, the project of bringing Judaism back to the land is more relevant and necessary today than ever. Can we find ways of enlivening Jewish worship by venturing out of our sanctuaries? Can we protect the eco-system that sustains and nourishes us every day?

Can Judaism find its way outdoors, back to the Sinai wilderness, back to the earth?

Distancing God from the World

The Jewish connection to the natural world dates back to the very roots of our tradition. When the mysterious, invisible God revealed God's self, moments of theophany were generally accompanied by natural phenomena such as storms, earthquakes, fire, or a burning bush. Revelation often occurred on mountains or other sacred sites in nature, such as Elon Morei (the Oak Tree of Moreh; Genesis 12:6–7). Ancient Israelite cult and early Rabbinic Judaism were closely tied to the earth through the main occupations of the day: farming and animal husbandry. Major holidays and many sacrifices celebrated agriculture and were correlated with the seasons.

But in late antiquity and the early Middle Ages, Jewish thought concerning the natural world shifted. Greek philosophers posited a realm of perfect forms and introduced an opposition between body and soul and between spirit and matter. As these ideas took hold in Jewish culture, God, too, came to be understood as perfect: All-knowing, all-powerful, all-good, and unchanging. The God of the Hebrew Bible, the God who physically appeared to Moses on Mt. Sinai, became a purely spiritual God untouched by the flawed, changing materiality of the world—a place marked by temptation and sin. Most thinkers reinterpreted Judaism accordingly, setting earthly pursuits and the human body as obstacles to be overcome in the religious quest.

The Enlightenment further distanced Jewish thought and practice from the land. With the rise of critical biblical scholarship, God-in-nature was read out of the Bible. Julius Wellhausen and other early Bible scholars claimed that the ancient Israelites separated themselves from their pagan neighbors by discovering God in history. Divine action, starting with the Creation of the universe and traveling toward the messianic period, was to be found in events, not natural processes. The Israelites, it was claimed, "desacralized" nature.

There is truth in this analysis, but it ignores or misinterprets the fact that ancient Israelite religion *was* primarily concerned with God's role in the aforementioned cycles of agriculture. The three major holidays (Pesach, Shavuot, and Sukkot) were organized around the three harvests in the Land of Israel (barley, wheat, and fruit). In a place where drought led directly to starvation, the central sacrifices were meant to ensure God's protection and care where it mattered most: the fertility of the soil and the timely coming of the rains. Nature was never desacralized by the Israelites. They had no need to choose God-in-history over God-in-nature or vice versa.[1]

The mind-over-body, spirit-over-matter dichotomy still pervades our thinking today. But, in our postmodern era, there is much room for critique. Postmodern thought pushes religious and theological dialogue to move beyond binaries and hierarchies. Today, most agree that the soul/body, spirit/matter divide is false. Research in medicine, evolutionary biology, quantum physics and other fields shows that there is a spectrum between the poles rather than a gap, and that invisible does not equal non-material. Current philosophy, particularly feminist thought, has changed our perception of materiality and taught us the critical role of our bodies in human thought and behavior.

But the soul-over-body, spirit-over-matter mindset is deeply engrained in our theological tradition, and that is especially problematic for contemporary Jews who find God in nature. If the spiritual is opposed to the material, the earth is the last place one should seek the divine. Fortunately, two of the most important Jewish thinkers of our time recognized the problem and responded to the challenge.

Martin Buber's *I and Thou*

Martin Buber and Rabbi Abraham Joshua Heschel contributed mightily to modern, Jewish theology. Not coincidentally, each found it necessary to re-envision the role of nature in Jewish spirituality as part of the process.

They asked: Do we *think* God, or do we *perceive* God? Do we continue to reason our way to God, like medieval philosophers, or do we, like our biblical ancestors, base our beliefs on our experience of divinity in the world?

Buber refused to talk about God at all in a discursive, philosophical manner, or in his terms, in I-it mode.

> If to believe in God means to be able to talk about him in the third person, then I do not believe in God. If to believe in him means to be able to talk to him, then I believe in God.[2]

Instead of reasoning his way to the existence of God, Buber wrote about the experience of encountering God through relationships. God-moments trump God-ideas. And while primarily a mode of engaging other humans, I-Thou is not limited to dialogue between people. The first example of genuine encounter Buber writes about in his influential book *I and Thou* is with a tree. In his essay, "Autobiographical Fragments," Buber recalls an I-Thou encounter with a horse.

Buber captures why I feel most spiritual in the most material of places. We don't need to overcome the natural world and our bodies to find God. Rather, we meet God when we are in concrete relationship with the other bodies of this world, when we are fully engaged with the earth and its beings.

A. J. Heschel's Radical Amazement

Heschel's *God in Search of Man* is a four-hundred-page treatise that engages revelation, commandments, and evil—the major topics of Jewish practice and belief. Rather than begin with these ideas, however, Heschel opens with what he calls the universal building blocks of faith: wonder and awe.

> Awareness of the divine begins with wonder. It is the result of what man does with his higher incomprehension.[3]

Curiosity, writes Heschel, leads to questions that have answers. Once we discover why some eyes are blue and others brown, we move on. But wonder is never satisfied by knowledge.

> Wonder or radical amazement is the chief characteristic of the religious man's attitude toward history and nature. . . . To find an approximate cause of a phenomenon is no answer to his ultimate wonder. He knows that there are laws that regulate the course of natural processes; he is aware of the regularity and pattern of things. However, such knowledge fails to mitigate his sense of perpetual surprise at the fact that there are facts at all.[4]

Scientific explanations do not satiate our thirst for wonder.

According to Heschel, wonder is a precious quality of the heart. To live well, we should treat it like a sapling that requires our attention and care. Growing our sense of wonder is a primary goal of Jewish ritual and prayer.

> Every evening we recite: "He creates light and makes the dark." Twice a day we say: "He is One." What is the meaning of such repetition? A scientific theory, once it is announced and accepted, does not have to be repeated twice a day. The insights of wonder must be constantly kept alive. Since there is a need for daily wonder, there is a need for daily worship.[5]

Wonder as a Virtue

Heschel takes wonder to an even higher level. To fully embrace wonder is to become a certain kind of person.

> To the prophets wonder is a form of thinking . . . it is an attitude that never ceases.[6]

Wonder as a mind-set, a worldview, a way of being.

In graduate school, I studied the basics of virtue education. Through reflection and practice over time, one can internalize a value such as trustworthiness or compassion. It never occurred to me, however, to view wonder in this way. Wonder, I thought, occurs when a person sees, for instance, a beautiful view from a mountain pass. It is a reaction. Wonder happens *to* me. It is the mountains that cause my wondrous response. But Heschel teaches that we have the ability to impress wonder into our very being.

Just as I can see the world as a cup half full, I can learn to walk this earth with "eyes of wonder." And as we saw above, a key purpose of Jewish practice—of saying blessings, celebrating the holidays, and praying the daily liturgy—is to train our eyes for wonder, to consciously develop our personalities so that we might experience the world in a wonderful way that helps us engage divinity.

Wonder Leads to Awe

In the Hebrew Bible, the word *yirah* means both fear and awe. What, asks Heschel, is the difference between *yirah*-as-fear and *yirah*-as-awe? If a lightning storm is right on you, you are justifiably afraid. The best response is to take shelter and distance yourself from the danger. But if you can safely see the lightning from afar, the natural inclination is to get closer. We want to see as much as we can. *Yirah*-as-fear repels; *yirah*-as-awe attracts.[7]

"Awe" is a composite term. Think of a paradigmatic, awesome event: the birth of a child. We experience wonder, beauty, possibility, amazement, excitement, humility, and more. We witness the miracle of a new life, and at the same time, there is danger. Both mother and child are at risk. Awesome moments confront us with the mystery of life and death.

In such moments we feel truly alive. Often, we intuit that there is something to be learned here about the meaning of a life, as we are compelled to see our existence in the deepest, widest context. It is in awesome moments, writes Heschel, that the divine shines through.

Awe is a sense for the transcendence, for the reference every-where to Him who is beyond all things.

The meaning of awe is to realize that life takes place un-der wide horizons, horizons that range beyond the span of an individual life or even the life of a nation, a generation, or an era. Awe enables us to perceive in the world intimations of the divine, to sense in small things the beginning of infinite sig-nificance, to sense the ultimate in the common and the simple; to feel in the rush of the passing the stillness of the eternal.[8]

Some insights shake you like an earthquake when they are revealed to you by a great visionary, because they articulate what you felt in your bones all along.

Awe precedes faith; it is at the root of faith. We must grow in awe in order to reach faith. We must be guided by awe to be worthy of faith. Awe rather than faith is the cardinal attitude of the religious Jew.[9]

Finding God in Nature

Both Buber and Heschel are clear and emphatic. We perceive God. Our bodies and the material world are a gateway to the spiritual realm. The place God dwells is right here—already here—if we know how to look.

I read Buber and Heschel in my twenties. I had always felt what they described, but I didn't truly understand their words until I read them after walking the desert in my forties, after learning to sit alone and be still in wilderness.

Once, while praying and meditating in a thicket of shrubs by a stream, I was nearly hit by a doe as she leapt across the water. She looked back from the other side, and I grabbed my flute. Her ears stiffened and flopped as we gazed at each other. Ten minutes later I was still playing. She moved on, and I threw a smile at the Grand Teton to share what I had no words for.

We tend to focus on such dramatic moments of I-Thou, wonder and awe, but a spiritual life is not a collection of epiphanies. The challenge is to train ourselves to see and feel divinity in the everyday routines of our lives. It is here where Jewish practice in nature can be so valuable. For many, there is no more inviting place than the natural world to cultivate wonder, to learn mindfulness, to express gratitude, to explore the yearnings of the heart, to let the soul speak without inhibition. In nature, one might learn to "hear" God in birdsong, or "see" God in the flow of water and light.

I have facilitated three- and four-day solo trips in the wilderness for some thirty Jews, over a third of whom were rabbis. Three uninterrupted days in the womb of God's creation—observing, listening, praying, davening, and dialoguing. Three days of playing with God.

Three days have the power to change the experience of davening in a synagogue forever. Three days can alter all past and future theological understanding. As Heschel might say it, three days of the ineffable, the mysterious, the indescribable that put substance and heart into a lifetime of Jewish acts and words.

Other than snuggling with my loved ones, I find that the easiest and most reliable way to experience awe is to touch a tree, see the sunset, follow a cloud, watch a bird, lay on the earth, or smell a flower. Anytime I want to invigorate my faith, I commune with my intimate partners and say as many blessings as I can.

Notes

1. The above paragraphs are based on Theodore Hiebert's study *The Yahwist's Landscape: Nature and Religion in Early Israel* (New York: Oxford University Press, 1996).

2. Martin Buber, "Autobiographical Fragments," in *The Philosophy of Martin Buber*, ed. Paul Arthur Schlipp and Maurice S. Friedman (La Salle, IL: Open Court, 1967), 24.

3. Abraham Joshua Heschel, *God in Search of Man* (New York: Farrar, Straus and Giroux, 1955), 46.

4. Ibid., 45.

5. Ibid., 48.

6. Ibid., 46.

7. Ibid., 77.

8. Ibid., 75.

9. Ibid., 77.

29

Creation

An All-You-Can-Eat Buffet

RABBI MARY L. ZAMORE

God then said, "Let the waters bring forth swarms of living creatures, and let the birds fly over the earth, across the face of the expanse of the sky!"

Genesis 1:20

Food has always been a theological experience for me. My God is Creator of all, but especially of food. My God is Creator who instills in humanity the wisdom to produce and prepare food. This knowledge is useful since the Genesis Creation narrative[1] seems to point to a human relationship with the rest of Creation as an all-you-can-eat buffet. Yet, that same narrative calls upon humanity and all animals to curb their food choices. Is all of Creation at our disposal to eat without limitation, or is our diet meant to be vegetarian? And what can the Creation narrative teach us about navigating our food choices?

After four days of staging the infrastructure of the universe, God finally starts to populate the world. On the fifth day of Creation, rather than beginning with humans, God fills the sky and waters with animals

(Genesis 1:20–23). Previously, on day three, vegetation had already been created, right after dry ground and collected waters were formed (Genesis 1:11–12). After day five, it would seem as if the proverbial table had been set for humanity's appearance and appetite, but day six brings more eating options, albeit with very important, concrete restrictions.

On day six, God fills the dry ground by ordering, "Let the earth bring forth living creatures of every type: domestic animals and creeping things and wild animals, each true to its type!" (Genesis 1:24). This is followed by finally making humans. With the entrance of people comes two defining instructions concerning the human/nonhuman relationship. First, at the end of six days of Creation, humanity is fashioned and immediately given control over the other creations. God underscores humanity's rule over the rest of Creation by declaring, "Let them hold sway over the fish of the sea and the birds of the sky, over the beasts, over all the earth, over all that creeps upon the earth" (Genesis 1:26). Two verses later, God reemphasizes this commandment by saying directly to the newly formed humans that they are to "fill the earth and tame it" (1:28). Control over Creation would seem to be for the sake of eating and reaping other benefits from the nonhuman world, but then comes the divine limitation, "I have given you all the seed-bearing plants on the face of the earth, and every tree that has in it seed-bearing fruit—these are yours to eat. And to every land animal, and to every bird of the sky, and to all that creeps on the earth in which is the breath of life, I [give] all green vegetation for food" (Genesis 1:29–30). With this, not only humans but also animals are put on a plant-based diet. However, this does not make sense, since God had just placed all of the animals under human control. If we were not eating them, why have domain over the animals? Strangely, here God does not prohibit eating meat; God only commands eating vegetation.

The Rabbis of the Talmud wondered about the first humans' relationship to the rest of Creation. Harping on the last-place creation of humanity, the Talmud poses the question "Humanity was created on Friday [right before Shabbat], for what purpose?" (BT *Sanhedrin* 38a). The text then shares a variety of answers, including that Adam was created and then immediately enjoyed a Shabbat meal. The Talmud offers the parable of a human king who builds a palace, decorates it, prepares a meal, and then brings in his guests. This Talmudic passage supports the parable with lines from Proverbs, stating, "Wisdom has built her house . . . killed her beasts for meat, she has mixed her wine." Finally, the Talmud drives its point home by reminding us that it is Adam and Eve who are the guests invited only after God has prepared Creation (BT *Sanhedrin* 38a). Notably, the Talmud uses a proof text that refers to serving meat when talking about the world being prepared for the human arrival. This may be a purposeful use of biblical text to leave open the possibility that the first humans were not fully vegetarian, but it is more likely that the Rabbis of the Talmud, who were definitely meat eaters, picked a text reflecting their typical Shabbat meal.

So when is meat eating introduced, according to Jewish tradition? While the Genesis Creation narrative defines the human diet as vegetarian, the Noah narrative clearly allows an omnivorous approach. The text states, "Any moving animal that is alive shall be food for you, like green grasses—I give you [them] all. But flesh whose lifeblood is [still] in it you may not eat" (Genesis 9:3–4). In fact, this restriction is part of the Seven Noachide Laws, incumbent upon all humans, not just Jews. Genesis 9:4 developed into a prohibition known as *ever min hachai*, "flesh torn from a living body," which is considered to contain two laws: (1) the prohibition against eating flesh or limbs from a live animal; and (2) not drinking blood from a live animal.[2] The vegetarian diet is now replaced with a restricted omnivorous one. The Torah will eventually add numerous dietary laws for the Israelites, and these laws will develop over time to become the system of keeping kosher that we know today. But why did the Torah give up on the vegetarianism of Eden?

The Bible holds up vegetarianism as the ultimate goal. A passage describing the messianic era promises, "The cow will feed with the bear, their young will lie down together, and the lion will eat straw like the ox" (Isaiah 11:7). In this bucolic image, the domesticated animals will live in harmony with predators, who will not seek to eat them. All will be sustained by the earth. The first chief Ashkenazic rabbi of Israel, Rav Abraham Isaac Kook, wrote about vegetarianism as Judaism's ideal diet. However, a well-known meat minimalist,[3] Rav Kook ate meat, albeit only on Shabbat and holidays. Kook, like many other Jewish authorities, believed that meat elevates the joy of holidays. This association with festivity is rooted in the Talmud text, "When the Temple was in existence, there could be no joy without meat" (BT P'sachim 109a). It is important to note that there are other Rabbinic authorities who believe that the second part of this Talmud text does not support an obligation to eat meat on holidays, as the text continues, "But now that the Temple is no longer in existence, there is not rejoicing save with wine."

While in his personal dietary practice Rav Kook found a balance between the vegetarianism of Gan Eden and the meat eating of Noah, he wrote A Vision of Vegetarianism and Peace, presenting vegetarianism as the perfect state of being, which would come with the Messiah. In Kook's writing, not only will vegetarianism be everyone's perfect diet in the world-to-come, but also working to ensure the proper humane treatment of animals and moving to cease their abuse and slaughter will hasten the Messiah's coming.[4]

The Talmud directly asks the fundamental question: why is Adam instructed to be vegetarian if at the same time he is given dominance over the animals (BT Sanhedrin 59b)? Rav Y'hudah in the name of Rav points out that the first man was not permitted to eat meat. Later, the Rabbis raise an objection, "And have dominion over the fish of the sea. Is it not for eating?" The text gives the answer, "No, for work." The passage asks in return, "Are fish fit for work?" Citing another legal case in which a fish was used for pulling a wagon, the answer is yes. The gemara then works through the types of animals, birds, and creatures that crawl on the earth, stating that each is permitted for Adam to use for work, not for food. Therefore, this section of Talmud reconciles early humans' control over the animals with their restriction on eating them.

Rav Kook, like other commentators, felt that permission to eat meat was granted as a concession to human weakness and imperfection. In the post-Flood era, humans are allowed to eat meat in order to give an outlet for our violent tendencies. Before the Flood, "the earth was filled with violence" (Genesis 6:11), with humanity showing no control over their most base instincts. Post-Deluge, God permits meat eating so that the humans can exert their self-control over more important impulses, like refraining from human murder. Twentieth-century rabbi Umberto Cassuto wrote about the compromise of eating meat:

> Your natural diet is vegetarian. . . . Apparently the Torah was in principle opposed to the eating of meat. When Noah and his descendants were permitted to eat meat this was a concession conditional on the prohibition of the blood. This prohibition implied respect for the principle of life ("for the blood of life") and an allusion to the fact that in reality all meat should have been prohibited. This partial prohibition was designed to call to mind the previously total one.[5]

According to Rav Kook, while eating meat is permitted, the laws of kashrut, especially *sh'chitah*, ritual slaughter, teach us to take the animals' lives in compassion, not to cause undue pain, and to recognize the life we are taking.[6]

The Talmudic discussion about why Adam was created right before Shabbat included another notable answer. *Sanhedrin* 38a teaches if the humans become haughty, God can put them in place with the reminder "The gnat preceded you in Creation." Being formed last in

Creation should teach humanity not to consider ourselves above the other creatures. Putting ourselves above the rest of the flora and fauna has inarguably led to disastrous results. We have taken such advantage of the rest of Creation that we have driven myriad species into extinction, twisted our food supply into a polluting machine, and accelerated global warming. Our love of meat contributes to all these ills. So the Talmudic reminder that we were created last is fitting, lest we continue to believe our privilege of dominance over Creation as permission to abuse the power given to us. Speaking to the tension between vegetarianism and meat eating, the twentieth-century Israeli modern Orthodox rabbi Pinchas Peli wrote:

> Accordingly, the laws of kashrut come to teach us that a Jew should prefer a vegetarian meal. If, however, one cannot control a craving for meat, it should be kosher meat, which would serve as a reminder that the animal being eaten is a creature of God, that the death of such a creature cannot be taken lightly, that hunting for sport is forbidden, that we cannot treat any living thing callously, and that we are responsible for what happens to other beings (human or animal) even if we did not personally come into contact with them.[7]

Like Rav Kook, Peli clearly sees vegetarianism as the ideal, yet recognizes that most humans crave meat. Drawing on the Jewish value of *tzaar baalei chayim* (kindness to animals), he argues that the laws of kashrut teach the sanctity of God's Creation by commanding Jews to raise and butcher meat in a particular fashion that seeks to reduce the pain of the animal. Regardless if we choose to keep kosher or not, taking an animal's life should not be done lightly whether we are directly or indirectly involved in the process.

While humanity was freed from a purely vegetarian diet after the Flood, we still have an important value to learn from the Genesis

Creation narrative. Whether today we choose to reach for the perfection of vegetarianism or the compromise of meat eating, we must be conscientious in our food production choices. Our dominion over the animals must be tempered and exercised judiciously. Otherwise, the consequences for flora and fauna alike will be disastrous.

Notes

1. For the purpose of this discussion, I am using Genesis 1:1–2:3 as a complete Creation narrative, for I believe the Torah provides two separate Creation narratives.

2. Lisë Stern, *How to Keep Kosher: A Comprehensive Guide to Understanding Jewish Dietary Laws* (New York: Morrow, 2004), 21.

3. Meat minimalist, flexitarian, and weekday vegetarian are different terms being used to describe omnivores who limit their consumption of meat but do not intend on becoming vegetarians or vegan. While many refer to Rav Kook as a pure vegetarian, many others believe he was not. See Martin I. Lockshin, "Rav Kook Was Not a Vegetarian!," MyJewishLearning.com, http://www.myjewishlearning.com/article/rav-kook-was-not-a-vegetarian/; and Nigel Savage and Anna Hanau, *Food for Thought: Hazon's Sourcebook on Jews, Food & Contemporary Life* (New York: Hazon, 2007), 105.

4. Rav Avraham Yitzhak Hacohen Kook, *A Vision of Vegetarianism and Peace*, ed. David Cohen, http://www.jewishveg.com/AVisionofVegetarianismandPeace.pdf, commentary by Jonathan Rubenstein, 2.

5. Nehama Leibowitz, *New Studies in Bereshit (Genesis)* (Jerusalem: World Zionist Organization, 1981), 76–77.

6. Kook, *A Vision of Vegetarianism and Peace*, 3.

7. Ibid.

30

Forging a Path Back to the Garden

A New Kashrut for Today

RABBI KAREN DEITSCH

God then blessed them, saying, "Be fruitful and multiply, fill the waters of the seas, and let the birds multiply in the earth!" And there was evening and there was morning, a fifth day.

Genesis 1:22–23

It is 11:00 a.m. on a foggy Tuesday morning in Venice Beach, California. I am sitting at a communal table made of reclaimed wood drinking a sprouted nut milk latte out of a recycled glass jug. After I place my order for a plate of locally grown micro greens and poached free-range eggs with a side of sprouted buckwheat bread, I take out my laptop and the Bible that my grandfather gifted me when I became a bat mitzvah.

I open to the text of Genesis chapter 1, upon which I have been asked to comment as it pertains to a new Reform approach to kashrut. Amidst my fellow patrons—clad in vintage t-shirts and jangling keys to electric cars—I look at the text:

God then said, "Let the waters bring forth swarms of living creatures, and let the birds fly over the earth, across the face of the face of the expanse of the sky!" God then formed the great sea monsters, and every living creature that creeps, with which the waters swarm, all true to their types, and every winged bird, each true to its type; and God saw how good it was. God then blessed them, saying, "Be fruitful and multiply, fill the waters of the seas, and let the birds multiply in the earth!" And there was evening and there was morning, a fifth day. (Genesis 1:20–23)

I imagine how happy my grandpa would be, if he were alive today, to see me studying the pages of this sacred book. My choice of doing so in this restaurant, however, would surely have invited some contention.

I can almost hear him saying, "To sit on a dilapidated bench next to people in *shmattes*, drink from an old jar, and eat vegetables someone picked from their backyard, you pay extra? What—are you *meshugeh*?"

To which I would attempt to explain: "Grandpa, things have changed since you have been gone. This is a big part of my spiritual practice. In fact, this is how I keep kosher now. I eat things that are grown locally and raised sustainably." "Local, shmocal. This has nothing to do with our tradition," he would most likely reply.

Indeed, I can see how for some members of my grandpa's generation, the notion that sustainability has something to do with the observance of Judaism would seem as bizarre as the fact that my ripped vintage jeans cost considerably more than a new pair. In the aftermath of pogroms, world wars, concentration camps, immigration, and the Depression, Jewish life occurred for a long time much more in the context of individual surviving, and not collective thriving.

My grandpa used to answer my inquiries about why he wrapped *t'fillin* or refused to eat shrimp from the perspective of preserving Jewish identity, upholding tradition, and following the prescribed customs of obedience to the God who had almost been lost along with God's chosen people during the Holocaust. He held to the fact that the Torah offers no explanation for the dietary laws other than the holiness of God and God's chosen people ("You shall be holy to Me, for I the Eternal am holy, and I have set you apart from other peoples to be Mine" [Leviticus 20:26]), and he did not come from a paradigm that inspired in him the need nor the luxury to question the mandates of kashrut any further.

Things have since changed. The backdrop for why and how Jews observed dietary restrictions when my grandfather was my age do not resonate with life in the twenty-first century. That these regulations seem irrelevant is perhaps in some ways a testament to the fact that we have progressed beyond the need to react from fear of persecution and threats to our personal survival. A shift is occurring away from a paradigm of individual endurance against an opposing force and toward a standard of mutual durability in alignment with a common planet. The Internet has furthered this sense of commonality, creating a culture based on access to unlimited questioning, infinite knowledge, and endless choice. Conversations about universal spirituality, holistic health, mindfulness, and the state of the environment pervade both the mainstream and the domain of Judaism out of what I perceive to be a return to the source: the notion of one God that exists beyond and within everything. As such, choosing to eat salads from vegetables that have been dowsed in pesticides, soup from chickens that have been pumped with hormones and raised inhumanely but slaughtered by a *shochet*, and coffee served with artificially flavored nondairy creamer—albeit certifiably kosher—have become, in some circles, obsolete parameters for authentic Jewish adherence.

I believe that what constitutes a *hechsher* needs to be deeply reconsidered. What if conversations and regulations around kashrut reflected a deeply passionate and informed stance on the environment and the ways in which we treat our food? As a society, we are now being called to *proact*—to make choices based on a desire to fortify and sustain our collective thriving as a species—rather than *react* from a need to protect and maintain our individual survival. This work of proaction, however, is not so much an endeavor to progress or align with modern times, but rather it is a willingness to return to the basics of Jewish religious integrity—by hearkening back to days that long preceded those of our grandparents and the rules that were invented to support their Jewish practices. With the memories of our oppression thankfully a few generations behind us, we have not only the opportunity, but also the necessity to return our attention to a time before humans were actually capable of dreaming up inventions like insect repellent, partially hydrogenated soybean oil, dipotassium phosphate, and genetically modified foods.

Back in the days before we ate from the forbidden fruit of knowledge of good and evil, prior to our being even an utterance of creation by God, the fifth day of Genesis existed as a state of perfected intention and blessed existence. When we humans showed up the following day as an addition to this world of prolific fertility, it was with the clear and simple assignment to replenish and govern the thriving system containing "every living creature that creeps, with which the waters swarm, all true to their types" (Genesis 1:21). Mass marketing of NutraSweet—albeit kosher—was not mentioned in the text as part of our job description.

Somewhere in between the fifth day of Creation and today, we seem to have lost sight of the perfection of that primordial ecosystem, along with the reason we were made to be a part of it. We forgot that our task—our *only* responsibility—was to act as custodians and re-creators of the fruitfulness and multiplication of God's flawless formation. And so, these many generations later, we find ourselves with a plastic ocean that brings forth bottles that swarm the earth, while the waters lose their capacity at an alarming rate to replenish the living creatures that move. As lox and bagels become a health hazard, we are being compelled to reconsider how we act—both as Jews and as the human beings who have fallen far away from our creative blueprint.

The laws and acts of observance in our tradition were developed and enforced as an attempt to help us maintain our righteous alignment with Creation. They have not, unfortunately, succeeded in activating that righteousness as an inherent choice. Whether we believe that Jewish dietary guidelines were primarily expounded upon for ethical, practical, philosophical, hygienic, cultural, or religious reasons, as of 2013, they were estimated to be kept by less than 22 percent of the American Jewish population. According to that percentage and given the lack of positive impact on our well-being as a species or as a planet, it seems clear that kashrut needs to be redefined and reintegrated such that it can help us return to functioning effectively according to the divine design.

We now have not only the capacity but also the necessity to realize that it has been true from the beginning that we are what we eat. The time has come to take responsibility for having consumed from the Tree of Knowledge and recover our role in what preceded that act. While the serpent was right about our eyes becoming opened and our power becoming godlike at the moment we ate, knowing to distinguish between good and evil did not translate for us into choosing good. We became caught up in a collective emotional adolescence that rendered us unaccountable for our capacity to know and to act on the distinction we got at that moment. The ignorance of our predecessors when it came to the environment and food choices is no longer an option for the way we live, relate, consume, or worship. In order to make the memories of our grandparents a blessing, we must be willing to declare that we chose to become awakened consumers when we bit into that forbidden fruit and to embrace our knowledge of what is—and always was—good.

Returning to the source, the word *kasher* (kosher) literally means "good, pure, and proper." And what was "proper," according to the fifth day of Creation, was the abundant and fruitful expression of life exponentially filling the waters and the heavens. What was "good" on this day—as on all of the days of Creation—was what God *saw* and affirmed as such; to the degree that we endeavor to see and maintain the organic and perpetually regenerating order of the system within which we were created to sustain, we retrieve access to this most basic definition of keeping kosher and return to functioning *b'tzelem Elohim*—in God's image and likeness.

"Kosher" evolved from its rudimentary definition to also mean, as per Merriam-Webster's, "clean, lawful, legitimate, genuine, authentic . . . fit to be eaten according to Jewish blessings and ritual preparations." Applying these definitions to the fifth day of Creation, we now have the opportunity to question: How can we live and procreate in a way that is truly pure and clean? What is lawful in accordance with the sacred acts of Creation? How must we treat animals and their natural habitats in order to restore our authenticity and legitimacy as their custodians? What will inspire in us a willingness to live such that blessings and sacred rituals become significant to our existence? How can we re-create our presence on this planet such that it is a stand for fruitfulness and multiplication of our natural resources?

In my experience, the answers begin to come when we do something like taking a seat at a communal table made of recycled wood and choose to live sustainably. "Sustainability" is defined by Merriam-Webster as "of, relating to, or being a method of harvesting or using a resource so that the resource is not depleted or permanently damaged . . . involving methods that do not completely destroy or use up natural resources." In other words, it is an alignment with the fifth day of Creation: a means for being a blessing for fruitfulness and multiplication of the living creatures that move and the elements within which they swim and fly.

Reforming or even taking on an approach to kashrut can work like a declaration of faith and devotion to the perfection of Genesis and its infinite sustainability. It can function as the reintegration of all that we have come to know and understand, unified with our newly awakened sense of responsibility and our realization of ourselves as co-creators with the Divine. It can show us the path back to Eden. With every dollar we contribute to organic farmers, every bite we take of ethically raised poultry, every glass we reuse and wash with biodegradable soap, every wild-caught fish we bless for giving us energy and sustenance, we come a step closer to the benedictions that were declared by God on the fifth day. A world that works for everyone is waiting to be reclaimed with each piece of wood we recycle.

This is a kind of kashrut that extends far beyond food. It is a legitimate, genuine, and authentic way of living that can also inspire purity in the clothes we wear, the cars we drive, the stocks we buy, and the thoughts we think. It is a practice that signifies our being part of a great movement backward and forward toward awakening—within which we reclaim responsibility for what we ate that granted us the knowledge of what is right and what is wrong and how to choose accordingly. It is an invitation of intent to being ever more accountable for everything we consume existing as a declaration of our devotion: to the fifth day of Creation, to everything that has transpired since that day, to our grandparents and ancestors seven generations back, and to the God who made us in the divine image.

As I take my last bite of eggs, I have a distinct feeling of faith that after a long and destructive departure from doing what we were put here to do, many of us are at last feeling inclined to clean up the many ways in which we violated the fundamentals of God's thriving pattern of Creation and to return ourselves and our planet back to the Source. I glance down again at the text and allow the words to come alive in me: "And God saw how good it was" (Genesis 1:21). And so it is. And so may it be.

Day Six

✦

PEOPLE

God then said, "Let the earth bring forth living creatures of every type: domestic animals and creeping things and wild animals, each true to its type!"—and so it was. Thus God made the wild animals, each true to its type, and the domestic animals, each true to its type, and every creature that creeps on the ground, each true to its type; and God saw how good it was. God now said, "Let us make human beings in our image, after our likeness, and let them hold sway over the fish of the sea and the birds of the sky, over the beasts, over all the earth, over all that creeps upon the earth." So God created the human beings in [the divine] image, creating [them] in the image of God, creating them male and female. God then blessed them, and God said to them, "Be fruitful and multiply; fill the earth and tame it; hold sway over the fish of the sea and the birds of the sky, and over every animal that creeps on the earth." And God said, "Look, I have given you all the seed-bearing plants on the face of the earth, and every tree that has in it seed-bearing fruit—these are yours to eat. And to every land animal, and to every bird of the sky, and to all that creeps on the earth in which is the breath of life, I [give] all green vegetation for food."—and so it was. God then surveyed all that [God] had made, and look—it was very good! And there was evening and there was morning, the sixth day.

Genesis 1:24–31

31

Finding Meaning as
God's Servant

Consulting the Design Specs
for Humankind

RABBI DAVID E. S. STEIN

*God now said, "Let us make human beings in our image, after
our likeness; and let them hold sway over the fish of the sea and
the birds of the sky, over the beasts, over all the earth, over all
that creeps upon the earth."*

Genesis 1:26

*And the man said, "This time— / bone of my bone, flesh of
my flesh! / Let this one be called ishshah, / for this one is taken
from ish."*

Genesis 2:23

What gives your life meaning?

You may not be used to articulating an answer to that question. But perhaps—now that I mention it—you may wish to formulate a response. If so, then it might help to use a certain answer from the *Tanach* as a springboard. Namely: *you exist to serve your Creator.*

At first sight, the above suggestion may seem bizarre. You may have misgivings about submitting to anyone—especially God. If so, don't worry, I will address that! But first, to show where the notion comes from, this essay will interpret two mutually reinforcing passages at the start of Genesis. Then I will discuss the implications and challenges for liberal Jews.

Born to Serve

The Torah's depiction of the sixth day features the creation of *adam*—the human species (Genesis 1:27). Just prior to carrying out that culminating act of Creation, God states its purpose:

> God now said, "Let us make human beings in our image, after our likeness; and let them hold sway over the fish of the sea and the birds of the sky, over the beasts, over all the earth, over all that creeps upon the earth." (Genesis 1:26)

Namely, humankind (collectively) will have the authority to act *on God's behalf*. In effect, God has delegated us to have dominion on earth, like a vizier or regent. How so?

The key term in verse 26 is the noun *tzelem* (image). The text's original audience would have reliably construed that term in light of concepts that prevailed throughout the ancient Near East. A *tzelem* functioned to represent a ruler or deity when the latter was unavailable (or at least, not otherwise perceptibly present).[1]

Hence, according to this biblical account, humankind was created to act as God's representative for whenever God might not be around (so to speak). In other words, we humans are supposed to manifest God *concretely* in this created world—on behalf of the transcendent deity who generally remains *abstract* in the everyday world of things.[2] We are to function in this world as God's eyes, ears, and hands. In its plain sense, this is the import of Genesis 1:26–27: *you are called to live in service to something greater than yourself.*[3]

Beyond Gender: On a Mission from God

A similar sense of mission underlies the Torah's second story about the creation of humankind, which is again referred to as *adam*. The theme of rendering service is expressed most forthrightly in Genesis 2:15:

> So God Eternal took the man, placing him in the Garden of Eden to work it and keep it.

More precisely, when the verb *haniach*—which Stern rendered as "placing"—is used in the context of a stated task (*l'ovdah ulshomrah*, "to work it and keep it"), the sense evoked is of "assignment to a particular station."[4] (Hence we might render *haniach* as "stationing.") From the start, humankind is assigned to operate on God's behalf.

According to Genesis 2:18, God soon decides that it is *lo tov*, "not good," to have a staff of only one; the *adam* needs a partner (*eizer k'negdo*, "counterpart") in order to carry out the assignment properly.[5] So a formal search is conducted. Numerous candidates are interviewed, but all outside candidates are rejected (2:19–20). The story culminates when God opts to "promote from within"—to produce the desired addition to God's staff by expanding a piece of the original *adam*.

At that point (Genesis 2:23), the nouns *ish* and *ishshah*[6] are used— the first two of the nearly three thousand individual occurrences of those words in the *Tanach*. As these key terms are spoken by "the *adam*," they get the royal treatment—literally speaking. This initial pair of instances features no fewer than six of the various ways that the biblical Hebrew composer could invest a word with special significance (see facing page for details). Such a concentration of focused attention is rare in the Bible.

This climactic pronouncement by the *adam* is usually understood to point to the differentiation of "woman" and "man"—which are the usual understandings of the terms *ishshah* and *ish*, respectively.[8] However, all the textual fuss here about those two words suggests that much more than gender is being conveyed!

Specifically, it appears that the *adam* recognizes at the same time another new reality: the ability to properly render service to God. For the context of agency that had been established in Genesis 2:15 now evokes the occasional sense of our terms *ish* and *ishshah* as "agent" (that is, a party who represent the interests of another party—who in this case is God).[9] Yet we learn that one agent, acting alone, is not good enough. Indeed, the label of "agent" is not applied to the first human being until the second one has been created. In other words, the first agent (*adam*) cannot serve as a true representative (*ish*) without the second agent (*ishshah*).

Two related points are being made. First, human existence is not just for its own sake; rather, human beings are on a mission from God (as earthly regents, per Genesis 1:26, as noted above).[10] Second, that mission can be carried out only via teamwork. Joint action and cooperation are required.[11]

Criteria for Evaluation

In Genesis, the nature of humankind's mission is not spelled out. There's no employment contract. No written job description. No list of duties. Apparently we are supposed to focus upon the *concept* of mission, rather than on its details. Proper orientation is paramount.

Even without details, the Torah's imagery implies a fairly specific measure of job performance. By definition, any agent must meet certain expectations. Implicitly, the Bible evaluates humankind according

continue on page 238

Six Ways of Highlighting *ish* and *ishshah* in Genesis 2:23

1. Our two nouns appear at the episode's climax. (That makes them as memorable as appearing in the punch line of a joke.)
2. They appear within a burst of poetry, which is how biblical characters express their inner emotions and state of mind. (That's much like the way that characters in a Broadway musical break into song when they are at their most passionate.)
3. Within each clause, *ish* and *ishshah* are in the most prominent position in terms of syntax; this is especially true of *ish*, which is highlighted by what some linguists call "fronting" before the verb. (The point seems to be one of contrast: she was taken from the *ish* rather than from somewhere else.)
4. The two clauses together reinforce each other via structural mirroring; our terms are then spotlighted at the heart of a symmetrical ("chiastic") pattern formed by three corresponding pairs of demonstrative pronouns, passive verbs, and our two nouns:

"This one shall be called *ishshah*, for from *ish* was selected this one."

This structure doubles the impact of the focusing structure within each separate clause.

5. The label *adam* has already been established in this passage as the default way to refer to the first human; the sudden switch of label to *ish* now calls attention to itself.
6. Our two words of interest resonate with each other by their very proximity—by virtue of their similar sound and nearly equivalent meanings.

to how *faithful* we are in rendering our service. What does it mean to be faithful agents in representing our principal?

First and foremost, faithful servants are *ready to perform* their duties (e.g., Isaiah 6:8). Readiness requires that we engage in self-care, show presence of mind, and possess tenacity. A decision to be "at the ready" may sound obvious—but it is actually the most difficult part of being faithful.

In addition to reporting for duty, faithful servants possess other vital qualities: they *listen* attentively (I Samuel 3:10); they *report back* truthfully (II Kings 4:31 versus 5:25); and they refrain from taking their delegated authority and *lording it over* others (I Samuel 2:12–17, 2:22–25). At the same time, they do not engage in *self-dealing* (gaining personally at their principal's expense; Numbers 16:15; I Samuel 12:3).

The modern dedication to the tenet of *tikkun olam* (repairing the world) can be an expression of "service to God." To qualify, it should avoid a desperate tone and a frantic quality. It should measure success not only in terms of tasks accomplished. And it should be a daily way of engaging life, not only an annual Mitzvah Day activity.

A Challenging Notion

Many liberal Jews prefer a world in which nobody (not even God) can tell them what to do. In their view, living a life of service may not even sound Jewish. Some tell me that the notion of "giving oneself over to one's deity" is, well, Christian. Similarly, the core idea of Islam—namely, to "surrender" to the Almighty's will—strikes some Jews as oppressive. Ironically, those liberal American Jews who are somehow attracted to "a life of service" tend to become Buddhists—or to join Chabad.

Probably all of us have at some point personally experienced mistreatment at the hands of our superiors (in social hierarchies that include the family). Some of us have been traumatized by abuse or neglect. And historically speaking, anti-Semitism has been most dangerous when it was sanctioned by the state. As a result, we may have developed a kind of allergy to hierarchies.

Meanwhile, our cultural context discourages anyone's being submissive. Born of revolution, American society has always been reflexively on guard against "tyranny." And in recent decades, it has become even less hierarchical. Nearly everyone is now on a first-name basis with everyone else. Outside of the military and of religious cults, American authority figures get precious little deference—let alone devotion.

It's Not About You

Nonetheless, maybe hierarchy and submissiveness have their place; perhaps they can make our lives more meaningful. How might that work in practice? I have begun posing the following set of three questions to myself each morning: (1) *How might I prepare myself to be of service today?* Perhaps, for example, I need to attend to some vital aspect of self-care. (2) *How can I be of service to God, and with whom?* Then I listen quietly for what ideas may surface—especially ones that might take me out of my comfort zone. (Just asking such a question in a spirit of faithfulness is helpful even without getting an answer, for it helps me to avoid being taken over by anxiety or a sense of victimhood.) (3) *How faithful was my service yesterday?* This last question is intended to notice any room for improvement.

Noble Servants

The biblical ideal of service to God is a metaphor. It is not the only guiding metaphor offered by our Bible. We are also told that God is a protector (e.g., Genesis 28:15, 49:24; Psalm 18:3), a committed and caring parent (Isaiah 54:10; Jeremiah 3:4), life-sustaining water (Psalms 42:2–3, 63:2), and more. These images coexist because none of them captures the whole picture of spiritual reality.

If we reject the image of our being devoted servants to the Master of the universe, our ability to enjoy a meaningful life is impoverished. For it points toward the possibility of our nobility—a nobility that arises both from selflessness and from being accountable. Perhaps, then, we should aspire to that lowly station!

Notes

1. For example, in Egypt, the god Amen-Re is reported to have declared to Pharaoh Amenhotep III (ca. 1370 BCE): "You are my beloved son . . . *my image*, whom I have put on earth. I have given to you [authority] to rule the earth in peace." For the source and extended discussion, see David J. A. Clines, "The Image of God in Man," *Tyndale Bulletin* 19 (1968): 55–103; reprinted in his *On the Way to the Postmodern: Old Testament Essays 1967–1998*, vol. 2, JSOT Supplement series 292 (Sheffield: Sheffield Academic Press, 1998), 447–97.

2. Regarding the phrase *b'tzelem Elohim* in Genesis 1:26–27, Rabbi Gunther Plaut, *z"l*, gives three interpretations; none of them involves submission to God (W. Gunther Plaut and David E. S. Stein, eds., *The Torah: A Modern Commentary*, rev. ed. [New York: URJ Press, 2005], 35). Likewise submission is not mentioned in Rabbi Tamara Cohn Eskenazi's comment on that passage in *The Torah: A Women's Commentary*, ed. Tamara Cohn Eskenazi and Andrea L. Weiss (New York: Women of Reform Judaism, 2008; now available from Reform Judaism Publishing), 7–8. The alternative explanation that I offer here comes from Clines, "The Image of God in Man," cited in the previous note.

3. Granted, Genesis 1:28 then depicts God as directing humankind to "tame" the earth and to "hold sway over" the animal kingdom. This does not mean, however, that humankind is given free reign (pun intended). As God's representatives, humankind must answer to God for its actions—and for its inaction.

4. In biblical Hebrew, in general when the action expressed by the verb *haniach* is applied to a person, its sense is equivalent to the English "to position (that person in a specific place)" (Genesis 19:16, 42:33; Leviticus 24:12; Numbers 15:34; Joshua 6:23; Ezekiel 37:1); but in the context of assigning that person a task or role, the sense is closer to "to station (someone in a particular post)," as in I Chronicles 16:21; II Chronicles 1:14, 9:25. In other words, this verb's use in Genesis 2:15 presupposes an agency relationship: the verb's grammatical subject refers to the principal, while its object refers to the agent (i.e., the representative).

5. Additional reasons are implied for God's creation of a second person: explaining the origin of Israelite social structure, and addressing human needs for reproduction and companionship. Even so, the only reason that is stated explicitly—and which therefore remains in view throughout the *Tanach*—is that humankind has a duty to serve divine interests.

6. Transliteration of the Hebrew term as *ishshah* is admittedly unusual and hard to read. I prefer it here in order to remind us that this term is not simply the grammatically feminine form of *ish*. Rather, it derives from a different root (*alef-nun-shin*),

and in ancient times it was pronounced with a distinctive pause before the second syllable. (In writing, that pause is represented as a doubling of the letter *shin*.)

7. My translation, which distorts English idiom so as to better reflect the Hebrew structure.

8. Rabbi Plaut commented that the biblical text claims that the word *ishshah* is derived from *ish* (*The Torah: A Modern Commentary*, 24). That claim seems imprecise. Surely the story presupposes that the two words are not inherently related, and the point is that nonetheless those words are mutually supporting—just like the characters whom they refer to. Otherwise, the *adam*'s pronouncement would be trivial—which seems unlikely, given that it is the story's climax.

9. The nouns *ish* and *ishshah* appear to always function relationally; that is, they regard their referent in terms of his/her/its relationship to something else. Their most common meaning is roughly equivalent to the English noun "participant." What I call their "agency use" is a more intensive (but perhaps original) sense. It regards the referent as a "participant's participant"—that is, as an agent of one of the other participants. Such usage occurs hundreds of times in the Bible. A prominent example is "Now Moses the *ish* was very humble" (Numbers 12:3). There, Moses's authority as God's representative is being challenged by Miriam and Aaron; in such a situation, "the *ish*" is a title that refers to Moses's office as God's agent. (See also Exodus 11:3, 32:1, 32:23; Deuteronomy 33:1.) See my article "The Noun אִישׁ in Biblical Hebrew: A Term of Affiliation," *Journal of Hebrew Scriptures* 8, art. 1 (2008), purl.org/net/ish-2008. This view of *ish* (and *ishshah*, as the counterpart feminine term) is employed in the current URJ translation of the books Exodus through Deuteronomy, although it is presently a minority view among biblical scholars.

10. Within the episode of Genesis 2–3 itself, humankind's express mission changes. Their initial assignment is as stewards of the Garden of Eden (2:15); but after they engage in self-dealing (3:6) and prove unwilling to take responsibility for having done so (3:11–13), they are reassigned to farm the earth's land outside the Garden (3:23).

11. In Genesis 2:23, the *adam* pronounces what amounts to a triple entendre, for the context of cooperation also evokes the frequent sense of the terms *ish* and *ishshah* as "partner." The implication is that we humans need to cooperate because all of us are God's agents collectively. One could elaborate on this point by discussing how through harnessing human *diversity*, we not only gain valuable perspective but also accomplish our mission. And of course one could also discuss the more specific need for cooperation among all human genders.

32

In the Image of God

God Is the Queer Role Model
I Always Wanted

RABBI RACHEL GRANT MEYER

So God created the human beings in [the divine] image, creating [them] in the image of God.

Genesis 1:27

When I was thirteen years old, I came out for the first time. In the presence of a trusted adult, I all but whispered, "I think I'm bisexual." The person I'd told responded innocently enough by asking me what that meant. I froze. I knew how I felt, but I didn't have words beyond describing the attractions I felt to explain what that meant to me.

As a child of the 1990s, I spent a good deal of my free time in AOL chat rooms for LGBTQ teens, which is how I found the label for the feelings I was having. I came to understand that I identified not as bisexual but instead as queer—an "umbrella" term for anyone outside the heterosexual norm.[1] Identifying as queer felt more inclusive of the fact that gender exists on a spectrum, rather than as a binary. My connection to queer community, though, was limited to these chat rooms, to digital words on a computer screen. At that time, there were no visibly queer adults or teens in my life, so when confronted with the question of what my identity meant to me, I did not know how to answer the question.

There was no source from which I could draw to color in the black and white lines of what it meant to be a queer person. The simple question "What does that mean to you?" produced myriad complicated practical and theoretical questions for me. What was queer love beyond a feeling? What did it look like to love someone who identified as your same gender or no gender at all? What did it look like to build a home with that person or to have children with that person? I had absolutely no idea where to look for answers to these questions. There was precious little representation of LGBTQ people in the media, art, literature, and film that I encountered as a child, and there were no out-and-proud LGBTQ people—that I knew of, anyway—in my everyday life. If I was learning how to be a person in the world based on the examples of the grown-ups around me in every other arena of my life, how would I learn how to be a grown-up queer person without queer role models?

As a young person who spent a tremendous amount of time in the organized Jewish community while growing up, I knew that no matter who I was, I was created in the image of God. Throughout my childhood, I learned and relearned the Creation story and the pronouncement that when God created humankind, God "created the human beings in [the divine] image" (Genesis 1:27). The way this piece of Torah got translated into practice in my Jewish education was that we were taught to treat other human beings with dignity and respect because if we are all created in God's image, then we are all imbued with a spark of divinity. To disrespect or mistreat another human being would be tantamount to disrespecting or mistreating God. It never occurred to me, nor was it offered to me in any theological discussion, that this verse from the Torah might point me in the direction of the queer role model I always wanted: God.

If human beings are created *b'tzelem Elohim* (in the likeness of God), this means that when we look at our own reflection, we are also looking at a reflection of divinity, and in coming to understand the essence of who we are, we also come to understand the essence of who God is. The reverse can also be true: if we come to better know God, we can come to better know ourselves. As a young queer person, I could have looked to God to be my queer role model. If I am queer, some part of God must also be queer. Now, as an adult, when I reflect on the God I have studied, the God I pray to, the God I wrestle with, this makes perfect sense to me.

God's love expresses itself as queer love. God loves flamboyantly and dramatically, and God loves intimately. God's love affair with the people of Israel is erotic and electric, and God's love for the people of Israel is also kind and quiet. Rabbi Art Green writes about the complexity bound up in God's love. In certain texts, we read about a tender God who "longs for His wayward children to return to Him."[2] In other texts, "the erotic metaphor [for the love between God and the people of Israel] is rampant."[3] There are moments when God dramatically threatens to end it all, when God accuses God's great love of incomprehensible evil, as in Sodom and Gomorrah and the Flood of Noah's generation. There are still other moments when God lovingly places humanity in the cleft of a rock, that God's presence may surround us without leading to our death.

God is genderqueer—of all genders and no gender at all. We describe God both as *Shechinah*, the sheltering female presence of the Divine, and as *Avinu*, "our Father." According to Jewish mystical tradition, God is *Ein Sof*, without end and without boundaries. The idea of a God that is *Ein Sof* suggests that there is no spectrum that contains God's gender identity as a finite point and that God exists in all the spaces in between the points on that spectrum.

Just as much as God loves simplicity, God also loves sparkle and pizzazz. From the prophet Micah we learn that all God requires of humanity is to "do justice, to love goodness, and to walk humbly with [our] God" (Micah 6:8). Yet, at the same time, God gives the Israelites a blueprint for a *Mishkan*, a place where they will meet God, that is to be built of acacia wood and overlaid with pure gold, with gold cherubim flanking the ornate Ark, and laden with dolphin skins, the finest threads of blue and crimson, oil, spices, and precious stones. When the priests make sacrifices to God, they are to wear intricate finery: a linen robe made of gold, purple, and scarlet and a beautifully woven breastplate set in gold.

In coming to more fully understand God, I have come to understand that God defies classification as definitively "this" or "that." Jay Michaelson writes of queer theology that "the farther we get from our preconceived notions of what 'identity' is supposed to be and the more open we are to categories beyond our imagination or experience, the closer we are to realization."[4] Queering the theological concept of *b'tzelem Elohim* means expanding the notion of what it means to be created in God's image beyond male and female or heterosexual. This means that God is so much more than male or female or heterosexual; queering this concept means that we come to understand God, and therefore ourselves, as beyond categorization. As a young person, I longed for a proper box into which the different parts of myself could be neatly folded. My queerness, though—the expansiveness of my love, my recognition that human gender does not exist in a binary, my affection for the flamboyance of queer art and culture—defied such compartmentalization. I did not know to look to God for an example of what might be possible. I did not know that the same way that God exists "beyond our imagination or experience," the joy my queer identity could bring to my life and to the world would be beyond my imagination or young experience. If I could have seen the way that God loved, the way that God inhabited (or didn't) gender, and God's flair for the fancy as part of God's *tzelem*, I may have been better able not just to imagine but also to embody my own *tzelem*.

Notes

1. Nikki Lyn DeBlosi, "Blessed Is God Who Changes Us: Theological Que(e)ries," in *Sacred Encounter: Jewish Perspectives on Sexuality*, ed. Lisa J. Grushcow (New York: CCAR Press, 2014), 178.

2. Arthur Green, *Radical Judaism: Rethinking God & Tradition* (New Haven, CT: Yale University Press, 2010), 51.

3. Ibid., 57.

4. Jay Michaelson, "Towards a Queer Jewish Theology," *Sh'ma: A Journal of Jewish Ideas*, December 2005, http://shma.com/2005/12/toward-a-queer-jewish-theology/.

33

Male and Female
God Created Them

The Everyday Life
of the Creation Myth
in Israeli Society

RABBI NOA SATTATH

*So God created the human beings in [the divine] image,
creating [them] in the image of God, creating them male and
female.*

(Genesis 1:27)

Creation myths provide us with an essential understanding of our
foundation—the reason for our existence. As such, they always serve
to establish and enforce power structures within our societies and specifically define gender roles. In this chapter I will explore the roles of
Creation myths and the influence of the Creation story in Genesis 2
on Israeli society today.

Every society for which there are records has its version of a Creation myth. These myths serve as important allegories and help the
society tell its own story. Products of the unique curiosity of the human

mind, origin myths tell us more than how a particular people might have gotten here. They inform people how they should behave now that they are sentient beings. These stories also help to give meaning, purpose, and direction with regard to relationships. Many such myths posit the existence of forces beyond the earth that shaped the world around us.

Creation myths are prescriptive, not just descriptive. They present a microcosm of society, of the way men and women relate to one another, and of the place of humans in the world of nature. It is not surprising, therefore, that ever since there evolved in the human mind that unique quality of consciousness, origin myths have been central to the intellectual lives and societal structures of people everywhere. [1]

The retelling of the story over generations gives it additional power. This retelling of a creation myth has the power to either reinforce or topple an existing power structure. It is essential that we understand the values projected in creation myths in order to transform power imbalances.

One way of examining the power structures revealed in Creation myths is through the specific elements of *how*, *when*, and *why* men and women are created.

The first element worthy of examination in a culture's Creation myth is the how of Creation. This line of questioning explores which substances humans are made from and whether those substances have any special physical connection to their god.

Second, the when aspect of Creation sheds light on the culture's self-perception in relation to its place in the larger order of the world.

The third and final element in Creation myths is the why, which relates the culture's specific purpose for existence.

While Jewish tradition has several Creation stories, I will focus first on the ways in which the Creation story in Genesis 2 establishes the patriarchal order of our Jewish history by answering all three questions. In terms of how, man is created by God from the earth, and God breathes life into him, emphasizing the direct and intimate relationship between man and God. The woman, by contrast, is created from the first man's rib, implying that her value is less than that of the man.

While the man is created (from the verb *y-tz-r*), implying a spiritual as well as a physical construction, the woman is made, or constructed (from the verb *b-n-h*), implying a more physical construction. The creation of man emphasizes both body and soul, while the construction of woman is more removed and technical and doesn't include an element of soul, regarding her soul as less significant.

In terms of when, the chronological hierarchy of the second Creation story allocates primary significance to the first creations; man is created after heaven and earth. He is charged with naming the animals, partnering with God in completing the Creation process. Woman is created last, after all Creation is complete. This order makes her the final missing piece of Creation, while making man an essential foundation to Creation. Man is independent of woman, and his role is to serve God. Woman is totally dependent on man and is created to serve him. Man names woman as part of the process of her creation and as part of his relationship with the animal kingdom, thus placing woman closer to the rank of animals in the hierarchy of significance, and man closer to God.

In terms of why, the first Creation story speaks about the essential nature of man to the project of Creation. Plants could not grow because man was not there to till the ground, which is why God created the mist to water the earth, and man to cultivate it. Following the creation of the garden, plants, and rivers, God guides man around the Garden of Eden and instructs him on cultivating and keeping the earth. God then attempts to build a companion to help man and save man from being alone. God creates all the animals. Man sees and names them and finds no help through them. So God creates woman from man's rib. According to this story, man has an essential role in Creation, designated to him by God. The entire plant and animal kingdom is dependent on man, while woman is created to support man's welfare.

After eating from the Tree of All Knowledge, Adam and Eve become aware of duality (which had been not present before)—of the knowledge of the pairs of opposites—and man and woman realize they're different. God and man then come into conflict, as they, too, are different. In that conflict, woman (paired with nature) is the cause of the first sin.

Knowledge therefore comes not only out of the realization of good and evil, but also out of the differences between male and female.

It is astounding to see that in Israel today, the concept of knowledge embodying sin still plays a role in society with regard to gender roles.

For thousands of years the second Creation story was used as the foundation for the paradigmatic relationship between men, women, and God in Jewish society. This paradigm led to the establishment of a society in which women were regarded as property of men, a society in which women could exist and function only in relation to their fathers, husbands, sons, or brothers.

The paradigm has also led to the evolution of two separate sets of rules within our halachic systems, one for men and one for women, excluding women from all religious leadership roles, from major events within the Jewish community, and from the close and intimate disciplines of religious practice that are related to time and season.

In Israel today we are witnessing an extremist trend that reflects and stems from the dualities of the second Creation story. Since 1999, there have been repeated demands made by members of the ultra-Orthodox leadership to segregate men and women in the public sphere in Israel. The attempts to segregate public bus lines and cemeteries, post offices and libraries, all draw from the perceived inferiority of women. The expectation that men and boys can, and should, exist in a world that is "cleansed" of women is an attempt to replicate man's initial, created state in which he was innocent and closer to God. These demands, following a decade of work by the Israel Religious Action Center, are now, thankfully, being rejected by the Israeli government.

But they have created an ethos that at once objectifies women and accommodates the welfare of men. These demands also lay the foundation for a paradigm that sees women as obstacles to men in their dedication to *avodat HaShem*, "God's work."

In Israeli society, this duality also echoes another element of the Creation story, which is the connection between women and knowledge. In the story of Creation, the "basic" state of man is one of ignorance. He is commanded to refrain from eating from the fruits of the Tree of All Knowledge (Gen. 2:16–17). The only limitation placed on man is the restriction of knowledge. Woman (being tricked by the snake) tempts man to eat from the fruit, committing the first sin, and shattering his divine-intended ignorance.

In Israeli society today, religious and political rhetoric perpetuate this particularly misogynistic reading of sin, knowledge, and gender roles. The ultra-Orthodox community is the fastest growing in Israel (averaging 6.9 children per family). Ultra-Orthodoxy's social structures are entirely dependent on the rejection of and separation from modernity: members of the community read newspapers supervised by rabbis and are forbidden from reading other news sources, using the Internet, listening to secular radio stations, or watching TV. The most critical element of preserving ultra-Orthodox society is the separate education system that instills the values of ultra-Orthodox society; Torah study (for men) is valued above all else. The effort to prevent adults from leaving the closed society begins in a gender-segregated school system that deprives boys of the educational tools that would enable them to sustain themselves and lead lives outside the ultra-Orthodox world. Through the political pressure of ultra-Orthodox parties, the Israeli government sponsors such schools that in essence teach traditional Jewish studies only—no English, no math, no science, no civics. The political goal of the system is to render male graduates unemployable and dependent on the welfare that is allocated to men through the system controlled by the ultra-Orthodox rabbis. This echoes the

Creation story—man is connected to God in a basic state. It also leads to a society in which women are the main breadwinners. In order to support their growing society, ultra-Orthodox women have broken new ground in the past two decades. Previously, ultra-Orthodox women worked only inside ultra-Orthodox society (mostly as teachers and caregivers). Since the late 1990s ultra-Orthodox women have been leading a quiet revolution. They are lawyers, accountants, and software engineers. They are more educated and are earning more money than ever before.

We in Israel therefore find ourselves living with the Creation metaphor as an everyday reality: man in a primal state, connected to God, and woman holding the forbidden fruit of knowledge, thus threatening the innocence of man. This ongoing reenactment of the Creation story is a major threat to the future of Israel. Twenty-seven percent of Israeli boys in first grade study in a public educational system that ostensibly sentences them to a life of poverty and binds them to the ultra-Orthodox community. As we continue to lead the legal and political struggle to improve the education of ultra-Orthodox boys, we need to both recognize the elements of our tradition that provide support for the current situation, as well as utilize the various traditional responses to support knowledge, education, and gender equality.

Note

1. Roger Lewin, "Man's Place in Nature," *Missouri Review* 11, no. 3 (1988): 16–32.

34

Created in God's Image

Protecting Even the Least Deserving of Protection

RABBI JILL JACOBS

God now said, "Let us make human beings in our image,
after our likeness; and let them hold sway over the fish of the
sea and the birds of the sky, over the beasts, over all the earth,
over all that creeps upon the earth." So God created the human
beings in the divine image, creating them in the image of God,
creating them male and female.

Genesis 1:26–27

These words define the essence of humanity, form the basis of the divine-human relationship, and set the stage for the establishment of halachah, the Jewish legal system.

By this point in the Torah, we know God as a creator and a maker of order, who exerts power over the universe. The human being, created in the divine image (*b'tzelem Elohim*; Genesis 1:27), therefore inherits this power. For the first time since the beginning of Creation, a hierarchy emerges, with God presiding over humanity, and human beings being given responsibility to preside over the rest of the earth's inhabitants. In this essay, we will examine the nature of *tzelem Elohim*, with an emphasis on how this concept informs Jewish law on criminal justice.

Creation *b'tzelem Elohim* simultaneously endows human beings with a divine level of honor and dignity and imposes on us obligations for stewardship of God's Creation. Rabbi David Kimchi (1160–1235, known as the Radak) writes, "The human being is exalted over all of the other lower creations, so much so that God created humanity in the divine image, with the intelligence that God gave humanity. For this reason, the other creations should be in awe of the human being—as should one person toward another—such that a person will not destroy another's body or image."[1]

Judaism most often speaks in the language of obligation, while international law speaks in the language of rights. However, per Kimchi, the concept of *tzelem Elohim* unites these two discourses by insisting that obligations and rights present two sides of a coin: as creations in the image of God, we have the right not to be killed and the right to be treated with dignity and awe. And, as creations in the image of God, we are obligated and empowered to protect the life and dignity of other human beings.

The first and primary obligation that emerges from the human being's status as a *tzelem Elohim* is the prohibition against murder. Just a few chapters later in Genesis, the Torah tells us, "The shedder of human blood, / that person's blood shall be shed by [another] human; / for human beings were made / in the image of God" (Genesis 9:6). Murder is wrong because it constitutes a destruction of the divine image.

The midrash offers a parable to explain this connection between murder and the divine image:

A king of flesh and blood entered a province and the people set up portraits of him, made images of him, and struck coins in his honor. Later on they upset his portraits, broke his images, and defaced his coins, thus diminishing the likeness of the king. So also if one shed blood, it is accounted to him as though he had diminished the divine image. For it is said: The shedder of human blood . . . for human beings were made in the image of God (Genesis 9:6).[2]

After the human king in this parable loses power, for reasons and by means not explained here, his former subjects respond by erasing any trace of this ruler. Specifically, they destroy the images that would have been worshiped as manifestations of the king and deface the coins that lose their value with the end of the regime. These actions demonstrate that the king no longer wields power and perhaps prevent the king from again gaining a foothold in the kingdom. Similarly, one who murders a human being diminishes God's presence and power in the universe. The destruction of a human being constitutes not only a human tragedy, but also a divine one.

If the death of every human being diminishes the Divine Presence, then the biblical mandate for capital punishment presents a paradox: why should we respond to the loss of one divine image by destroying a second?

Kimchi, in a continuation of the commentary cited above, attempts a resolution:

Similarly, God commanded that the killer's blood be shed for his sin . . . since the perpetrator destroyed the image of God in him/herself first in transgressing the divine command.[3]

In order to murder a human being, Kimchi says, one must first deny the very existence of the image of God in humanity—including in oneself. Otherwise how could one possibly bring oneself to murder? Therefore, capital punishment is enacted only on a person whose divine image has already been irretrievably damaged.

While perhaps psychologically astute—as evidenced by the phenomenon of "suicide by cop" or murder suicides, in which a person
plans to kill or to be killed as part of his or her suicide plan—this
justification does not ultimately resolve the paradox of the biblical
command to kill a second human being to make up for the murder
of the first.

Rather, the response to—if not resolution of—this paradox comes
in the deep ambivalence among the Talmudic Rabbis to capital punishment, their efforts to legislate it out of existence through strict rules
of evidence, and the multiple references to *tzelem Elohim* as a guiding
principle for addressing those accused of wrongdoing.

One of the most oft-quoted lines of Rabbinic literature declares,
"Whoever destroys a single soul, Scripture holds guilty as though this
person had destroyed a complete world; and whoever preserves a single soul, Scripture ascribes [merit] to him as though he had preserved
a complete world" (*Mishnah Sanhedrin* 4:5). Often lost in the citation
of this passage is the fact that it appears within the context of a capital
case, in which a person accused of a serious crime—perhaps murder—
stands to lose his or her life:

> How are the witnesses intimidated in capital cases? Witnesses
> in capital cases are brought in and intimidated [in this way]:
> Perhaps you are only repeating hearsay or what another wit-
> ness said, or what a trustworthy person said. Perhaps you don't
> know that we will check your testimony by inquiry and cross-
> examination. You should know that capital cases are not like
> civil cases. In civil cases, [the witness] can make atonement [for
> false testimony] through payment. In capital cases, the witness
> is held responsible for the blood [of the convicted] and of his
> [potential] descendants until the end of time. We find this in
> the case of Cain, who killed his brother. The Torah teaches
> [that God says to Cain]: "The bloods of your brother shriek to

Me" (Genesis 4:10). It doesn't say "the blood of your brother," but rather "the bloods of your brother." That is to say, "his blood and the blood of his [potential] descendants." . . .

For this reason was the human being created alone, to teach you that whoever destroys a single soul, Scripture holds guilty as though this person had destroyed a complete world; and whosoever preserves a single soul,[4] Scripture ascribes [merit] to him as though he had preserved a complete world. Furthermore, [Adam was created alone] for the sake of peace among people, that one might not say to another, "My father was greater than yours," and that heretics might not say, "There are many ruling powers in heaven"; again, to proclaim the greatness of the Blessed Holy One: for if a man strikes many coins from one mold, they all resemble one another, but the supreme Sovereign, the Blessed Holy One, fashioned every individual in the stamp of the first human being, and yet not one of them resembles another. Therefore every single person is obliged to say: The world was created for my sake. And lest one should say, "What do I need with this trouble?" the Torah says, "If one is able to testify as one who has seen or knows of the matter, and does not give information, that person is liable for a sin" (Leviticus 5:1). Or lest one say, "Why do we need this responsibility for another person's death?" Behold, it is said, "When the wicked are destroyed, there is rejoicing" (Proverbs 11:10).

In the Rabbinic system of law, conviction requires two eyewitnesses. Unlike the U.S. standard of guilt beyond a reasonable doubt, halachah requires proof of guilt beyond *any doubt*. This means that witnesses are grilled not only on the circumstances of the crime, but also on unrelated details, famously whether the stalks of the figs growing near the crime scene were thick or thin, and whether the figs themselves were black or white. (Babylonian Talmud, *Sanhedrin* 41a). Any contradiction between the testimonies invalidates both witnesses. In practice, this means that it becomes virtually impossible to carry out capital punishment. Every story of a death-row inmate absolved of guilt through DNA testing or other means reinforces the Talmud's insistence on eliminating any possibility of error.

Witnesses who conspire, successfully, to bring about a false conviction stand to receive the punishment that they brought on the accused. As the Mishnah notes, in civil cases in which the punishment is a monetary fine, the witnesses can make good by paying restitution to the one they helped to convict. In capital cases, however, the witnesses pay with their lives—but can never restore the life of their victim. Therefore, the examination of these witnesses begins with a reminder that they will be held responsible not only for the life of the accused, but also for all of his or her potential descendants—the worlds that might have emerged from this person. (We should note that strict rules of evidence also apply to the false witnesses, whose guilt will have to be proven beyond any doubt.)

Within this text, *tzelem Elohim* imposes an obligation on the court to take every precaution not to kill an innocent person—or even a guilty person whose guilt cannot be proved beyond a sliver of doubt. *Tzelem Elohim* also serves as a reminder that each human being carries the divine power of creating complete worlds and that each human being is both equal to every other and entirely unique. Finally, the insistence at the end of this text that a person not shirk his or her responsibility to testify, even when stakes are high, reminds us that the protection of human beings requires a functional legal system, not only good wishes or theological constructs.

As evidenced by this mishnah, the true test of human rights comes through our treatment of those whom we might be inclined to despise, including those who have committed horrible crimes. Thus, another early Rabbinic text insists that when the blood of the wicked is spilled, God says, "My head is too heavy for Me, My arm is too heavy for Me"

(*Tosefta Sanhedrin* 10:7). The destruction of a human being—even one who has done evil—causes direct pain to God. Here, even the most wicked human being is not only a reflection but an extension of God.

For this reason, Jewish law mandates dignified treatment of those accused of a crime. Excessive punishment, the Torah warns, runs the risk that "your peer be degraded before your eyes (Deuteronomy 25:3). Or, in the words of Rav Abraham Isaac Kook (1865–1935), "In the case of a corrupt person, it would be appropriate to hate him/her as a result of his/her faults. But from the perspective of his/her *tzelem Elohim*, it is appropriate to treat this person with love, and also to know that the precious nature of this person's worth is more essential to him/her than the lower characteristics that have developed through his/her circumstances."[5] No matter what someone may have done, the person should be defined not by his or her worst action, but by his or her essence as a creation *b'tzelem Elohim*, deserving of the protections owed to any image of God.

The implications of destroying an image of God go far beyond the loss of a single person. One surprising text hints at the potentially devastating effects of a world that engages in the degradation of human beings:

> Rabbi Meir used to say: What does "one who is hanged is a curse against God" mean? This is compared to two twin brothers, identical to one another. One ruled over the whole world, and the other took to highway robbery. After a while, the robber was caught, and they were hanging him. All passersby said: "The king is on the cross." For this reason, the Torah says, "one who is hanged is a curse against God" (Deuteronomy 21:23). (*Mishnah Sanhedrin* 6:5)

Imagine the consequences of the execution in this parable. The townspeople walk by and see their king (they think) hanging in the town square.[6] What do they do next? Do they destroy the king's images or their coins, as in the midrash cited earlier? Do they cease observing the laws of the land? Certainly, they believe—at least for some time—that there is no ruler in the kingdom. Similarly, if we are God's identical twin, per the bold suggestion of the parable, then any injury to a human being—even one guilty of a capital crime—not only diminishes the divine image, but may even lead to the conclusion that God no longer exists in the world. Such a conclusion threatens to lead to widespread murder, or at least a failure to treat others as images of God.

The concept of *tzelem Elohim*, therefore, creates both rights and obligations. Every human being merits the protection of his or her life and dignity and simultaneously bears the responsibility of protecting other images of God. The true test of our society's success in protecting the image of God in each person comes through our treatment of those we find the least sympathetic—particularly those accused or convicted of heinous crimes. If we succeed, perhaps we increase the presence of God in the world. But if we fail, we may find ourselves living in a world with a diminished divine presence and without the protections of *tzelem Elohim* that the Torah demands.

Notes

1. Rabbi David Kimchi, commentary on Genesis 9:6.

2. *M'chilta D'Rabbi Yishmael*, Tractate *BaChodesh*.

3. Kimchi, commentary on Genesis 9:6.

4. The printed edition of the Talmud inserts the word "of Israel." However, this word does not appear in manuscripts and does not make sense in context, as Cain and Abel were not Jewish.

5. Abraham Isaac Kook, *Midot HaRaayah, Ahavah* 9.

6. This text also contains a clear anti-Christian polemic, especially when we consider that hanging probably actually referred to crucifixion. Just because a person—who looks like God—is seen crucified in the public square does not mean that God has actually been killed.

35

The World As It Is

RABBI DR. RACHEL S. MIKVA

*So God created the human beings in [the divine] image,
creating [them] in the image of God, creating them male and
female. God then blessed them, and God said to them, "Be
fruitful and multiply; fill the earth and master it; hold sway
over the fish of the sea and the birds of the sky, and over every
animal that creeps on the earth."*

Genesis 1:27–28

J ust one kind. Animals and plants are created with diverse species,
but there is no different kind of human. We are one species, all graced
by a likeness with the Divine. Genesis 1 presents us with a radical egalitarian vision that we have yet to realize in our world, where human
dignity attaches to all people regardless of race, gender, religion, eth-
nicity, sexual orientation, nationality, class, or physical ability.

With other details of our creation, we have been overachievers:
"Be fruitful and multiply; fill the earth and master it" (Genesis 1:28).
This we have determinedly pursued. The verse has become a target of
critique for appearing to advocate our heedless assault on the planet,
but it wasn't meant to be controversial. Inscribed in antiquity, it was

an invocation against extinction and an aspiration for some measure of control over an uncertain world. How could one imagine that humanity would multiply so greatly as to overload the earth's resources, and control our environment to the extent that we might threaten Creation itself?

Mastery can mean many things. One way to read day six is as the culmination of a divine plan in which all of Creation exists in balance, where the creature of the divine image holds sway in minding the store. Waters above and below, lights of day and night—all support the life-generating force of the universe. Humans and animals live as vegetarians in harmony with one another. "Very good," indeed—at least in our imagination as a world that could be, a world we can almost taste each Shabbat, but release as the Sabbath sun sets and we reenter the world as it is.

Our world is illuminated in the second Creation narrative, beginning with Genesis 2:4 and its recasting of Creation as a story all about us. Androcentrism run amok, earth and heavens serve merely as a backdrop, with plants and animals apparently awaiting our arrival. We are then created from the dust of the earth; the breath of God animates our being but does not describe our nature.

This world reveals a dialectical struggle embedded in our DNA, where our kinship with the rest of Creation opposes our tendency to hold ourselves apart. Genesis 2 signals both aspects of our being. We are created as *adam* (human) from the *adamah* (earth), words linked to the same Hebrew root. Yet, as we give names to all the animals, we find no fitting partner among them. We also receive a sacred task to till and tend the garden, but stewardship does not come naturally and our appetites are difficult to contain—so the command that follows (the only command in the passage) is about what we can and cannot take, rather than what we might give.

At the same time, the text portrays our deep need for companionship, with a willingness to sacrifice some part of ourselves to make it possible: "This one at last is bone of my bones and flesh of my flesh" (Genesis 2:23). As the narrative unfolds, however, it illustrates the all too familiar unsettling of human relationship. Genesis 3:6 shows how we can be driven by desires—physical, aesthetic, and intellectual: the fruit of the forbidden tree is good to eat; it is a delight to the eyes and a potential source of wisdom. Why not take a bite, despite the consequences for ourselves and others? The discrepancy between God's command about the tree as given to Adam (Genesis 2:16–17) and Eve's description of it to the serpent (3:3) forces us to wonder about our struggles to communicate honestly with one another: is it Adam's exaggeration or Eve's distraction that leads her to believe they are not allowed to touch the tree? Most telling of all is the heartbreaking illustration of human beings failing to take responsibility: Adam blames it on Eve, and Eve blames it on the serpent. It's hard to go a full day without a savory rationalization. Yet somewhere in our bones, we know what we have done. After they eat from the forbidden tree, Adam and Eve try to hide when God draws near (Genesis 3:8–13).

In the world as it is, sometimes even such minimal awareness evades us. We often cannot be sure if we are doing the right thing. Maimonides asked why God would not want us to obtain knowledge of good and evil; is it not a requisite part of our moral responsibility? He postulated that prior to eating from the tree, we had superior knowledge, knowledge of true and false. One does not say that the concept of the earth as flat is "bad," but rather that it is false. Yet with many of life's most important questions, he lamented, we have been reduced to relativism, arguing from our own limited cultural context and perspective whether something is right or wrong (*Guide for the Perplexed* I:2). It becomes one more source of conflict.

The second Creation story concludes by describing a series of profound alienations that permeate our reality (Genesis 3:14–16). The world as it is struggles with spiritual impoverishment, for the Divine Presence (or its secular parallel, a transcendent sense of purpose) too often feels distant or absent from people's lives. The world as it is suffers a rampant sense of homelessness, with countless individuals physically or emotionally stripped of their place. The world as it is evokes enmity between human beings and the animal world, fighting for space and food and security. The world as it is perpetuates patriarchy and a host of other hierarchical relationships that infect the body politic. The world as it is admits a fundamental alienation between humanity and the earth. Not only have we had to eat by the sweat of our brow (or someone's brow, anyway), we stand on the precipice of catastrophic climate change.

These are not commanded ways of being. They are not the eternal punishment for sin. Torah is not merely describing this world; it is critiquing it with a cautionary tale of what happens when we continue to miss the mark, when we repeatedly demonstrate our origin in dust rather than the divine image.

Historical criticism assigns authorship of the two Creation narratives to different documentary sources, Genesis 1 to the Priestly tradition and Genesis 2–3 to the Yahwist tradition, each with its own historical context and conceptual emphases. Yet they speak together in our Torah, and we are forced to reckon with their collision. Rachel Adler writes: "The goodness of creation and mastery conferred in Genesis 1 are complicated by pain, alienation and defeat. The redemptive truth offered by this grim depiction is that patriarchal social relations construct a world that cries out to be mended."[1]

Is patriarchy the foundational hierarchy of human society, as Adler's comment would suggest? It certainly reaches beyond our remembered past and operates on us beyond the realm of consciousness. There are multiple systems of power, however, that enable some people to dominate others and allow humanity to destroy the ecosystem that sustains us. As the quick succession of curses in Genesis 3 suggests, the problems of our world are bound up together. We cannot repair one piece while leaving other forms of oppression and alienation in place. Too often, this truism of intersectionality is paralyzing; the cumulative task is too immense. Yet its corollary is that we can begin in one place and thereby contribute to the reweaving of the entire social fabric. So let us begin at our creation on the sixth day, which does seem to emphasize gender in unraveling systems of domination. Judaism neither invented patriarchy nor eliminated it, but the foundational anthropology in Genesis 1 is a building block for constructing right relation, relations of mutuality and tenderness, equality and empowerment—the world as it could be.

It is difficult to translate the verse of our creation in a way that captures its radical vision, however. The first edition of the Plaut commentary used the New Jewish Publication Society translation, "And God created man in His image, in the image of God He created him; male and female He created them" (Genesis 1:27). There is no hierarchy and no essentialized ideas about what men do and what women do. Even though *adam* (human) has been rendered as "man," there is no codified difference in our existence; we are each created in the image and "likeness" of God. If we of diverse genders are so fashioned, then how can we call the Creator "he"?

Using "they" would reflect the plural-form name of God, *Elohim*, inscribed in the first Creation narrative—and it is the commonly preferred way to finesse gender binaries and male privilege when talking about people in English today. In our multi-faith world, there is even something attractive about lifting up the multiplicity of the Divine. The Hebrew Bible itself flirts with such language, as in the previous verse, which states, "Let us make human beings in our image, after our likeness" (Genesis 1:26). It cannot be sustained, however, without seriously undermining clarity of expression and the text's emphasis on monotheism.

The Plaut commentary's more recent gender-sensitive version opts for a less verbatim translation and adds bracketed words to accommodate our egalitarian perspective: "So God created the human beings in [the divine] image, creating [them] in the image of God, creating them male and female." That works fairly well. For our study, however, I propose something more destabilizing: "God created humankind in zher image; in the image of God did zhe create it, male and female zhe created them" (Genesis 1:27).

Resorting to the already outdated and never-popular neologism of "zhe" and "zher" highlights our struggle. How do we liberate our imagination from the blasphemous grip of patriarchy that idolizes maleness as representative of the Most High? Can we do it without stripping God of gender altogether and accidentally desexing the Divine? The Hebrew verse is also a bit stilted, ensuring that we stop to notice the astonishing nature of our creation.

Might the blended pronoun also empower us to recognize that "male and female" need not be two utterly distinct and static genders in binary relation? The Rabbis of late antiquity knew it; they discerned a minimum of six genders within the community, overlapping and fluid. The Sages' interest was in guiding these individuals toward a fulfilled Jewish life, not in judging them. My favorite comment is "The intersex person, he is a creature unto herself" (*Mishnah Bikurim* 4:5). Our minds are wired to discern difference, but they are not computers, limited to thinking in ones and zeroes.

The experience of endless diversity within Creation should blow open the limits on our theological imagination. Pulling at the thread of gender polarity, we glimpse a world without the hierarchies that separate person from person, humanity from the earth, and Creation from its Creator. This is not "the world as it is," but part of what makes us human is the capacity for abstract thought, to explore and to fashion even things we have not seen. The world of Creation in balance is yet a possibility.

And God saw all that he had made and found it very good.
And there was evening and there was morning, the sixth day.
(Genesis 1:31)

Note

1. Rachel Adler, *Engendering Judaism* (Philadelphia: Jewish Publication Society, 1998), 123–24.

36

Paradise on Earth

DR. RACHEL HAVRELOCK

God then said, "Let there be an expanse in the midst of the waters, and let it divide water from water!" So God made the expanse, separating the waters beneath the expanse from the waters above the expanse—and so it was.

Genesis 1:6–7

Human life transpires in a fragile state between efforts toward a perfect order and the possibility of an overwhelming flood. In the beginning, water is as potent as God, who contains it in order to bring distinct life-forms into being. On the second day of Creation God separates water into the lighter elements that form the sky and the heavier ones that run beneath the earth. The boundary is the *rakia*—the firmament or expanse—which the Rabbis describe as a tunnel at the horizon where surface water and rain turn like buckets in a waterwheel. It is clear that Genesis 1:7 knows how blue skies and azure waters are connected in a cycle of evaporation and precipitation and sees the interconnection as an essential component of the world. However, this is the only day of Creation not deemed "good" by God, as if to acknowledge the great struggle between the Creator and the water only perhaps temporarily won. Water, of course, not only nourishes our land and our bodies but can overwhelm human structures through the force of a flood. So God only calls the creation of bodies of water "good" in association with fertile earth (Genesis 1:10–12).

This passage corresponds with the two larger visions of human dependence on water. Genesis chapter 1 is concerned with the possibility of a flood that washes away the work of Creation, whereas Genesis chapter 2 imagines the world amid a sustained drought before God causes a dew to soften the parched earth. Many commentators have recognized the longings of water-strapped farmers in the lush imagery of Eden's trees and rivers. Humanity emerges in the balance struck between flooding and drought.

Genesis 1 envisions the initial state of the world as entirely covered by water, which is then pushed back into seas, lakes, and rivers bounded by land. On the second of six days of Creation, God separates the waters into the heavy waters that remain on earth and the light waters that compose the sky. Never assessed as "good," water maintains its force, can break its limits at any point, and return the ordered world to its primordial chaos. On the third day, God separates the land from the water. The land emerges fertile with plants that are able to constantly regenerate. On the first, second, and third day, realms are created. These realms are the day, the night, the water, the sky, and the earth. On the fourth, fifth, and sixth days, the population of these realms is created. There is even greater symmetry because the sun, moon, and stars that inhabit the day and night are created on the fourth day; the fish and birds that inhabit the waters and the sky are created on the fifth day; and the animals and humanity are created on the sixth day. Order reverberates on every level of Creation, but water can always break its bounds and transform it instantly to chaos.

The second chapter of Genesis finds the world stuck in a rainless state of drought. Not until a mist rises from the parched earth can humanity flourish among vegetation and trees. The Garden of Eden is planted by God in the east (Genesis 2:8), and a single river emerges from Eden and branches out in four directions (2:10–14). Headwaters enable both a Tree of Life and a Tree of All Knowledge to grow at the center of Eden. The spring, in turn, nourishes a river that branches out into four streams that sustain the sites of human habitation. The emerging streams—the Pishon, the Gihon, the Tigris, and the Euphrates—divide the world into quadrangles. Mention of the Tigris and Euphrates, known geographical waterways, suggests that Eden is part of the known world, and the mention of the Gihon and Pishon, at least one of which has no corollary in geography, suggests that Eden belongs to an unknown world. The intersection of the known and the unknown rivers designates Eden as place where mythic topography and historical geography meet.

Josephus understands the singular river of Eden to be the ocean-river that encircles the earth's landmass and laps up at its edges to give rise to the world's great rivers. He believes the Pishon to be the Ganges, and the gold-filled land of Havilah (Genesis 2:11) to be India. In his map, the Tigris and Euphrates filter into the Red Sea, which Josephus understands as including the Persian Gulf and forming the southern limb of the world ocean. The headwaters of the Tigris and Euphrates are found at the northern stretch of the world ocean, and the rivers flow from north to south across the entire landmass and pour into the ocean's southern sphere. Josephus locates Eden, the source of such great rivers, beyond the discs of both the inhabited world and the ocean. By conflating the river of Eden with the concept of the world ocean, Josephus merges Jewish utopia with the Greek concept of universal geography. The meeting of Jewish tradition and Hellenistic thought indeed motivated Josephus's whole interpretive project. Here he avoids the question of where on earth Eden might be by placing it beyond the limit of the world ocean.

The First Book of Enoch locates paradise somewhere similar. It describes earth in terms of three circular divisions: the inhabited earth at the center, with the ocean around it surrounded by a desert wilderness (I Enoch 77). Paradise is situated in the northeastern edge of the wilderness in a region of darkness beyond earth and ocean. The enormous distance between the inhabited world and paradise seems to represent the significant disparity between the current actions of humanity and the righteous acts required to gain entrance to paradise. The remoteness of Eden thus conveys how very long it will take for humanity to take action worthy of paradise. Meanwhile, Eden awaits far beyond our world.

The Rabbinic authors of *B'reishit Rabbah* had no investment in Eden as a geographical site. The midrash takes the word *mikedem*, "to the east" (Genesis 2:8), to mean "earlier" and then applies this chronology in order to reduce the discrepanies between Genesis chapters 1 and 2. "Rabbi Shmuel ben Nachmani said: You may think that it means before [*kodem*] the creation of the world, but this is not so; rather it is, before Adam, for Adam was created on the sixth day, whereas the Garden of Eden was created on the third" (*B'reishit Rabbah* 15:3). Rabbi Shmuel ben Nachmani explains that the Garden of Eden was planted on the third day of Creation when God caused the grasses and fruit-bearing trees to sprout from the earth. The Garden of Eden, a place of trees, was created along with all trees, three days prior to the creation of humanity. More textually oriented, the Rabbis favor reconciling biblical chapters over geographical speculation.

The Rabbinic explanation for the four rivers of Eden likewise avoids locating them in physical space and instead associates them with Israel's top four enemies. Punning on the word *rashim*, "heads," used for the four branches of Eden's river, Rabbi Tanchum explains that these are the four heads—leaders—of empires. Through ever more clever wordplay, Rabbi Tanchum links the name of each river with the qualities of a specific empire, so the Pishon represents Babylon, Gihon represents Media, Tigris is Greece, and the Euphrates is Rome. Rather than providing a clue to the site of primordial beginnings, the names of the four rivers indicate Israel's historical fate—to be buffeted by the conquests of empire. Like the ancient river, Israel stems from a source in its homeland and flows through the kingdoms of the world subject to the raging waters of empire. But, just as rivers eventually pour into the sea, so Israel will one day stream into the world-to-come.

These texts are maps to paradise, although like the Rabbis we shouldn't read them too literally and go looking for some distant location. The tragedy involved in such an act, I believe, is illustrated in the film *Mad Max Fury Road* when Imperator Furiosa hits the road in search of "the Green Place," only to find old women with some seeds. Eden, in other words, must be found locally where we are. Water seems key to this equation. We need only think of the peace and sense of connection achieved by splashing, paddling, or sitting by lakes and rivers. As foretold in Genesis, our contemporary glimpses of paradise likewise transpire between moments of flooding and drought and should compel us to change our behaviors to pursue conservation. It is vital for each of us to examine our water use, what sorts of pollutants we wash down the drain, and the mountains of plastic bottles left after we pay corporations to extract our local waters. However, these important actions alone do not suffice.

On the social level, we must protect our local waters from privatization. Such privatization takes many forms—water bottled by the Nestle, Coke, and Pepsi corporations; corporate purchase of our water intake and pipes from struggling municipalities; even the takeover of our sewage treatment. Studies show that corporate ownership leads to higher water bills, greater leakage, and more infrequent repairs. Investors, not the public, become the party to be satisfied through profit. From a Jewish point of view, the very idea of owning water is paradoxical. It flows beneath us, past us; it evaporates bearing our traces and returns to us as rain. Water crosses the very boundaries between nations, ethnicities, social classes, and races. Water would then seem to be the perfect unifier, the ideal system that reflects balance and interconnectedness.

So, in addition to changing behavior and protecting water for future generations, we need to attend to how water both connects and divides communities. Even as everyone present in a place depends on shared sources of water for life itself, communities are divided by access, pricing, exposure to toxins, and a voice in water allocation. Because water constitutes such a necessary public good, we need a new approach that engages everyone in the question of how water is managed. First of all, people need to see where their water goes, through clear maps of the pipes and channels that redirect the flow of water and define areas of prosperity and poverty. Secondly, the allocation of water to corporations, agriculture, and municipalities needs to be publicized so that the public can weigh in on the primary beneficiaries of water resources. In addition, we need to talk about water and energy needs in the same breath. Here we can gain inspiration from the water protectors of Lake Oahe, the Missouri River, and the Standing Rock Sioux Reservation. In the Great Lakes basin—site of 20 percent of the world's freshwater— Alberta tar sands slog through pipelines on the floor and shores of the lakes. In March 2014, a spill of tar sands and likely some of the highly toxic chemicals used to send it down pipelines spilled from the Whiting, Indiana, BP refinery into Lake Michigan, the water source for *over ten million people*. The story was hardly reported.

Also barely recorded is the rupture of an Enbridge pipeline that released around 1.1 million gallons of tar sands and its chemically heavy diluent into the Kalamazoo River, which feeds Lake Michigan. The EPA—may it live long and prosper—spent four years addressing the damage and enlisting Iraq veterans in the oil cleanup. Even in the wake of the disaster, most residents of the Great Lakes region do not know that similarly aging pipelines encircle most of our freshwater sources. What we need immediately is open dialogue about the best sources and sites of energy processing, what sorts of energy producers are funded and subsidized by the government, and the most vital water stores that need to be free of refineries, pipelines, and oil train crossings. We need a public forum where these matters can be discussed among residents whose concerns will not be drowned out by commercial rhetoric. Perhaps people will decide that a pipeline supporting lower gas prices is worth the risk to their drinking water. Perhaps protecting water will inspire transition to a renewable energy source. Whatever collective decisions about water management may be, they cannot continue to be driven from corporate chambers alone.

Finally, we must address inequality in terms of who is most exposed to toxins. The environmental justice movement teaches us how poor and underserved communities coincide with the most polluted landscapes and have the highest rates of environmental illness. Addressing such dangerous inequality is not an act of charity, but an occasion of a new politics that crosses the borders of race, gender, and class by engaging everyone present in the assessment of resources and pollutants, the sharing of benefit and risk, and the establishment of socioeconomic systems with clean water at the center.

An example of this new politics, interestingly, emerges in the famously water-scarce and war-torn region of the Middle East. In the absence of peace treaties or national frameworks for cooperation, the trilateral NGO EcoPeace Middle East brings together Palestinian, Jordanian, and Israeli communities along the same watershed. Together, they learn the path of their water, what compromises it, and the culture of those from whom they are separated by elaborate borders. As these "Good Water Neighbors" build trust, they plan together what to do with waste and pollution and how to sustainably develop their shared land.

EcoPeace's Good Water Neighbors project builds upon "mutual dependence on shared water resources" to support cooperative engagement and peace building, with tangible results. Communities on opposite sides of political divides come together and plan a shared future. Their work offers a concrete strategy to repair injustice and promote equality while saving the Jordan, one of the world's holiest rivers, now carrying a mere 4 percent of its historical flow. Like Eco-Peace, the prophet Ezekiel envisioned a restored Jordan River as key to healing his embattled homeland. God let Ezekiel down on "a very high mountain," where he saw a new Eden with abundant trees (Ezekiel 47:7; Genesis 2:9), swarming creatures (Ezekiel 47:9; Genesis 1:20), and potential immortality offered by leaves that heal and fruits that never rot (Ezekiel 47:12). The replenishing fruit trees beside sanctified waters indicated an imminent and inclusive paradise.

Water is the dominant feature in Ezekiel's vision of paradise. As a river rises from Eden and branches out into four courses (Genesis 2:10), so a single stream bubbles from beneath the Temple and swells into an uncrossable river (Ezekiel 47:5). The surging waters of Jerusalem symbolize a future of overcoming oppression, a collective purification, and a national revival in a restored Temple (Isaiah 33:21; Joel 4:18; Zechariah 14:8). The redemptive river that heals staid waters and revives fish and fruit trees (Ezekiel 47:9–12) morphs into the Jordan as it flows in the eastern region through the Aravah and Dead Sea (47:8). Just as the prophet Ezekiel envisioned a river coursing through the land in order to purify the earth and usher in a new beginning, EcoPeace Middle East envisions a "flood event" to wash the toxins from the Jordan River Basin, restore the vital ecosystem, and bring together all communities of the Jordan Valley to plan a sustainable future.

These Good Water Neighbors in a parched valley show how water sharing can form the basis of a bioregional culture that thinks in terms of neighbors along a waterway rather than as enemies or economic competitors. For them, water is shared and public. Drawing from public resources like precious water can support local economies, and conserving it can ensure the health and well-being of all riparian communities. Ideally, water in all of its forms will remain a commons held in public trust and not become a commodity traded by financiers or exploited by industry. Together with the prophet Ezekiel and Eco-Peace, let us envision an open, flowing Jordan River in a valley where monotheism and humanity itself began. Let us learn about our water and what contaminates it, then halt those toxins in order to drink, fish, and swim together with our neighbors. This seems the most viable map to Eden.

◆

SHABBAT

Completed now were heaven and earth and all their host. On the seventh day, God had completed the work that had been done, ceasing then on the seventh day from all the work that God had done. Then God blessed the seventh day and made it holy, and ceased from all the creative work that God had chosen to do.

Genesis 2:1–3

37

What a Group of Cloistered Nuns Taught Me About Shabbat

RABBI SHOSHANAH CONOVER

*Completed now were heaven and earth and all their host. On
the seventh day, God had completed the work that had been
done, ceasing then on the seventh day from all the work that
God had done. Then God blessed the seventh day and made
it holy, and ceased from all the creative work that God had
chosen to do.*

Genesis 2:1–3

The Torah proclaims a stark break between the six days of Creation
and Shabbat. The six days of Creation fill chapter 1 of the Book of
Genesis. The description of Shabbat is reserved for Chapter 2. For a
long time, the break between the weekdays and Shabbat felt equally
stark in my own life. However, a transformative encounter last summer
changed all that.

During most days of the week, my clock awakens me with alarming news—tuned as it is to my local NPR station. I wake in a hurry, put out clothes and breakfast for my young sons, pack their lunches, and get myself ready. After dropping them at school, I glance at my schedule for the day that shows appointments calendared to the minute, no breaks between. From teaching to meetings, from hospital visits to writing, hours pass in a flash. After an intense day working, I pick up my children and enjoy a meal with our family filled with brief accounts of our days and playful word, math, and musical games. We clear dinner, and then bath time and bedtime rituals commence. Soon, my spouse and I wind down . . . not to be wound up again until the next day begins with alarm. Each day brings spectacular moments, varied and holy—yet, so many of them they are each hard to savor!

Shabbat begins in a wholly different way. Instead of with alarm, it begins with the lighting of two candles—one to remember and one to protect this *z'man kodesh*, this sacred time of Shabbat as separate and unique. As Rabbi Abraham Joshua Heschel, *z"l*, wrote:

> In the tempestuous ocean of time and toil there are islands of stillness where man may enter a harbor and reclaim our dignity. The island is the seventh day, the Sabbath, a day of detachment from things, instruments and practical affairs as well as attachment to the spirit.[1]

The constant rush of the week robs me of the time it takes to give each moment—and each person in each moment—the honor they deserve. I overuse my phone, my computer, and my car while underusing my spiritual focus and presence. This shifts profoundly on Shabbat. As rabbis we need Shabbat, and some of the ways that I have attached to the spirit of Shabbat are through my community and my family.

Most often, I light two tea candles on a large, round table with dozens of other candles on my way into the sanctuary. This table of candles serves as our community's repository of Shabbat wishes as we light these candles collectively. When I circle my hands around these tiny flames, I begin this time of the spirit with prayer. Opening my eyes afterward, I greet everyone I see, "*Shabbat shalom.*" We receive each other with a warmth and almost giddiness that surface so naturally at this time. Singing, swaying, meditation, deep learning, silence, and gratitude infuse these Shabbat hours. Morning dawns with promise. I enter our synagogue's *beit midrash* to a small minyan gathered, singing in a round. Regulars arrive at varied times, all greeted with huge smiles, winks, hugs. The non-verbals say everything. The late-morning hours open into early afternoon as my prayer moves to the sanctuary to enjoy *b'nei mitzvah*, burgeoning Torah readers and teachers shyly asserting themselves in their new roles on the bimah. I return home as leisure and laughter fill our family home in the waning Shabbat hours. *Shavat vayinafash*, I rest and become refreshed. As the stars appear (or just before that in spring and summer), our sons grab juice to fill the cup in our *Havdalah* set. The braided candle, spices, and melody by Debbie Friedman all add to the allure of this ritual of separation: bidding farewell to Shabbat and greeting the week ahead. As I look at my hands in the flickering light of the candle's enormous flame, I think about my obligations in the week ahead. I ready my hands for the work of the week ahead that will begin as soon as the morning's news awakens me once again with alarm. These two modes of time: *kodesh* (sacred) and *chol* (ordinary) had stayed starkly separate for most of my adult life, meeting only occasionally. Thank God, an encounter last summer changed all that.

On a learning trip last summer with two dozen rabbis in Jerusalem, I visited a sprawling monastery of sequestered nuns who had taken vows of silence.[2] For educational purposes, a few of the nuns were given permission to speak to individuals and groups seeking knowledge. The nuns spend much of their time alone in contemplation, engaging in various tasks to support the monastery—including creating magnificent pottery sold in a small shop. Through meals, yard work, and other daily activity spent in silence, they acknowledge each other's presence without ever having to speak. Yet, even as they spoke with us that day, they intoned their words with a kind of quiet and calm that I associate with silence. More than that, their love for each other and us shone through as they answered our questions. (And, I have to say, that is a rare feeling when someone addresses a group of rabbis!)

A highlight of our visit was observing the nuns of the monastery in prayer. From a loft above, we watched the women silently enter a small sanctuary with vaulted ceilings and a completely open center. Each found a place behind a kneeler lining the sides of the bare space. Soon, they lifted their voices in the transcendent harmonizing of utter devotion. Moments mingled between song, spoken word, and silence. I stood mesmerized at one point when they walked slowly, one by one, to a portrait of Jesus and tenderly kissed each one of his wounds.

The entire afternoon spent with them was a lesson in humility—as they lived with such commitment, vulnerability, and openness. In some sense, their daily life is a Sabbath, consumed as it is with devotion, singing, and silence in a constant cultivation of the perfected sacred environment. Few if any of them go outside the monastery for any length of time. They have chosen a sequestered life—an island of stillness where these women have detached from material things and attached to the spirit.

This four-hour encounter changed me in subtle and profound ways. From these sequestered nuns, I learned to infuse my daily life with more of a sense of Shabbat. I now indulge in daily moments of intentional silence, of savoring and appreciating. I pay special attention to what I communicate to and receive from others by focusing not on what has been said, but on what someone is attempting to convey. I try to lovingly coax the best out of others as the nuns lovingly coaxed us in our encounter in Jerusalem. To do this requires an inner calm, an attachment to the spirit.

I used to dread the ending of Shabbat, shoring myself up for the pace of the week ahead. However, my experience with these nuns reminded me that, at its core, the ceremony of *Havdalah* is not about separation of *kodesh* and *chol*, as its name implies, but an integration of the sacred into our daily lives. Shabbat awakens us to the inner Eden available to us daily in life's mundane moments, and the rituals of *Havdalah* beckon us to take note of them. Spices stir our sense of smell with the promise that sweet and savory moments during the week will bring us back to this sense of Eden. As the great flame of the intertwined wicks of the candle illumine our hands with shadow and light, we recognize our potential to bring about a world more reflective of the divine light through the work of our own hands. The juice from the fruit of the vine reminds of the week's sweet potential. We don't need peak moments, but peak attention to notice life's daily blessings both big and small. Now, as I look at my hands in the light of the *Havdalah* candle . . . I imagine Rabbi Mordecai Kaplan, *z"l*, encouraging me with his well-known quote:

An artist cannot be continually wielding the brush. The artist must stop painting at times to freshen the vision of the object, the meaning of which is to be expressed on canvas. Living is also an art. Shabbat represents those moments when we pause in our brushwork to renew the vision of the object. Having done so, we take ourselves to our painting with clarified vision and renewed energy.[3]

Our lives, in all their varied moments, are works of art. We, through our intentions and attention to the sacred, become greater artists of the spirit.

Notes

1. Abraham Joshua Heschel, *The Sabbath* (New York: Farrar, Straus and Giroux, 1951), 29.

2. Yossi Klein Halevi wrote about this community in *At the Entrance of the Garden of Eden: A Jew's Search for God with Christians and Muslims in the Holy Land* (New York: Harper Perennial, 2002).

3. Mordecai Kaplan, *The Meaning of God in Modern Jewish Religion* (Detroit: Wayne State University Press, 1962), 59.

38

Determining the Path Ourselves

What Might Shabbat Look Like for Us?

RABBI JACK P. PASKOFF

Completed now were heaven and earth and all their host. On the seventh day, God had completed the work that had been done, ceasing then on the seventh day from all the work that God had done. Then God blessed the seventh day and made it holy, and ceased from all the creative work that God had chosen to do.

Genesis 2:1–3

It's Saturday. The kids have soccer, the lawn needs to be mowed, and I think we have plans tonight. Maybe I can catch a few minutes of the game on TV. With any luck, I'll nap for twenty minutes. It's not so much that I choose all of these activities. They just pile up over time. Could I really tell my child that he can't play soccer?

And with that, Shabbat is done. And so what? Why would I voluntarily choose a whole list of things I can't do when there's so much that

I want to do, that I need to do? I can't take a day off. All week long I'm
at work. The other things pile up. Don't shop, don't drive, don't spend
money, don't turn my computer on. It can't be done. I'm not Orthodox, and I don't want to be. The Orthodox live in the past. I need to
live in today.

But something tugs at me. Is it the desire to reconnect with a distant, primal memory? Or is it the desire to connect with a simpler
time? A time when life wasn't ruled by so much technology that was
supposed to make life easier, but in fact, complicates things even more?
Do I need an oasis in a world that can so often be barren, yet takes so
much from me? I know I can't do it the way the Orthodox do, but is
there something that I can derive from Shabbat? Something that can
add meaning and purpose to my life? Something I can find to nourish
me, to reenergize me?

Shabbat wasn't really all that hard in the Torah. Don't gather sticks
(Numbers 15:32–36), don't start fires (Exodus 35:1–3), and don't work
on the *Mishkan*, the Tabernacle (Exodus 31:12–15). Then the early
Sages made it harder. Now there were thirty-nine things you couldn't
do on Shabbat (*Mishnah Shabbat* 7:2). Each generation added layers of
restrictions and requirements. Rabbi Eugene Borowitz, *z"l*, offered us
an antidote to this kind of legalism. He taught us to seek out the meta-
ethic. What is the principle that stands behind and informs the law?
Perhaps we can find meaning in that, if not in the laws of Shabbat that
have multiplied through the ages. Let's examine a number of terms,
seek out an understanding of them on the meta-level, and see if we can
create a meaningful way to conceive of and observe Shabbat as Reform
Jews today.

Before we can think about observing any kind of Shabbat, we have
to know that it *is* Shabbat. In the version of the Ten Commandments
that appears in Exodus, we are told to remember the Sabbath day:
zachor et yom hashabbat (Exodus 20:8). It sounds simplistic, but we can't
create any kind of Shabbat if we're not aware that it is Shabbat. If we

allow that twenty-five-hour period from sundown Friday to darkness on Saturday merely to be "the weekend," we'll never see the potential of what Shabbat is and can be. In Hebrew, only one day each week has a name. The others are assigned numbers. There is no Sunday, Monday, Tuesday—just First Day, Second Day, etc. But Friday night begins Shabbat. We greet each other with *"Shabbat shalom."* In every sense, the week builds toward Shabbat. We must raise this in our consciences as well. We have to train ourselves to say the word *Shabbat.* Nothing else can happen until we do.

The fourth commandment continues, adding the verb *vay'kadsheihu.* It tells us we have to make the day *kadosh,* "holy" (Exodus 20:11). Fundamentally, the word merely means "set apart." Yet we know we want it to mean more. We want it to indicate some kind of elevated reality. We want it to feel like something other than "different." We need not talk about the rules here. We need to ask what we could do that would elevate us personally on Shabbat. For some, it may be Torah study and services. Others may find it on a hike or in spending time with family. Whatever the choice, our goal should be *k'dushah,* "holiness." We may not achieve it each week, but we must consciously choose to do the things that at least make it possible.

Before the Rabbis latched onto this commandment and complicated it with the multiple layers of law, the commandment was simple: "Six days you shall labor and do all your work" (Exodus 20:9). How might we understand "your"? Can we make a case that Shabbat is a day to avoid only the work of your occupation? If working in my garden helps me achieve *k'dushah,* must I still cross it off my list? If a lawyer finds *k'dushah* working with wood in his shop, is it still work? Yes, the commandment does go on to say *any* work, but I think we can argue for "occupation" instead.

Shabbat is about more than the cessation of work, though. In the story of Creation, the Torah tells us that God finished the work of Creation on the seventh day, not at the end of the sixth, as we would expect (Genesis 2:2). What did God create on the seventh day? God created rest. That runs counter to our typical definition of rest. Rest is the absence of something, namely work, not the presence of something. Yet we know that unless we proactively schedule rest, it rarely happens. We too have to work to create rest. But how can we define "rest" in this context? Later on in Exodus, in the passage that we more typically identify with the Shabbat service, we read *V'shamru* (Exodus 31:16–17). There we gain an insight into what rest is intended to be as we see its pairing with the word *vayinafash*. We don't just rest, we breathe and, as I prefer to translate it based on the Hebrew, we get our souls back. Some may question what a soul is, but I think we know when something has touched our souls. It's not just a thought or a feeling. It's something deeper yet; nothing we can point to, but an affirmation of something more.

V'shamru points to two other matters as well. The first is *b'rit*, the covenant. The wonder of Judaism in general, and Reform Judaism specifically, is that we have room for many understandings of God, the Divine, a Power greater than ourselves. However we may define it, we seek a relationship with this Power, and that relationship places expectations on us, as we do on it. Even for avowed atheists, perhaps Shabbat can become a day to seek out divinity, if not the Divine; godliness, if not God, in a covenantal relationship.

While the Hebrew grammar of the biblical text reveals that the Ten Commandments are given to us as individuals, *V'shamru* tells us that the covenant is between God and the Children of Israel (Exodus 31:17). It is about us collectively. As much as we may crave the autonomy to say that I get to decide if and how to observe Shabbat, there is a sense of the peoplehood of Israel here. What is my connection to my people? What is my obligation to my people? Yes, as Reform Jews we demand the right to make personal, informed choices, yet on some level we must know that we stand as part of something more. As a people, we share a history, we share a destiny, and we share the task of creating that destiny for ourselves, for our descendants, and for the sake of the repair of the world. What might it mean for me to connect with my people—be it my family, my community, or my congregation, on Shabbat?

Let's take a look at one last thought about Shabbat. As part of our liturgy, we read, or most often sing, the passage *Yism'chu*. The word itself tells us that Shabbat is a time to be happy. Echoing Isaiah 58:13, it refers to *korei oneg*, "the ones who call Shabbat a delight." What must I do to make Shabbat delightful? Where can we find delight? What do we do to achieve it? We call the refreshments after services *oneg*, but that is only one way to enjoy Shabbat. Listening to the cantor, singing along, finding new meanings in a prayer, being inspired by a sermon, debating the meanings of words of Torah, a long quiet walk, a nap in a hammock in the shade on a sunny day, all can help us experience this sense of *oneg*.

Remembering Shabbat, seeking holiness, avoiding the work of my occupation, catching my breath, recovering my soul, acknowledging a covenant, placing myself as a part of our people, and finding happiness and delight must be the goals of our contemporary Shabbat observance. We may find suggestions for specific behaviors to engage in or refrain from to help us achieve these goals in traditional halachah and other sources, but in our Reform way, while we may have suggestions, ultimately the individual will decide on the appropriate mechanisms. The formula may not be the same every week. We can't experience any of this, though, if we allow the day to be consumed by that which is *chol*—everyday, mundane, secular. There is ample time to return to that after *Havdalah*. Our tradition guides us to something more, not for the sake of obedience, but for our own sakes, physically, emotionally, and spiritually. We determine the path ourselves.

37

The Loneliness of Time

What We Can Learn from That First Shabbat

RABBI RICHARD F. ADDRESS

Completed now where heaven and earth and all their host. On the seventh day, God had completed the work that had been done, ceasing then on the seventh day from all the work that God had done. Then God blessed the seventh day and made it holy, and ceased from all the creative work that God had chosen to do.

Genesis 2:1–3

Time. No doubt, time is one of the great creations of humanity. Before primordial humankind decided to divide it into days, time was, in a very real sense, eternal. Humankind existed in the world and created time as a means, perhaps, of ordering its interaction with space. The creation of Shabbat remains one of the Jewish people's great contributions to humankind, but we have no conclusive idea of how this concept emerged. An essay in *The Torah: A Modern Commentary* reviews several well-known ideas. One is the pre-Hebrew *shapattu*, a day dedicated to the planet Saturn, yet

> We do not really know how and when the Sabbath developed
> into the central institution of Judaism—and why it alone of
> all cultic observances merited inclusion in the Decalogue. According to the Torah, it was instituted in the wilderness; many
> modern scholars believe that it took form only later on when
> Israel came in contact with the agricultural calendar of Canaan,
> and that only after many centuries it grew into a day of rest.[1]

The repetition of the Shabbat commandment in Exodus 20:8 and Deuteronomy 5:12 links the concept to two different words: in Exodus, *zachor*, "to remember"; and in Deuteronomy, *shamor*, "to observe." "To remember" implies that this concept existed before the writing of the chapter in Exodus, while "to observe" links Shabbat to the ideals provided by God. The remembering and observing speak to a larger value that is inherent in the beginning of Genesis that sees this idea of cessation as part of Creation. It is not as if Shabbat "completes" Creation in Genesis 1; rather it serves as a symbolic pause while we examine our place in the ongoing process of Creation.

The idea of linking Shabbat to Creation has become part of our belief system. We take the moment in the space of our weekly life, and we link it to Creation. By doing so we become part of the eternal process of Creation, a process in which we are charged to find our own path of life. This special, separated time becomes a way of creating, within the space of our life, moments of meaning. Heschel understood it through viewing Creation as an ongoing manifestation of our relationship with the Eternal:

> Creation, we are taught, is not an act that happened once upon
> a time, once and for ever. The act of bringing the world into

existence is a continuous process. God called the world into being, and that call goes on. There is this present moment because God is present. Every instant is an act of creation. A moment is not a terminal but a flash, a signal of Beginning. Time is perpetual innovation, a synonym for continuous creation.[2]

What can we take from this idea of continuous Creation? This concept has direct application for us. The technology-centered culture in which we live is mainly about, as Heschel wrote, the conquest of the world around us. This view of the world is focused on "man's conquest of space" and our desire to "subdue and manage the forces of nature."[3] Humankind is managing to do so despite the catastrophic costs. In the process of this conquest, however, we are confronted by the flip side of space, that of time. It is the one thing that despite any advances in technology, we cannot subdue. It is as if we created the concept of time in order to master the space of the world, yet time itself is beyond our ability to master. Our lives are a testimony to that very reality. We are born, we live, and we die; our time is finite, no matter how many material objects we have. This is the great religious concern: how do I bring meaning to the time I have?

Shabbat is not only a means to sanctify time in general, but also a means through which we can sanctify our time in particular. Marking Shabbat allows us to see ourselves within a larger context of history. It reminds us that our "time" is but part of time eternal and asks us to see the choices of how and why we do things within the context of a larger framework. It sends a message that time is given to us as a gift and that we are charged to see in this gift the ability to continually create and renew our own life and the time we have. The gift of Shabbat is the opportunity to use this sacred time not to produce but to reflect, not to acquire but to reenergize our soul, and in doing so, to create a better understanding of the holiness of our own existence.

There is another aspect of this linkage between Shabbat and the idea of ongoing Creation. Few cohorts are more aware of the eternality of time and our finite place within it than those of us who are confronting our own aging. There is a moment that slowly dawns on each of us that our place in this time continuum is limited. That realization is a profound spiritual moment. It changes us, often in not-so-subtle ways. A contributor to a website on aging recently described her "moment." She wrote of her lifelong relationships with time as a commodity, something that was measured and used to mark the to-do lists of life. "But in my late sixties, the relationship began to change. And now I am seventy-one, we are barely on speaking terms. The truth is, time terrifies me. And all the clichés seem to be true. Time flies."[4] She goes on to explore the shift in her relationship with time, commenting on the idea of an "obituary clock"—the feeling when she hears of people close to her age who die. She also explores the struggle of trying to figure out her relationship to time as she transitions from full-time work to the next chapter in her life. So many share this transitional stage in which we confront the limitations of our time while coming to accept that time itself will continue without us. She seems to echo a line from Heschel—"Living is not a private affair: it is what man does with God's time"[5]—when she asks, "Why can't I learn that I am a human being, not a human doing?"[6]

Creation implies a sense of doing. It is active. Many look at Shabbat as a somewhat passive event. It is a day of rest—a cessation from the rest of the week's pressures, of the desire to subdue and conquer space. Yet it is also a moment in time that we designate as "holy"—as something special and, in a way, unique. It is a time that we are asked to focus on things beyond our own selves and on our place within a larger historical continuum. It is a time when we are asked to forgo the rush of personal ego and satisfaction to reexamine our place in the universe. It is a moment when we light Shabbat candles and say the blessings, to be reminded that we are part of this eternal unfolding of Creation.

The moment of rest is not to retreat from the world. Rather, it is a time to reimagine how we can best create a world and a life of blessing. It is a time when we are asked, "What are you doing with God's time?" It is a reminder that Jewish tradition says to us, no matter what our age, that every day is another opportunity to sanctify the time we have.

That creation of the Sabbath day as a symbol that highlights the creative aspect of life also speaks to another very personal need. One of the great fears of people as they age is that of isolation. The literature associated with spirituality, health, and aging is filled with examples of studies that prove that being in community, celebrating personal relationships, and continuing to foster and create those relationships are necessary methods to ensure a sense of meaning. This sense of meaning provides balance, texture, and purpose to life. The Jewish tradition knew this, which is why it is so difficult to practice Judaism in isolation. Shabbat echoes Genesis 2:18, in which God sees that it is not good for the first human to be alone. The power of community is part of Shabbat, be it with family, friends, or congregation. We are at our best and our most creative when we engage with people and nurture relationships. As we experience more of life, this reality becomes ever more present. The loneliness of too much time spent without people and relationships that once were so important destroys the sacred aspect of life. Too many people exist in a space that is isolated and alone, marking time rather than celebrating the time they have with others. Shabbat is a symbolic example of the need for community and the necessity to have no one exist alone, our own selves included.

As Shabbat begins in homes and congregations around the world, the melody of *L'chah Dodi* is often heard. That mystical song begins with the *shamor v'zachor* of Torah. While the historical origins of Shabbat may be unknown to us, the symbolic power of the day, and all that it represents, is a constantly evolving reality. This is a concept that speaks to each of us, calling us to remember and to observe; to celebrate the time we have been given and to always be open to the creative possibilities that have been given to us as a sacred gift.

Notes

1. Gunther Plaut and David E. S. Stein, eds., *The Torah: A Modern Commentary*, rev. ed. (New York: URJ Press, 2005), 492.

2. Abraham Joshua Heschel, *Between God and Man* (New York: Free Press, 1959), 229.

3. Ibid., 214.

4. Carole Leskin, "Tick Tock, I Hate The Clock!," Jewish Sacred Aging, March 22, 2016, http://jewishsacredaging.com/carole-leskin-tick-tock-i-hate-the-clock/.

5. Heschel, *Between God and Man*, 27.

6. Leskin, "Tick Tock."

40

Shabbat and Parenting

RABBI BENJAMIN DAVID

Completed now were heaven and earth and all their host. On the seventh day, God had completed the work that had been done, ceasing then on the seventh day from all the work that God had done. Then God blessed the seventh day and made it holy, and ceased from all the creative work that God had chosen to do.

Genesis 2:1–3

Every time I walk through its towering gates, Camp Harlam returns me to my childhood. Harlam is where I saw a Reform Judaism that was vibrant and fresh. There were rabbis who inspired me with their wit and empathy, an environment that celebrated great imagination. I can close my eyes and picture it still, years removed from those days. When I was a kid, Harlam took me to the most fundamental version of myself and my Judaism.

If camp offers us the space to return to who we are at our core and to truly embrace our Judaism, then Shabbat at camp, stripped of pretense and fanfare, does so to an even greater degree. My friends and I felt free to pray, sing, and discuss in ways that were different from the rest of the week. There was no worry about being judged. Shabbat was rooted in music, food, and fun. I remember how the rabbis' *divrei Torah* summoned such luminaries as Jacob, Moses, and Miriam, encouraging us to go find our own unique place in Judaism too.

Now, as a parent, I think about what Shabbat might mean not only for me, but for my children. Ours is a world that relentlessly pushes kids to adulthood. It is a world where technology rules, the fleeting sound bite runs rampant, schedules are crammed, and clothing is constantly going out of style. But Shabbat can provide them with an antidote to this harried life, offering the kind of freedom and reassurance that I felt as a camper. Maybe Shabbat can allow a twenty-first-century kid to be a kid again.

In her acclaimed book *The Blessing of a Skinned Knee*, author Wendy Mogel writes, "The sages advise us to study Torah *lishma*—'for its own sake'—rather than to impress others with our scholarship. A paradox of parenting is that if we love our children for their own sake rather than for their achievements, it's more likely that they will reach their true potential."[1]

In a time obsessed with achievement, SAT scores, and the number of AP courses our teens are taking, can Shabbat give us the space to "love our children for their own sake"? What if, after the dire busyness of the week and the never-ending quest for tangible accolades, Shabbat brought us back to those most sacred elements of parenting and, with that, the most pure and enduring connection with our loved ones?

Shabbat need not be set at Jewish overnight camp or around the most traditional Friday night table to be meaningful. Rather, it can be lived fully through time spent outside, a break from screens, or opportunities to reflect and learn at synagogue with family and community. Indeed our twenty-first-century synagogues offer so much more than worship services. There are family education programs, book discussions, study groups, and myriad social action projects that infuse today's Shabbat with great breadth and power. The "cathedral in time," referenced by Rabbi Abraham Joshua Heschel, thus becomes a vital alternative to our increasingly hectic lives, offering room to deeply connect with one another and ground ourselves firmly in tradition.

Wendy Mogel continues:

Unsure how to find grace and security in the complex world we've inherited, we try to fill up the spaces in our children's lives with stuff: birthday entertainments, lessons, rooms full of toys and equipment, tutors and therapists. But material pleasures can't buy peace of mind, and all the excess leads to more anxiety—parents fear that their children will not be able to sustain this rarefied lifestyle and will fall off the mountain the parents have built for them.[2]

While the first six days of Creation emphasize the production of materials, this seventh day introduces something else entirely. Shabbat is a mind-set, a revolution in the way that we conceptualize of ourselves and those around us. Our prayer book reminds us that on Shabbat we "are called upon to share in what is eternal in time, to turn from the results of creation to the mystery of creation, from the world of creation to the creation of the world."[3]

How can we tap into and embrace the mysteries of Creation, the glowing aura of our Sabbath? The midrashic work *B'reishit Rabbah* teaches that God "blessed the Sabbath with radiance in one's face; hallowed it with radiance in one's face. The radiance on weekdays is not like that on the Sabbath" (11:2).

Whether or not our Sages had it in mind, we might wonder whether the radiance waiting to be discovered on Shabbat is a totally different type of radiance than we could ever attain in the boardroom or our kids could earn in the classroom, on the basketball court, or in the dance studio. The reward of Shabbat spent with family—a Shabbat infused with meaning and love—could never be likened to any grade or aptitude test. The blessing of a child coming to look forward to Shabbat and see it as very much their own cannot be quantified like a math final.

Finally, Shabbat also takes on new meaning in an age that is too often defined by divisiveness. When our kids grow up painfully aware of the countless shootings and acts of violence that fill our news feed, Shabbat comes to mean more. It becomes a safe haven, a place of comfort and acceptance far removed from a world of too prominent hatred. Sitting with our child in the synagogue pew on Shabbat offers stability and calm in a world marked by gross acts of violence. Putting a hand atop our child's at the end of a long week offers our chaotic world's best version of reassurance. These are ways of conveying to our young ones that they are loved, and not only by us, but by a Jewish community forever embodying empathy and peace.

Anne LaMott shares the following reflection in *Operating Instructions: A Journal of My Son's First Year*:

I heard an old man speak once, someone who had been sober for fifty years, a very prominent doctor. He said that he'd finally figured out a few years ago that his profound sense of control, in the world and over his life, is another addiction and a total illusion. He said that when he sees little kids sitting in the back seat of cars, in those car seats that have steering wheels, with grim expressions of concentration on their faces, clearly convinced that their efforts are causing the car to do whatever it is doing, he thinks of himself and his relationship with God: God who drives along silently, gently amused, in the real driver's seat.[4]

In a world that is desperately unpredictable, Shabbat provides us and our children predictability and consistency: the rhythm of *L'chah Dodi* and the pulse of our liturgy, the familiar faces, the calm of silent prayer, the familiar flow of the processional, and the rhythmic cadence of the Mourner's *Kaddish*. Shabbat has the power to bless our lives with tranquility and community precisely when we need it most. Anchored in moments of reflection and prayer, blessing and song, we find a chance to revel in the glow of our children, the peace of our tradition, and the beauty of pause.

Notes

1. Wendy Mogel, *The Blessing of a Skinned Knee* (New York: Scribner, 2001), 60.

2. Ibid., 32.

3. *Mishkan T'filah: A Reform Siddur* (New York: CCAR Press, 2007), 329.

4. Anne LaMott, *Operating Instructions: A Journal of My Son's First Year* (New York: Pantheon, 1993), 113.

41

Shabbat and Social Justice

RABBI JONAH DOV PESNER

God then surveyed all that [God] had made, and look—it was very good!

Genesis 1:31

Shabbat is a day of rest. It is a day of joy. It is a day of peace. When we think of Shabbat, we think of the savory smell of challah baking, festive singing, time with family, delicious meals, and sweet wine. The Sabbath is a day of such joy, that as Rabbi Theodore Friedman has shown, the classical Rabbis understood it as a taste of *olam haba*, "the world-to-come"[1]—a messianic time of perfection in which "every man will sit under his vine and beneath his fig tree, and none will make them afraid" (Micah 4:4). Some examples from Rabbinic literature include a Talmudic reference to a time when *yom shekulo Shabbat*, "every day is Shabbat."[2] Another reference states, "Israel said before the Holy One of Blessing, 'Master of the world, if we observe the commandments, what reward will we have?' God said to them, 'The world-to-come.' They said to God, 'Show us its likeness.' He showed them the Sabbath."[3] Finally, the classical commentator Nachmanides comments on Genesis 2:3

301

saying, "The seventh day is an indication of the world-to-come that is all Sabbath."

The point is, Shabbat is much more than a day of rest, celebration, and joy. Shabbat is arguably the Jewish practice that may embody the essence of Judaism more than any other. It would be tempting to limit the power of Shabbat to a day of eating, drinking, and sleeping. Because Shabbat is a taste of *olam haba*, the world-to-come that is perfected and repaired, observing the Sabbath invites us individually and collectively to experience the world as it should be—a world made whole. At its best, the world we inhabit one day a week is one of abundance, equality, and freedom. Grounded in the Genesis story of Creation, it is a day in which the entire world and all its inhabitants experience a taste of Eden-like tranquility.

It is for this reason that I would argue that ultimately Shabbat is a call to action. Though on the seventh day we experience the world as it should be, the other six days a week we inhabit the world as it is. The "real world" is broken. It is a world of scarcity, inequality, and oppression.

Therefore, while Shabbat is a day of rejoicing, it also has the power to agitate. As we celebrate the earth's abundance and our own Shabbat bounty, we recognize humanity's failure to steward Creation and listen for the cries of those who suffer in hunger; as we rejoice in our freedom, we also witness the ongoing oppression, injustice, and hate that plague humanity. Shabbat pushes us to see injustice in our world—to worry for those who cry out in hunger around us, to mourn the loss of our natural resources, and to rage against the forces of oppression and injustice that plague humanity. We cannot see these evils and not act. This is why Shabbat is a call to action. It is as important to be outraged by all that is broken as it is to rejoice in all that is good on God's earth.

Rabbi Abraham Joshua Heschel wrote in *Moral Grandeur and Spiritual Audacity*: "Prayer is meaningless unless it is subversive, unless it seeks to overthrow and to ruin the pyramids of callousness, hatred, opportunism, falsehood. The liturgical movement must become a revolutionary movement, seeking to overthrow the forces that continue to destroy the promise, the hope, and the vision."[4]

I would argue that Shabbat embodies what Heschel calls "the promise, the hope, and the vision." Our rituals, observances, and celebrations of the seventh day all seek to fulfill the promise of Creation, to inspire our hope for redemption, and to depict a vision of *tikkun olam*, a world repaired. Yet, as Heschel notes, our prayers must also be subversive and revolutionary, calling us to confront the forces of destruction and hate.

I believe that through prayer and ritual, Shabbat calls us to action regarding three clear themes: stewardship of Creation, freedom (for all people), and equality.

The Rabbis understood the connection between appreciating God's Creation and the human responsibility for stewardship. They taught in the classical midrash: "When God created Adam, God led him around the Garden of Eden and said to him, 'Behold my works. See how wonderful and beautiful they are. All that I have created, for your sake did I create it. Now see to it that you do not spoil and destroy My world, for if you do, there will be no one to repair it after you.'"[5]

Notice the artful connection the Rabbis make between appreciating the beauty of Creation to the call to action, in defense of the planet. If Shabbat is the time to rejoice in the grandeur, the miracle of the universe, it is also the time to recommit to our role as stewards.

The human responsibility to steward Creation is made clearer in a critical passage found in the Torah, Leviticus 25:2–5, which teaches:

When you enter the land that I assign to you, the land shall observe a Sabbath of the Eternal. Six years you may sow your field and six years you may prune your vineyard and gather in the yield. But in the seventh year the land shall have a Sabbath of complete rest, a Sabbath of the Eternal: you shall not sow your field or prune your vineyard. You shall not reap the aftergrowth of your harvest or gather the grapes of your untrimmed vines; it shall be a year of complete rest for the land.

The text is teaching us that just as humans need the restorative power of Shabbat, the land itself needs it as well. Rabbi Noam Yehuda Sendor has argued that "the earth needs to rest as an ecological necessity, just as people need to rest as a spiritual necessity." He continues, writing that *Sh'mitah* (the Sabbatical year) "represents an ideal, an expanded perspective which seeks out meaning in all experiences and moves us to treat the world around us, and its fruits, with the sanctity they deserve."[6] Shabbat, like *Sh'mitah*, represents that "ideal" of Creation, well-tended and in balance.

Just as Shabbat calls us to provide rest for the earth, it reminds us that rest for human beings is an imperative of social justice. The opposite of freedom is slavery, the ultimate form of oppression by some human beings over others. The Rabbis made the link clear between Shabbat and freedom in the traditional blessing over the wine, recited on Friday night: "You [God] made the holy Shabbat our heritage as a reminder of the work of Creation. As first among our sacred days, it recalls the Exodus from Egypt." Shabbat reminds us that we are children of God (created in God's image), not instruments of Pharaoh or any other oppressor.

The Rabbis' connection between Shabbat and freedom from the slavery of Egypt is first made in the Torah, Deuteronomy 5:12–17:

Observe the Sabbath Day and keep it holy, as the Eternal your God has commanded you. Six days shall you labor and do all your work, but the seventh day is a Sabbath of the Eternal your God; you shall not do any work—you, your son or your daughter, your male or female slave, your ox or your ass, or any of your cattle, or the stranger in your settlements, so that your male and female slave may rest as you do. Remember that you were a slave in the land of Egypt, and the Eternal your God freed you from there with a mighty hand and an outstretched arm; therefore the Eternal your God has commanded you to observe the Sabbath Day.

The Torah text issues several critical commands related to Shabbat that amplify the underlying values of the sacred day. First, in connecting Shabbat to the Exodus from Egypt, we are reminded that freedom is a gift, and we are obligated to celebrate Shabbat in part to affirm God's redemption of us from slavery into freedom. Second, Shabbat applies to everyone in the community—Jew and non-Jew alike—including servants. Finally, similar to the land itself observing Shabbat through the Sh'mitah (Sabbatical year), animals also rest on the Sabbath Day. The inclusion of animals reinforces the notion of human stewardship of all Creation through Shabbat.

Perhaps the most radical aspect of the Deuteronomy text is that every human being enjoys the Sabbath, including slaves. Clearly the ancient Israelites significantly reformed the notion of servitude and the justice due to even to those whom we would call slaves. It is important to note that in historical context, slaves in Israel were more like indentured servants who entered into service for financial reasons, and in the Jubilee year the Torah required that all slaves were freed and debts annulled. Since its very inception, Shabbat obligates the Children of Israel to treat all workers ethically and, even more radically, to see every human being (Jew and non-Jew alike) as deserving of freedom, equality, and justice.

In conclusion, let us return to what Rabbi Abraham Joshua Heschel wrote in the seminal source The Sabbath:

The meaning of the Sabbath is to celebrate time rather than space. Six days a week we live under the tyranny of things of space; on the Sabbath we try to become attuned to holiness in *time.* It is a day on which we are called upon to share in what is eternal in time, to turn from the results of creation to the mystery of creation; from the world of creation to the creation of the world.[7]

Let us remember that Heschel was also the very same rabbi who marched with Dr. Martin Luther King, Jr. in Selma and described it as if "my legs were praying." He famously wrote, "Morally speaking, there is no limit to the concern one must feel for the suffering of human beings, that indifference to evil is worse than evil itself, that in a free society, some are guilty, but all are responsible."[8]

On Shabbat we taste perfection—and then we are called to action, responsible for the well-being of the earth itself and for all those who suffer amidst the brokenness of injustice.

Notes

1. Theodore Friedman, "Shabbat as a Preview of the Perfected World," *Judaism* 16, no. 4 (Fall 1967).

2. *Mishnah Tamid* 7:4.

3. *Otiot D'Rabbi Akiva.*

4. Abraham Joshua Heschel, "On Prayer," in *Moral Grandeur and Spiritual Audacity: Essays*, ed. Susannah Heschel (New York: Farrar, Straus and Giroux, 1996), 263.

5. *Kohelet Rabbah* 7:13.

6. Noam Yehuda Sendor, "Lessons from *Shmita*, the Sabbatical Year," Aytzim, http://aytzim.org/resources/articles/276.

7. Abraham Joshua Heschel, *The Sabbath* (New York: Farrar, Straus and Giroux, 1951), 10.

8. Abraham Joshua Heschel, *Moral Grandeur and Spiritual Audacity: Essays* (New York City: Farrar, Straus and Giroux, 1996), 225.

42

Shabbat And Workers' Rights
RABBI ELLEN LIPPMANN

Completed now were heaven and earth and all their host. On the seventh day, God had completed the work that had been done, ceasing then on the seventh day from all the work that God had done. Then God blessed the seventh day and made it holy, and ceased from all the creative work that God had chosen to do.

Genesis 2:1–3

As we go marching, marching, in the beauty of the day
A million darkened kitchens, a thousand mill lofts gray
Are touched with all the radiance that a sudden sun discloses
For the people hear us singing, bread and roses, bread and roses.

The song "Bread and Roses" originated with a speech given by Jewish labor leader Rose Schneiderman; a line in her speech ("The worker must have bread, but she must have roses, too") inspired the title of the poem "Bread and Roses" by poet, novelist, and editor James Oppenheim, first published in the *American Magazine* in December 1911.

It was later set to music most famously by 1960s' songwriter Mimi Farina.

The intertwined themes of bread and roses—sustenance and dignity, the mundane and the sacred—recur again and again in all labor struggles. We Jews might call these themes "Bread and Shabbat," our own intertwining of the workday and the Sabbath, of labor and sacred service, of perspiration and aspiration.

The Intertwining

It is Shabbat morning at Kolot Chayeinu/Voices of Our Lives, the congregation I founded and serve in Brooklyn, New York. We gather every Saturday morning to have breakfast together before services. It is a time to make a transition from home and street to prayer, song, and reflection—an acknowledgment of the need for additional elements of Shabbat for today's busy working people. As we gather, we join hands, and I say, "We are linked up like this for two reasons: One, to remember that when we join with others to break bread together, we can cross the divides that might otherwise separate us. Look around at the beautiful faces of the people you are breaking bread with—we are bridging that divide right now. And two, we honor the chain of work it takes for the bread—these bagels, this challah, this pita—to get from the way God created the wheat to the way it shows up here on this table. From God to whoever made or bought the bread, there is an important chain of work. And because workers in this country are not much honored these days, we add a bit of honor this way and recommit ourselves to helping them regain an honored place in society." Then we say *HaMotzi*, the prayer thanking God for having brought that bread from the ground.

Because Shabbat and workers' rights are intertwined, we celebrating Shabbat in Brooklyn, New York, each week decide to emphasize the connections. The word *avodah* means "sacred service," and it means "labor" or "work." Our prayer weaves in labor on our all-important day of rest, allowing or enabling Jews everywhere to recommit to the task of actively honoring workers here and now. For our progressive Jewish community in the twenty-first century, the workers we especially keep in mind are low-wage workers in the fast-food industry, car "washers," domestic workers like nannies and house or office cleaners, and warehouse workers for major companies. We keep them in mind as we move into our Shabbat prayer and rest, thus fortified by our food, our declared intentions, and our joining in community.

A Day of Rest: Foundation of Workers' Dignity

Dr. David Sperling of Hebrew Union College–Jewish Institute of Religion in New York used to say that Jews are the people who invented the week by creating a day that ended it. Without Shabbat, time might just unfold endlessly, unmarked, unbounded. That possibility undergirds many modern workers' grievances: seemingly endless days in endless weeks in endless years of work. Workers' rights originate in Jewish thinking with the idea of a day of rest. That rest is in the realm of the "roses," the dignity workers yearn for, while pushing for wage increases, like the recent "fight for $15" (dollars an hour) is the "bread," the sustenance, for the labor.

From the idea of a day of rest flows the possibility of a lunch hour, family leave, even bathroom breaks—time away from the work itself that offers some dignity to workers, especially those engaged in apparently menial tasks. These workers are not simply the means of labor, but human beings with their own physical and emotional needs. The day of rest also offers overworked professionals the chance for a break; initiatives like "Shabbat Unplugged" (an adaption of our ancestors' ritual of carving out one day per week to unwind, unplug, relax, reflect, get outdoors, and connect with loved ones) give the opportunity for a day without e-mail or Facebook or any social media, a day to rest brains and eyes and spirits.

God's own rest on the seventh day after six days of the work of Creation (Genesis 2:1–3) offers our original model: we understand that we, created in God's image, can imitate God's work ethic and take a day of rest. We too must have a time to *shavat vayinafash*—to rest and refresh our souls. Life is not all drudgery; each week we can return to Eden by resting, eating well, praying our gratitude, spending time with loved ones. Shabbat is, as Abraham Joshua Heschel wrote, "the first holy object in the history of the world . . . on the Sabbath we try to become attuned to holiness in time."[1] But that holiness in time does not just happen. It must be stated, allowed for, entered with intent: "He [*sic*] who wants to enter the holiness of the day must first lay down the profanity of clattering commerce, of being yoked to toil. . . . The world has our hands, but our soul belongs to Someone Else."[2]

Jews have a particular historical memory that leads us to identify with and support the downtrodden workers of today. The first "workers" to benefit from the foundational Jewish understanding of Genesis were those whose story lives most deeply in Jewish hearts thanks to millennia of Passover seders: the ancient Hebrew slaves, groaning under the harsh bondage inflicted by Egyptian taskmasters. For these slaves, the gift of a day of rest was an unheard-of luxury, a yearned-for possibility in a place of no-possibility. When they were freed from slavery, their first attention was to the need for food. In watching them gather God-given manna, God reminds them—have they heard this before?—"Mark that it is the Eternal who, having given you the Sabbath, therefore gives you two days' food on the sixth day. Let everyone remain in place: let no one leave the vicinity on the seventh day. So the people remained inactive on the seventh day" (Exodus 16:29–30). This initial Shabbat instruction has strict boundaries; the Sabbath is so important that it must be enforced, an uncomfortable irony for the modern non-Orthodox reader grappling with the dual desires for a self-defined day of rest and a communally defined Sabbath. But for our ancient, recently freed ancestors, the enforcement made rest possible for those who had never known it. Manna and Shabbat, bread and roses.

How sadly surprising, then, to learn from labor lawyer Liz Vladeck[3] that in the United States, a country often described as Judeo-Christian (and we might add Muslim, to complete the three-part definition of "Abrahamic faiths"),

> federal law has no blanket prohibition on requiring employees to work seven days a week. . . . . Maine is actually the only state that puts a cap on total hours that can be required to be worked in a two-week period. In New York, nurses cannot be required to work mandatory overtime. And New York requires one day off in seven for certain categories of workers. None of this addresses the issue of religious accommodations whereby due to a person's faith, they may have an entitlement to observe a day of rest as prescribed by their religion.[4]

Commandments

I asked Vladeck if there are any sort of commandments for labor organizing today. The commandments for Shabbat in Jewish tradition, most especially in the Ten Commandments and in the many labor laws that developed in Talmudic and later sources, speak to an ethical foundation for such undertakings. Her answer:

> A good place to start might be the International Labor Organization, the closest thing the world has to a global oversight body on labor issues. Since their founding they have promulgated a number of what are called "Core Conventions."
>
> What has always been interesting to me is that the Core Conventions don't relate to substantive/material labor standards—minimum wages, health and safety, time off, etc.,—but rather to structural/process issues. They relate to the right of both individuals and workers acting collectively to take action, have liberty, have agency with regard to the terms on which they will labor.

Forcing employers to follow labor "commandments" remains one of the greatest challenges. In most cases, employers
will definitely *not* do the right thing *unless* that thing is written
down, and then *unless* the writing is accompanied by a meaningful enforcement mechanism.

For Jews, the writing down of the "labor commandments" and the
possibility of their enforcement comes in the Talmud and later Rabbinic texts. Rabbi Jill Jacobs, in her *t'shuvah* "Work, Workers, and the
Jewish Owner," reminds us of a well-known story in the Talmud that
for her was "one of the best-known and most powerful statements of
the responsibility of employers toward their workers' demands that
employers go above and beyond the letter of the law in caring for their
workers"[5]:

> Some porters working for Raba bar bar Hanan broke a jug of
> wine. He seized their clothes. They came before Rav, and Rav
> said to Raba bar bar Hanan, "Give them their clothing." Raba
> bar bar Hanan said to him, "Is this the law?" Rav said, "Yes,
> because of the principle 'You should walk in the ways of the
> good' (Proverbs 2:20)." He gave them back their clothes. They
> said to him, "We are poor, and we troubled ourselves to work
> all day and we are needy—do we receive nothing?" Immedi-
> ately, Rav said to Raba bar bar Hanan, "Go, give them their
> wages." He said to Rav, "Is this the law?" Rav said, "Yes—'you
> should keep the ways of the righteous' (ibid.)" (Babylonian Tal-
> mud, *Bava M'tzia* 83a)

Responsibility

Our responsibility, then, as modern Jews who observe Shabbat in a
range of ways, is multidimensional:

1. As workers ourselves, we must push ourselves to take a day of rest each week, combining physical rest with spiritual nourishment.
2. As employers, we must remember the roses as well as the bread. We must remember that at the beginning of the world, as Torah tells it, we humans were created *b'tzelem Elohim,* "in the image of God" (Genesis 1:27). It is said that we combine the traits of angels and animals, heaven and earth, aspiration and determination. So too every human worker, and we employers must never forget that our employees, be they our nanny or our secretary or our deputy, need the roses as well as the bread.
3. As advocates, we must organize and urge raising wages (bread) and conditions that foster dignity (roses).

Dr. Jonathan Gold of Princeton University, teaching about *Vayikra* in a recent Torah study session, brought some of the work of Georges Bataille, a twentieth-century French intellectual and literary figure. This text reminded the group that the sacrifices enumerated in Leviticus were an early attempt to connect to the Divine at times of joy and sorrow, guilt and error, profound well-being. This divine connection, he posited, is one way that human beings try to escape a life of unbroken drudgery and its dehumanizing degradation:

> The first labor established the world of *things,* to which the profane world of the Ancients generally corresponds. Once the world of things was posited, man [*sic*] himself became one of the things of this world, at least for the time in which he labored. It is this degradation that man has always tried to escape.[6]

Similarly, the Passover Haggadah reminds us, "Our story begins in degradation and ends in praise." As we move through the Haggadah's tale, we move with our ancient ancestors as they suffer under slavery and eventually celebrate the astonishment of freedom. We are asked to see ourselves as if we had been slaves; as if we had escaped to freedom. Only by doing so can we become confident workers, just employers, and fair advocates.

Our freedom is exemplified by the gift of a day of rest every week. Shabbat is a taste of Eden once again, the blessing of rest after hard work, the bouquet of roses when expecting only bread.

No more the drudge and idler, ten that toil where one reposes,
But a sharing of life's glories, bread and roses, bread and roses.

Notes

1. Abraham Joshua Heschel, *The Sabbath* (New York City: Farrar, Straus, Giroux, 1951), 9-10.

2. Ibid., 13.

3. At the time of this writing, Vladeck was an attorney with the firm Cary Kane. She is now Head of Labor Policy and Standards for the City of New York.

4. E-mail correspondence with Liz Vladeck, March 2016.

5. Jill Jacobs, *There Shall Be No Needy: Pursuing Social Justice through Jewish Law and Tradition* (Woodstock VT: Jewish Lights Publishing, 2009), 105.

6. Georges Bataille, *The Accursed Share: An Essay on General Economy*, vol. 1, *Consumption*, trans. Robert Hurley (New York: Zone Books, 1988), 57.

Contributors

Rabbi Richard F. Address, DMin, is founder and director of Jewish Sacred Aging (jewishsacredaging.com). He was ordained by Hebrew Union College–Jewish Institute of Religion in 1972 and has served congregations in California and New Jersey, as well as serving as regional director of the Union for Reform Judaism and founder and director of the URJ Department of Jewish Family Concern.

Rabbi Dr. Yehoyada Amir, is a theologian, educator, and a scholar of Jewish thought. He is professor of Jewish thought at Hebrew Union College–Jewish Institute of Religion in Jerusalem and the president of MARAM (the Israel Council of Reform Rabbis). His academic works deal with a wide range of modern Jewish philosophers, including some of the major European, Israeli, and American thinkers who designed modern and postmodern Judaism. His theological work takes this treasure of human and Jewish thought as a point of departure for the making of an up-to-date Jewish, dialogical constructive theology, fruitful for enhancing contemporary Jewish and Israeli life as well as responsible and sincere interfaith dialogue. He is the author of *Reason out of Faith: The Philosophy of Franz Rosenzweig* (Hebrew, 2004); *Small Still Voice: Theological Critical Reflections* (Hebrew, 2009); and *The Renewal of Jewish Life in Nachman Krocmal's Philosophy* (forthcoming, 2017).

Alex Cicelsky is a founding member of Kibbutz Lotan, established by the Reform Movement as a vanguard for pluralistic and egalitarian Jewish expression in Israel. He studied agriculture at Cornell University, established the dairy on Lotan, and then completed his BSc in soil and water science at the Hebrew University Faculty of Agriculture. He worked in science education at the Weissman Institute of Science and developed some of the first hands-on environmental education programs for the Havayeda—Israel's Experiential Science Museum. This experience led him and other Kibbutz Lotan members to establish the Center for Creative Ecology, a pioneering research, development, and education center, which garnered national attention for its work in recycling, construction of energy efficient housing from natural materials, and development of a nature reserve for migratory birds. Alex continues researching energy-efficient construction with Ben Gurion University while teaching on Lotan and lecturing worldwide on Judaism, sustainable technologies, and the connections between environmental protection and peace.

Rabbi Mike Comins is founding director of the Jewish online education center Lev Learning (LevLearning.com), teaches the Making Prayer Real course and curriculum he created (www.MakingPrayer-Real.com), and directs the TorahTrek Center for Jewish Wilderness Spirituality (www.TorahTrek.org). A yeshivah-trained, Israeli-ordained Reform rabbi and a licensed Israeli desert guide, he holds an MA in Jewish education (Hebrew University) with an emphasis in contemporary philosophy. He is the author of *Making Prayer Real: Leading Jewish Spiritual Voices on Why Prayer is Difficult and What to Do about It* and *A Wild Faith: Jewish Ways into Wilderness, Wilderness Ways into Judaism*.

Rabbi Shoshanah Conover serves as the Associate Rabbi at Temple Sholom of Chicago. She is a Senior Rabbinic Fellow of the Shalom Hartman Institute and a vice-chair of Chicago's Jewish Community Relations Council. She serves on the Executive Committee of the Chicago Board of Rabbis, as well as the Union of Reform Judaism's Commission on Social Action. She received AVODAH's Partner in Tzedek Award and enjoys co-hosting the podcast *The Chosen Films*.

Rabbi Benjamin David is the senior rabbi of Adath Emanu-El in Mount Laurel, New Jersey. He previously served as associate rabbi at Temple Sinai in Roslyn, New York, and has taught and interned at such places as the 92nd Street Y, the Jewish Guild for the Blind, Temple Shaaray Tefila of Manhattan, and Temple Beth Am of Monessen, Pennsylvania. A competitive marathon runner, he is a co-founder of the Running Rabbis, a social justice initiative that aims to bring attention to important causes across the religious spectrum. His wife, Lisa, is the director of URJ Camp Harlam, the same camp where the two of them met as kids. They are the proud parents of Noa, Elijah, and Samuel.

Rabbi Karen Deitsch attained her bachelor's degree in psychology in 1996 from the University of California, Los Angeles, and was ordained by Hebrew Union College–Jewish Institute of Religion in New York in May 2004. In between her BA and her ordination, she received certification as a clinical hypnotherapist, classical homeopath, and Aura-Soma color therapist, trained in Chinese medicine at the Emperor's College in Los Angeles, and worked as an educator and adviser at schools in both California and Sydney, Australia. Following her ordination, she served Congregation Ahavat Shalom in Northridge, California, taught at the Milken Day School and the American Jewish University, and was a contributing writer for the *Jewish Journal of Greater Los Angeles*. She has since been working in Venice Beach, California, as a spiritual adviser/educator for individuals, couples, families, and conscious businesses and as a ritualist and holistic facilitator with the members of her growing community.

Rabbi Fred Scherlinder Dobb, DMin, has served Adat Shalom Reconstructionist Congregation since his ordination from Philadelphia's Reconstructionist Rabbinical College. He is the chairperson of the Coalition on the Environment and Jewish Life, a past President of the Washington Board of Rabbis, active with the National Religious Partnership for the Environment and Interfaith Power and Light, and the proud father of two.

Loui Dobin is the executive director of the URJ Greene Family Camp, beginning as camp director in 1978. Prior to his arrival in Texas, Loui attended New York University. As a musician, Loui was one of the founding members of the Jewish musical group Kol B'seder, and participated in a number of recording projects. He's been a composer, song leader and performer. He has also found time to become a licensed pilot and emergency medical technician. Loui lives in Temple, Texas with his wife Sheila, a geneticist, and his dog Shayna. Loui and Sheila are the proud parents of Jonathan and Zachary, both longtime campers and staff members at Greene, now all grown up.

Cantor Ellen Dreskin (www.ellendreskin.com) is an innovative leader in today's Reform Movement. Her expertise extends from music to synagogue transformation, from experiential education to enlivened liturgy and mysticism. She has worked as a scholar-in-residence with Jews of all denominations from Houston to Chicago and Los Angeles to Boston, has served as cantor and educator for congregations in Cleveland and New York, and has taught for many years at URJ Summer Kallot, Hava Nashira, URJ Kutz Camp Leadership Academy, and numerous other national conferences and educational seminars. Ellen is a graduate of Hebrew Union College–Jewish Institute of Religion's Debbie Friedman School of Sacred Music, has a master's degree in Jewish communal service from Brandeis University, and is proud to have received her honorary doctorate of music from HUC-JIR in 2011. She is a synagogue consultant and clergy coach in the areas of liturgical innovation, personal prayer practice, and communal worship skills. She is married to Rabbi Billy Dreskin and is extremely proud of their joint projects: Katie, Jonah (z"l), and Aiden.

Rabbi Denise L. Eger is the founding rabbi of Congregation Kol Ami in West Hollywood, California, and the immediate past president of the Central Conference of American Rabbis. She is a noted activist for civil and human rights. She is married to Rabbi Eleanor Steinman and is the proud mother of Benjamin.

Rabbi Rayna Gevurtz is currently serving Temple Bat Yahm in Newport Beach, California. She is married to Rabbi Gershon Zylberman, and together they rejoice in their three vegan daughters, Adira, Noa, and Mira, and their shnoodle, Elisheva Shnitzel. Rabbi Gevurtz wrote her rabbinic thesis on *tzaar baalei chayim* (the prevention of animals' suffering) and the issue of factory farming and is a passionate animal rights spokesperson in her community.

Rabbi Edwin Cole Goldberg, DHL, is the senior rabbi of Temple Sholom of Chicago. He served as coordinating editor of *Mishkan HaNefesh* and has published numerous books.

Alyssa M. Gray, JD, PhD, is the Emily S. and Rabbi Bernard H. Mehlman Chair in Rabbinics and professor of codes and responsa literature at Hebrew Union College–Jewish Institute of Religion in New York. She is the author of *A Talmud in Exile: The Influence of Yerushalmi Avodah Zarah on the Formation of Bavli Avodah Zarah* (2005) and the co-editor of *Studies in Mediaeval Halakhah in Honor of Stephen M. Passamaneck* (2007). Gray was also a contributor to *My People's Prayer Book* (vols. 6–10), *My People's Passover Haggadah*, and *The Torah: A Women's Commentary*. She has published numerous scholarly articles, as well as essays for wider audiences on topics such as *tzedakah*, history of halachah (Jewish law), and the formation of the Talmud. She has been a visiting professor at Yale University and the Jewish Theological Seminary and is a sought-after presenter at academic conferences as well as in synagogues and other Jewish settings.

Dr. Rachel Havrelock is associate professor of English and Jewish studies at the University of Illinois at Chicago. Long engaged with questions of gender and geography, she is the co-author of *Women on the Biblical Road* and the author of *River Jordan: The Mythology of a Dividing Line*. She served as the editor of the Early Judaism section for *The Oxford Handbook of the Bible and Gender Studies* and as a commentator for *The Torah: A Women's Commentary*. She is currently engaged with a monograph on political power and the Book of Joshua, tentatively titled *The Joshua Generation: Politics and the Promised Land*. She founded the Freshwater Lab, which focuses on the humanistic dimension of water management, and sits on the International Advisory Council for EcoPeace Middle East.

Rabbi Oren J. Hayon grew up in Columbus, Ohio. He received his undergraduate education at Rice University and was ordained by Hebrew Union College–Jewish Institute of Religion in 2004. He is the senior rabbi of Congregation Emanu El in Houston, Texas, and serves as a vice president of the Board of Trustees of the Central Conference of American Rabbis. He is an editor, translator, and author of Hebrew texts and poetry and an avid consumer of popular culture, literature, and technology.

Shaina Herring, RN, is currently a student nurse-midwife at Columbia University. She worked at ImmerseNYC, a community mikveh project, helping to educate the Jewish community about diverse and creative uses for mikveh. She is particularly interested in the intersection of women's health and religious practice and hopes to incorporate this interest into her professional work. She lives in New York City with her husband, Avi, and their son, Noam.

Rabbi Michael G. Holzman is the spiritual leader of Northern Virginia Hebrew Congregation. Before coming to Virginia, he was an associate rabbi and the director of youth learning at Congregation

Rodeph Shalom in Philadelphia, Pennsylvania. He is the editor of *The Still Small Voice: Reflections on Being a Jewish Man.*

Rabbi Jill Jacobs is the executive director of T'ruah: The Rabbinic Call for Human Rights, which mobilizes eighteen hundred rabbis and cantors and tens of thousands of American Jews to protect human rights in North America and Israel. She is the author of *Where Justice Dwells: A Hands-On Guide to Doing Social Justice in Your Jewish Community* (2011) and *There Shall Be No Needy: Pursuing Social Justice through Jewish Law and Tradition* (2009). Rabbi Jacobs has been named three times to the *Forward*'s list of fifty influential American Jews, to *Newsweek*'s list of the fifty most influential rabbis in America every year since 2009, and to the *Jerusalem Post*'s 2013 list of "Women to Watch." She holds rabbinic ordination and an MA in Talmud from the Jewish Theological Seminary, an MS in urban affairs from Hunter College, and a BA from Columbia University. She lives in New York with her husband, Guy Austrian, and their daughters, Lior and Dvir.

Cantor Amanda Kleinman serves as assistant cantor of Westchester Reform Temple in Scarsdale, New York.

Rabbi Kevin M. Kleinman is the associate rabbi, director of education at Main Line Reform Temple in Wynnewood, Pennsylvania. He previously served as associate rabbi at Reform Congregation Keneseth Israel in Elkins Park, Pennsylvania. He was ordained by Hebrew Union College–Jewish Institute of Religion in 2009. He was born and raised in Northern Virginia. After graduating from Brandeis University in 2002, he worked as a Jewish environmental educator at the Teva Learning Center in Falls Village, Connecticut, where he met his wife and life partner, Chana Rothman, a renowned Jewish musician. He and Chana are avid outdoor enthusiasts and passionate about working toward building a more sustainable and just world, guided by

Jewish values. They live in Philadelphia with their three children, Izzy, Yarden, and Misha.

Rabbi Jamie Korngold, known as the Adventure Rabbi, is the founder of Adventure Judaism, specializing in online education for bar and bat mitzvah students and outdoor retreats. She is an HUC-JIR ordained rabbi. Rabbi Jamie is the author of eleven books including *God in the Wilderness* (Doubleday) and the beloved Sadie and Ori series (Kar-Ben). Find her at www.AdventureRabbi.org.

Rabbi Ellen Lippmann is founder and rabbi of Kolot Chayeinu/Voices of Our Lives, building a progressive Jewish community in Brooklyn since 1993. She is the former East Coast director of MAZON: A Jewish Response to Hunger, and former director of the Jewish Women's Program at the New 14th Street Y in Manhattan. She was co-chair and still serves on the board of T'ruah: The Rabbinic Call for Human Rights. She is the founder of the Soup Kitchen at Hebrew Union College–Jewish Institute of Religion in New York and co-founder of the Children of Abraham Peace Walk: Jews, Christians and Muslims Walking Together in Brooklyn in Peace. She was ordained in 1991 by Hebrew Union College–Jewish Institute of Religion. Rabbi Lippmann and her wife are longtime Brooklyn residents and believe to be absolutely true what a Kolot Chayeinu member once said in jest: "It don't get any better than Brooklyn!"

Rabbi Sara Luria, founder and executive director of ImmerseNYC: A Community Mikveh Project, incorporates a passion for justice and feminist values into her work, as well as a belief in the transformational power of loving relationships. As a rabbinical student at Hebrew Union College–Jewish Institute of Religion (ordained 2013), she was a Tisch Leadership Fellow and is currently the program director for the fellowship. She graduated Phi Beta Kappa from Trinity College in

Hartford, Connecticut. She currently lives back in her hometown of Brooklyn with her husband, Isaac, and their young children, Caleb, Eva, and Judah.

Rabbi Jill L. Maderer is the senior rabbi at Congregation Rodeph Shalom in Philadelphia, Pennsylvania, where she has served since her ordination in 2001. She is immediate past co-chairperson of the Center City Kehillah, is immediate co-president of the Board of Rabbis of Greater Philadelphia, and currently serves on the Board of Trustees of the Jewish Federation of Greater Philadelphia. She proudly serves as a member of the faculty at URJ Camp Harlam.

Rabbi Rachel Grant Meyer is a social justice advocate, community organizer, rabbi, and educator. She hopes to help Jews of all ages live their most authentic life using Judaism as a guide. A graduate of Columbia University, she was ordained by Hebrew Union College–Jewish Institute of Religion in New York City. Prior to rabbinical school, she worked as a program associate in the KESHER College Department at the Union for Reform Judaism. After ordination, she served as assistant rabbi at Congregation Rodeph Sholom on Manhattan's Upper West Side. In June 2015, she joined HIAS as the director of education for community engagement, where she develops educational materials, resources, and programs that educate American Jews about the global refugee crisis through a Jewish lens. She also sits on the Steering Committee of Reform Jewish Voice of New York and is a rabbinic *chavera* of T'ruah: The Rabbinic Call for Human Rights.

Rabbi Dr. Rachel S. Mikva serves as the Herman Schaalman Chair in Jewish Studies and Senior Faculty Fellow for the InterReligious Institute at Chicago Theological Seminary. The institute and the seminary work at the cutting-edge of theological education, training religious leaders who build bridges across cultural and religious difference for the critical work of social transformation. She is the author of *Broken Tablets* (2000), *Midrash vaYosha* (2012), and *Dangerous Religious Ideas* (forthcoming).

Rabbi Geoffrey A. Mitelman is the founding director of Sinai and Synapses, an organization that bridges the scientific and religious worlds and is being incubated at Clal—The National Jewish Center for Learning and Leadership. His work has been supported by the John Templeton Foundation, Emanuel J. Friedman Philanthropies, and the Lucius N. Littauer Foundation, and his writings about the intersection of religion and science have appeared on the homepages of several sites, including the Huffington Post, Nautilus, Science and Religion Today, Jewish Telegraphic Agency, and My Jewish Learning. He has been an adjunct professor at both the Hebrew Union College–Jewish Institute of Religion and the Academy for Jewish Religion and is a sought-out teacher, presenter, and scholar-in-residence throughout the country. For seven years, he served as assistant and then associate rabbi of Temple Beth El of Northern Westchester in Chappaqua, New York, and appeared on *Jeopardy!* in March 2016. He lives in Westchester County with his wife, Heather Stoltz, a fiber artist, and their daughter and son.

Rabbi Scott M. Nagel is senior rabbi at Congregation Beth Ahabah in Richmond, Virginia. His love and passion for Judaism was fueled by the Union for Reform Judaism's youth and camping programs. He graduated from the University of Michigan in Ann Arbor and took a position as assistant director of the URJ's Kutz Camp, NFTY's National Leadership Center. He went on to Hebrew Union College–Jewish Institute of Religion, where he met his wife, Rabbi Randi Chudakoff Nagel. During his rabbinical training, he worked for HUC-JIR's Department of Youth Programs and had student pulpits in Rapid City, South Dakota, Selma, Alabama, and Piqua, Ohio, before coming to Temple Oheb Shalom in Baltimore, which he proudly served for twelve years until he was elected as the eleventh senior rabbi in the 225th year of Congregation Beth Ahabah in Richmond, Virginia. Rabbis Randi and Scott Nagel live in Richmond and have three sons, Daniel, Lev, and Ari.

Rabbi Aaron Panken, PhD, is president of Hebrew Union College–Jewish Institute of Religion, North America's premiere Jewish seminary, with campuses in Cincinnati, Jerusalem, Los Angeles, and New York. He has taught Rabbinic and Second Temple literature at HUC-JIR in New York since 1995. An alumnus of the Wexner Graduate Fellowship, he earned his doctorate in Hebrew and Judaic Studies at New York University, where his research focused on legal change in Rabbinic literature. Prior to teaching at HUC-JIR, he served congregations including Congregation Rodeph Sholom in New York City and Westchester Reform Temple in Scarsdale, New York. A native of New York City who graduated from Johns Hopkins University's Electrical Engineering Program, Rabbi Panken is also a certificated commercial pilot and sailor and lives with his wife and two children in the New York area. His publications include *The Rhetoric of Innovation* (2005), which explores legal change in Rabbinic texts, and numerous scholarly and popular writings.

Rabbi Jack P. Paskoff is the rabbi of Congregation Shaarai Shomayim in Lancaster, Pennsylvania, a position he has held since 1993. He is frequently called upon to speak at various community events, representing the Jewish community. He is also a voice in interfaith dialogue in Lancaster and is active in various social justice efforts in Central Pennsylvania. For eighteen years, he has served on the faculty of URJ Camp Harlam. He is married to Risa and is the father of Ari and Gadi.

Rabbi Jonah Dov Pesner has served as the director of the Religious Action Center of Reform Judaism since 2015. Rabbi Pesner also serves as senior vice president of the Union for Reform Judaism. Named one of the most influential rabbis in America by *Newsweek* magazine, he is an inspirational leader, creative entrepreneur, and tireless advocate for social justice. His signature accomplishment has been to encourage Jewish communities in efforts to reach across lines of race, class, and faith in campaigns for social justice. In 2006, he founded Just Congregations (now incorporated into the Religious Action Center), which engages countless clergy and professional and volunteer leaders in interfaith efforts for the common good. Ordained at Hebrew Union College–Jewish Institute of Religion in 1997, he was a congregational rabbi at Temple Israel in Boston and at Temple Israel in Westport, Connecticut. A graduate of Wesleyan University and the Bronx High School of Science, Rabbi Pesner is married to Dana S. Gershon, an attorney. They have four daughters: Juliet, Noa, Bobbie, and Cate.

Liya Rechtman is currently a dual-degree candidate for a Masters of Theological Studies at Harvard Divinity School and a Masters of Law and Diplomacy at the Tufts University Fletcher School as a Wexner Graduate Fellow/Davidson Scholar. She has published pieces in Lilith Magazine, Washington Jewish Week, JewSchool, The Energy Collective, and The Interfaith Observer. Previously, she was a Dorot Fellow '16-'17, a Legislative Assistant at the Religious Action Center of Reform Judaism and the Manager of the Coalition on the Environment and Jewish Life. She is a member of the Board of Trustees of the Association of Reform Zionists of American, the American Zionist Movement, and a member of the All That's Left Collective. She graduated from Amherst College Summa Cum Laude.

Rabbi Noa Sattath is the director of the Israel Religious Action Center, the social justice arm of the Reform Movement in Israel.

She is charged with leading the staff of the organization, developing and implementing social change strategies in the fields of separation of religion and state, women's rights, and the struggle against racism. Prior to her work at IRAC, she was the executive director of the Jerusalem Open House, the LGBT community center in Jerusalem. She was also the executive director of MEET, a nonprofit organization that uses technology to create a common language between Israeli and Palestinian young leaders. Prior to her work in civil society, she worked as a leader in the Israeli software industry. Rabbi Sattath is a graduate of the Hebrew University and Gratz College. She was ordained by the Hebrew Union College–Jewish Institute of Religion in 2014. She is a member of Congregation Kol Haneshama in Jerusalem.

Rabbi Kinneret Shiryon, DD, is the first woman to function as a rabbi in the history of the State of Israel. She was also the first woman to be elected as the head of a rabbinical organization; she served as the chairwoman of MARAM for two terms. She is the founding rabbi and leader of the community of YOZMA (Yahudut Z'maneinu Moreshest Ha'Am—Judaism of Our Time, Heritage of Our People). YOZMA is a progressive synagogue, community center, early childhood educational center, and elementary school in the city of Modi'in, Israel. It is one of the largest centers of Progressive Jewish life in the country. Rabbi Shiryon has also served communities in North America, Australia, New Zealand, and Thailand. She was married to Baruch Shiryon, z"l, and is the proud parent/grandparent of four children and three granddaughters.

Rabbi Matthew Soffer is a rabbi at Temple Israel of Boston, where he focuses on social justice work through community organizing, connecting young families to Jewish life, and worship innovation. Rabbi Soffer is the creator and host of *Pulpit on the Common*, a podcast on the dynamic intersection of faith and public life, produced by Temple Israel. As a musician and composer, Rabbi Soffer writes modern folk melodies for ancient liturgy, and as an amateur comedian he is part of "3 Rabbis Walk into a Bar," a comedy trio devoted to cultivating a sacred sense of humor. He serves on the board of the Jewish Alliance for Law and Social Action (JALSA), the Advisory Council for the Pluralism Project at Harvard University, and the Rabbinic Council of Hand-in-Hand Center for Jewish-Arab Education in Israel.

Rabbi Rifat Sonsino, PhD, born in Ankara, Turkey, is rabbi emeritus at Temple Beth Shalom in Needham, Massachusetts. He taught at Boston College and is now on the faculty of Framingham State University, Department of Philosophy/ Psychology.

Rabbi Joshua M. Z. Stanton is the rabbi of East End Temple in Manhattan. He serves on the Board of Governors of the International Jewish Committee for Interreligious Consultations, which liaises on behalf of Jewish communities worldwide with the Vatican and other international religious bodies. He is in the 2015–2016 cohort of Germanacos Fellows and was part of the inaugural group of Sinai and Synapses Fellows from 2013 to 2015. He served as associate rabbi at Congregation B'nai Jeshurun in Short Hills, New Jersey, and associate director of the Center for Global Judaism at Hebrew College. He was founding co-editor of the *Journal of Interreligious Studies*, a publication that has enabled interreligious studies to emerge as an academic field of its own.

Rabbi David E. S. Stein has been committed to enhancing American Jewish life via providing good tools for rabbis and supporting their efforts throughout his more than twenty-five years in the rabbinate. The most visible result is the stack of prominent books that he has helped to shape, most famously the *JPS Hebrew-English Tanakh* and the revised *The Torah: A Modern Commentary* (the Plaut *chumash*). Meanwhile, his well-honed analysis of texts has prompted original scholarship on a wide range of Jewish topics. Most recently he has been producing pieces on Biblical Hebrew for academic publications, displaying an abiding interest in the nouns אִישׁ and אִשָּׁה. He lives in Culver City, California, with his wife, Carole.

Rabbi Arthur Ocean Waskow, PhD, has since 1969 been one of the leading creators of theory, practice, and institutions for the movement for Jewish renewal, and has especially pioneered in developing the theology, practice, and activism of Eco-Judaism. He founded (1983) and directs The Shalom Center, a prophetic voice in Jewish, multi-religious, and American life—speaking for peace, eco-social justice, and healing of the Earth.

Rabbi Mira Beth Wasserman, PhD, bridges Talmud study, community building, and the pursuit of social justice through her work as a rabbi and scholar. She began her career as a congregational rabbi in Bloomington, Indiana, where she served for over a decade. Currently, she is assistant professor of Rabbinic literature at the Reconstructionist Rabbinical College, where her teaching and writing focus on bringing Rabbinic texts into conversation with contemporary life. Her recent book *Jews, Gentiles, and Other Animals* looks to Talmudic law and storytelling to investigate what it means to be a human being. Rabbi Wasserman's doctorate in Jewish studies is from the University of California at Berkeley, her rabbinic ordination is from Hebrew Union College–Jewish Institute of Religion, and she is an alumna of the Wexner Graduate Fellowship. She is the proud parent of four children.

Rabbi Dr. Shmuly Yanklowitz is the president and dean of the Valley Beit Midrash, a pluralistic Jewish learning and leadership center; the founder and president of Uri L'Tzedek, an Orthodox social justice movement; the founder and CEO of the Shamayim V'Aretz Institute, a Jewish vegan, animal welfare movement; and the author of ten books on Jewish ethics. *Newsweek* named Rav Shmuly one of the top fifty rabbis in America, and the Forward named him one of the fifty most influential Jews. He studied at the University of Texas as an undergraduate and at Harvard University for a master's in leadership and psychology, completed a second master's degree in Jewish philosophy at Yeshiva University, and completed his doctorate at Columbia University in moral development and epistemology. He was ordained as a rabbi by Yeshivat Chovevei Torah (the YCT Rabbinical School) in New York, where he was a Wexner Graduate Fellow, and he received two additional private rabbinic ordinations. As a global social justice educator, he has volunteered, taught, and staffed missions in about a dozen countries around the world. A film crew followed him for over a year to produce a PBS documentary (*The Calling*) about the training of religious leadership, which was released in the winter of 2010. He was born in Canada, was raised in New Jersey and Chicago, and now lives in Scottsdale, Arizona, with his wife, Shoshana, and three children.

Rabbi Mary L. Zamore currently serves as the executive director of the Women's Rabbinic Network. She also is the CCAR's manager of mentoring. She is the editor of and a contributing author to *The Sacred Table: Creating a Jewish Food Ethic* (CCAR Press, 2011), which was designated a finalist by the National Jewish Book Awards. Ordained by Hebrew Union College–Jewish Institute of Religion in New York in 1997, she graduated from Columbia College, also studying at Yad Vashem and Machon Pardes. Rabbi Zamore is a frequent contributor to the *Huffington Post*.

32, 33

13 meh
14 nice
15 to the point
16 self indulgent
17. nice
18 Eden/no Eden,
   Interplay ✳
19 - in Israel,
      everywhere
20 ✳✳ passionate
21
22 time not place
   Heschel
   cf c̄ 19

First & Second
   stories

CPSIA information can be obtained
at www.ICGtesting.com
Printed in the USA
LVOW13s0609190218
567105LV00018BA/546/P

9 780881 232905